JANE AUSTEN AND LORD BYRON

JANE AUSTEN AND LORD BYRON

REGENCY RELATIONS

Christine Kenyon Jones

BLOOMSBURY ACADEMIC
LONDON • NEW YORK • OXFORD • NEW DELHI • SYDNEY

BLOOMSBURY ACADEMIC
Bloomsbury Publishing Plc
50 Bedford Square, London, WC1B 3DP, UK
1385 Broadway, New York, NY 10018, USA
29 Earlsfort Terrace, Dublin 2, Ireland

BLOOMSBURY, BLOOMSBURY ACADEMIC and the Diana logo are trademarks of
Bloomsbury Publishing Plc

First published in Great Britain 2024

Cover design and illustration by Rebecca Heselton

A catalogue record for this book is available from the British Library.

A catalog record for this book is available from the Library of Congress.

ISBN: HB: 978-1-3503-8140-7
PB: 978-1-3503-8139-1
ePDF: 978-1-3503-8141-4
eBook: 978-1-3503-8142-1

Typeset by Deanta Global Publishing Services, Chennai, India
Printed and bound in Great Britain

To find out more about our authors and books visit www.bloomsbury.com and
sign up for our newsletters.

CONTENTS

ILLUSTRATIONS

ABBREVIATIONS

BLJ   Byron, George Gordon Noel, Lord, *Byron's Letters and Journals,* ed. Leslie A. Marchand, 13 vols (London: John Murray, 1973–94).

References to Byron's letters are given in footnotes as, for example, 1.234 (volume 1, page 234), followed by addressee and date.

JAFR   Le Faye, Deirdre, *Jane Austen: A Family Record,* 2nd edn (Cambridge: Cambridge University Press, 2004).

JAL   Austen, Jane, *Jane Austen's Letters,* collected and ed. Deirdre Le Faye (Oxford: Oxford University Press, 1997).

References to Austen's letters are given in footnotes by the relevant page number in this edition, followed by addressee or sender and by date.

LBCMP   Byron, George Gordon Noel, Lord, *Lord Byron: The Complete Miscellaneous Prose,* ed. Andrew Nicholson (Oxford: Clarendon Press, 1991).

LBCPW   Byron, George Gordon Noel, Lord, *Lord Byron: The Complete Poetical Works,* ed. Jerome J. McGann, 7 vols (Oxford: Clarendon Press, 1980–93).

References in footnotes to some of Byron's works are abbreviated: for example, *EBSR* for *English Bards and Scotch Reviewers*; *CHP* for *Childe Harold's Pilgrimage* and *DJ* for *Don Juan.*

References to cantos and other divisions in Byron's verse are given in Arabic numbering, followed by the line(s) concerned, for example 1.23–4 (canto 1, lines 23–4). References to plays are given as, for example, *Manfred* 1.2.34 (Act 1, scene 2, line 34).

References to volumes and pages in *LBCPW* are given as, for example, 1.23–45 (volume 1, pages 23 to 45).

References to Austen's works are quoted from *The Cambridge Edition of the Works of Jane Austen* (Cambridge: Cambridge University Press, 2005–8). The following abbreviations are used: *MP* for *Mansfield Park*; *NA* for *Northanger Abbey*; *P&P* for *Pride and Prejudice*; and *S&S* for *Sense and Sensibility.*

ACKNOWLEDGEMENTS

My warmest thanks to Peter W. Graham for his encouragement and help with this project; to Professor Emma Clery, Dr Trudi Darby, Monica Farthing, Professor Susan Allen Ford and Professor Rivkah Zim for their friendly assistance, close reading, corrections and support; to Ben Doyle at Bloomsbury for his enthusiasm, kind judgement and expertise; to Nasser Al Tell LRPS for photography and technical advice; to Dr Andrew Pitcairn-Hill for design of the family tree; to Christine Ayre for generous help with design and imagery; to Ben Chisnall for creative input and crafting the title; and to Geoffrey Bond, Emily Brand, Robin, Lord Byron, Nick Hugh McCann, John, Virginia and Ocky Murray and Natalie Shaw for their help in enabling me to reproduce photographs of artworks owned and connected with them.

Some of the material in Chapter 4 was originally published in Christine Kenyon Jones, '"He Is a Rogue of Course, But a Civil One": John Murray, Jane Austen, and Lord Byron', *Persuasions* 36, 2014, 239–54, and I am grateful to the editor for permission to reproduce it here.

The author and publisher gratefully acknowledge the permission granted to reproduce the copyright material in this book. Every effort has been made to trace copyright holders and to obtain their permission for the use of copyright material. The publisher apologizes for any errors or omissions and would be grateful to be notified of any corrections that should be incorporated in future reprints or editions of this book.

JANE AUSTEN AND LORD BYRON
SIGNIFICANT DATES

Year	Significant dates in the life of Jane Austen (JA)	Significant dates in the life of George Gordon Byron, Lord Byron (GGB)
1706	Marriage of Catherine Perrot (great-aunt of JA's mother) and the Reverend James Musgrave.	
1759		Marriage of Isabella (née Byron, widow of the Earl of Carlisle) and Sir William Musgrave.
1764	Marriage of JA's parents, the Reverend George Austen and Cassandra Leigh.	
1765–74	Births of JA's older siblings: James, George, Edward, Henry, Cassandra and Francis.	
1769		Separation of Isabella and Sir William Musgrave.
1775	Birth of JA at Steventon Rectory, Hampshire, on 16 December.	
1776	Jane Musgrave (1732–88) becomes JA's godmother.	
1778–9		Elopement of Captain John Byron (GGB's father) with Lady Camarthen, followed by their marriage.
1779	Birth of JA's younger brother Charles.	
1783	Edward Austen adopted by the wealthy Thomas and Catherine Knight of Godmersham, Kent.	Birth of Augusta Byron, GGB's older half-sister (later Augusta Leigh).

Year	Significant dates in the life of Jane Austen (JA)	Significant dates in the life of George Gordon Byron, Lord Byron (GGB)
1784		Death of Captain Byron's wife (Augusta's mother).
1785		Marriage of Captain Byron to GGB's mother, Catherine Gordon of Gight.
1787	JA starts writing her *juvenilia*.	
1788	JA first visits London.	Birth of George Gordon Byron in Holles Street, London, on 22 January.
1789		GGB taken to Aberdeen by his mother.
1791		Death in France of GGB's father, Captain John Byron.
1792		Birth of Annabella Milbanke (the future Lady Byron, great-niece of Elizabeth Musgrave).
1794	JA probably begins *Lady Susan*.	On the death of GGB's second cousin, William John Byron, GGB (aged six) becomes heir to the Barony of Byron.
1795	JA probably writes *Elinor and Marianne* (early version of *Sense and Sensibility*) and flirts with Tom Lefroy.	
1796	Tom Lefroy leaves for London. JA starts *First Impressions* (early version of *Pride and Prejudice*).	

Year	Significant dates in the life of Jane Austen (JA)	Significant dates in the life of George Gordon Byron, Lord Byron (GGB)
1797	JA finishes *First Impressions* and her father offers it for publication to Thomas Cadell, who rejects it sight unseen. JA starts converting *Elinor and Marianne* into *Sense and Sensibility.* Her brother Henry marries their first cousin Eliza de Feuillide (née Hancock).	
1798	JA probably starts *Susan* (early version of *Northanger Abbey*).	William, fifth Lord Byron, dies. GGB (aged ten) becomes sixth Baron Byron of Rochdale and inherits Newstead Abbey, Nottinghamshire. He and his mother move to England.
1799		GGB goes to London with his lawyer John Hanson and enters Dr Glennie's school in Dulwich.
1801	The Reverend George Austen retires from his parish. He and Mrs Austen, Cassandra and JA leave Steventon and move to Bath. Henry Austen sets up as a banker and army agent in London.	GGB enters Harrow School.
1802	JA accepts and then withdraws from a marriage proposal by her friends' brother, Harris Bigg-Wither. She revises *Susan* (*Northanger Abbey*).	
1803	Manuscript of *Susan* is sold to Benjamin Crosby for £10, who advertises it but does not print or publish it.	GGB falls in love with Mary Chaworth.

Year	Significant dates in the life of Jane Austen (JA)	Significant dates in the life of George Gordon Byron, Lord Byron (GGB)
1804	JA probably writes *The Watsons*. Henry Austen moves his office to Albany in Piccadilly.	
1805	Death of JA's father in Bath.	GGB enters Trinity College, Cambridge. He falls in love with the chorister John Edleston.
1806		GGB's first book of poems, *Fugitive Pieces*, printed and immediately destroyed.
1807	JA, Cassandra and Mrs Austen take lodgings in Southampton and Henry Austen moves from Albany to 10 Henrietta Street, Covent Garden.	GGB publishes *Hours of Idleness*.
1808		*Edinburgh Review* critically attacks *Hours of Idleness*. GGB is awarded his MA and leaves Cambridge.
1809	JA, Cassandra, their mother, and Martha Lloyd move to Chawton Cottage (part of Edward Austen's Hampshire estate).	*English Bards and Scotch Reviewers* published. GGB and his Cambridge friend John Cam Hobhouse visit Portugal, Spain, Malta, Albania (where they are received by Ali Pasha), and parts of Greece including Missolonghi and Athens. GGB completes first canto of *Childe Harold's Pilgrimage*.
1810		GGB and Hobhouse visit Smyrna and Constantinople and return to Athens. GGB completes canto 2 of *Childe Harold* and has an affair with Nicolo Giraud.

Year	Significant dates in the life of Jane Austen (JA)	Significant dates in the life of George Gordon Byron, Lord Byron (GGB)
1811	*Sense and Sensibility* published by Thomas Egerton. JA starts revising *First Impressions* as *Pride and Prejudice*.	GGB returns to London. Death of his mother and several friends.
1812	On Mrs Knight's death, Edward Austen and his family take the surname Knight. JA sells copyright of *Pride and Prejudice* to Egerton for £110.	GGB makes his maiden speech in the House of Lords, opposing the introduction of the hanging penalty for frame breakers, and his second speech in favour of Roman Catholic emancipation. *Childe Harold* cantos 1 and 2 published by John Murray. GGB instantly becomes famous. Has affairs with Lady Caroline Lamb and Lady Oxford.
1813	Publication of *Pride and Prejudice*. Death of Henry's wife Eliza.	GGB confides in Lady Melbourne about his affair with his half-sister Augusta. *The Giaour* and *The Bride of Abydos* published by John Murray.
1814	JA begins *Emma. Mansfield Park* published by Egerton. JA makes several visits to London, staying with Henry. The Hinton/Baverstock lawsuit against Edward begins.	*The Corsair* and *Lara* published. GGB proposes (for the second time) in September to Annabella Milbanke and she accepts him.
1815	Battle of Waterloo (18 June) finally ends the war with France. JA starts *Persuasion,* begins association with John Murray and by invitation visits the Prince Regent's residence at Carlton House. *Emma* published by John Murray (dated 1816).	GGB marries Annabella Milbanke (2 January) and their daughter Augusta Ada (later Lovelace) is born on 10 December. GGB becomes a member of the Drury Lane Theatre management sub-committee.

Year	Significant dates in the life of Jane Austen (JA)	Significant dates in the life of George Gordon Byron, Lord Byron (GGB)
1816	JA starts to feel unwell. Henry buys back from Crosby the manuscript of *Susan* (*Northanger Abbey*), which JA revises. Henry's bank fails and he leaves London. *Persuasion* completed in August.	In January Annabella leaves GGB, who has heavy debts and a scandalous reputation. After a brief affair with Clare Claremont he leaves Britain forever on 25 April. Spends the summer in Switzerland near the Shelleys. Writes *Childe Harold 3* and *The Prisoner of Chillon* and begins *Manfred*. Moves to Venice and has an affair with Marianna Segati.
1817	JA starts *Sanditon* but is increasingly unwell. She and Cassandra move to Winchester in May for medical care. She dies on 18 July and is buried in Winchester Cathedral. *Northanger Abbey* and *Persuasion* are published posthumously (dated 1818) with a 'Biographical notice' by Henry Austen.	GGB's and Clare Claremont's illegitimate daughter Allegra is born in London. GGB visits Rome. Writes *Lament of Tasso, Childe Harold 4* and *Beppo* and has a turbulent affair with Margarita Cogni in Venice. Newstead Abbey is sold to Major Thomas Wildman.
1818		GGB begins *Don Juan*. He and Allegra live at Palazzo Mocenigo, on the Grand Canal in Venice.
1819		GGB begins a liaison with Teresa, Countess Guiccioli. *Don Juan* cantos 1 and 2 are published anonymously by Murray. GGB writes *The Prophecy of Dante* and *Don Juan* canto 3 (later divided into *DJ* 3 and 4).

Year	Significant dates in the life of Jane Austen (JA)	Significant dates in the life of George Gordon Byron, Lord Byron (GGB)
1820		GGB moves to Palazzo Guiccioli in Ravenna with Teresa and her husband and remains there when Teresa is granted a separation from her husband by the Pope and moves away. He becomes involved with the revolutionary Italian 'Carbonari' who aim to expel the Austrians from Italy. Writes *DJ 5*.
1821		Places Allegra in a convent school at Bagnacavallo. *Marino Faliero* published. Writes *Sardanapalus, The Two Foscari, Cain* and *The Vision of Judgment* and begins *Heaven and Earth*. Moves to Pisa, where Teresa and her father, and the Shelleys are living.
1822		Finishes *Werner*, completes *Don Juan 6–12*. Allegra dies at the convent school. GGB moves with Teresa to Montenero and then Albaro, near Genoa. Leigh Hunt arrives to edit a journal with Byron and Shelley but Shelley is drowned at Lerici on 8 July. GGB severs his business relationship with Murray and offers his works for publication to Leigh Hunt's brother John.

Year	Significant dates in the life of Jane Austen (JA)	Significant dates in the life of George Gordon Byron, Lord Byron (GGB)
1823		Writes *The Age of Bronze, The Island* and *Don Juan 13-17*. Agrees to go to Greece as representative for the London Greek Committee and leaves Italy and Teresa on 16 July, reaching Cephalonia in August. Lends the Greek government £4,000. Falls in love with young Lukas Chalandritsanos.
1824		Arrives in Missolonghi in early January. Suffers severe convulsions in February. His final illness (probably malaria but exacerbated by medical treatments) begins on 9 April. Dies on 19 April. His body is taken to England and lies in state in London before burial at Hucknall Torkard Church, near Newstead, on 16 July.

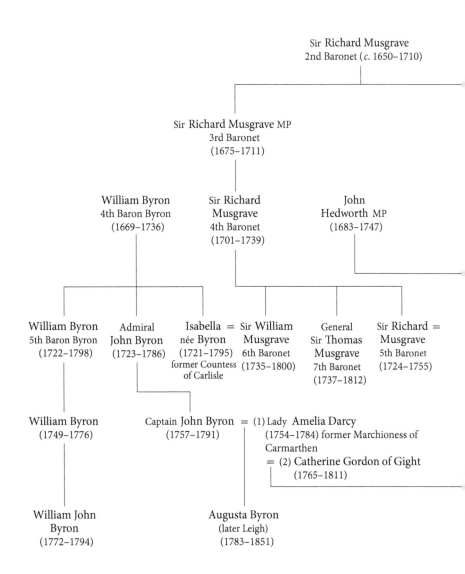

Sir Richard Musgrave
2nd Baronet (*c*. 1650–1710)

Sir Richard Musgrave MP
3rd Baronet
(1675–1711)

William Byron
4th Baron Byron
(1669–1736)

Sir Richard
Musgrave
4th Baronet
(1701–1739)

John
Hedworth MP
(1683–1747)

William Byron
5th Baron Byron
(1722–1798)

Admiral
John Byron
(1723–1786)

Isabella = Sir William
née Byron   Musgrave
(1721–1795) 6th Baronet
former Countess (1735–1800)
of Carlisle

General
Sir Thomas
Musgrave
7th Baronet
(1737–1812)

Sir Richard =
Musgrave
5th Baronet
(1724–1755)

William Byron
(1749–1776)

Captain John Byron = (1) Lady Amelia Darcy
(1757–1791)   (1754–1784) former Marchioness of
                       Carmarthen
                       = (2) Catherine Gordon of Gight
                            (1765–1811)

William John
Byron
(1772–1794)

Augusta Byron
(later Leigh)
(1783–1851)

Parts of the Musgrave,

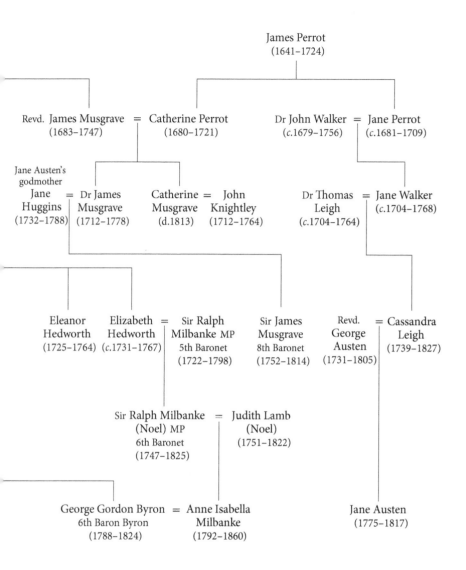

James Perrot
(1641–1724)

Revd. James Musgrave = Catherine Perrot   Dr John Walker = Jane Perrot
(1683–1747)   (1680–1721)   (c.1679–1756)   (c.1681–1709)

Jane Austen's
godmother
Jane   = Dr James   Catherine = John   Dr Thomas = Jane Walker
Huggins | Musgrave   Musgrave Knightley   Leigh   (c.1704–1768)
(1732–1788) (1712–1778) (d.1813) (1712–1764)   (c.1704–1764)

Eleanor   Elizabeth = Sir Ralph   Sir James   Revd.   = Cassandra
Hedworth   Hedworth Milbanke MP   Musgrave   George   Leigh
(1725–1764) (c.1731–1767) 5th Baronet 8th Baronet   Austen   (1739–1827)
                          (1722–1798) (1752–1814)   (1731–1805)

Sir Ralph Milbanke = Judith Lamb
(Noel) MP   (Noel)
6th Baronet   (1751–1822)
(1747–1825)

George Gordon Byron = Anne Isabella   Jane Austen
6th Baron Byron   Milbanke   (1775–1817)
(1788–1824)   (1792–1860)

Milbanke, Austen and Byron families

INTRODUCTION
A FAMILY AFFAIR: MUSGRAVES,
MILBANKES, AUSTENS AND BYRONS

Jane Austen and George Gordon Byron, sixth Lord Byron, were distantly related by marriage. In August 1759 Isabella Howard, the glamorous, recently widowed Countess of Carlisle, met Sir William Musgrave, a lawyer and art historian who had just become a baronet after the death of his brother. She was thirty-seven and, as portrayed by Thomas Gainsborough at the time, wonderfully elegant with a fashionable dusting of lavender hair-powder, while he was twenty-three and 'attractive in a willowy, studious sort of way'.[1] They met in Yorkshire and fell in love over a shared enthusiasm for books and botany, and were married at her house in Westminster on 10 December 1759.[2] Isabella, née Byron, was the sister of Captain (later Admiral) John Byron, the poet's grandfather, and her second marriage brought her into relationship with a flourishing family of Musgraves: one of whom, the Reverend James Musgrave (William's great-uncle), had married Catherine Perrot, Jane Austen's mother's great-aunt (see family tree on pages xviii–xix).[3] Their son was the wealthy Dr James Musgrave, Rector of Chinnor, Oxfordshire, and in 1776 his wife Jane Musgrave became Jane Austen's godmother.[4] A sprightly letter from Jane Musgrave to Sir William (her husband's first cousin once removed) apologizing that 'they *really* ware Unfortunately from home' when he had tried to visit them, indicates that they knew each other well.[5]

The Austens took godparenthood seriously, and Jane would certainly have known her godmother before Mrs Musgrave's death in 1788 when Jane was twelve. Jane Musgrave's son, also James, eventually inherited the Musgrave title as eighth baronet in 1812, sharing his financial inheritance from his uncle with a certain Mrs Clay, an impoverished widow who wrote obsequious letters to her future benefactor, while his aunt married a Mr John Knightley.[6] Austen's canny use of these and the Musgra/ove names in *Persuasion*, *Emma*, *The Watsons* and the 'Collection of Letters' in her early work makes it very clear that she was familiar with this part of her family.

Lord Byron seems not to have been so well informed. His great-aunt Isabella's marriage connected her not only with the Musgraves but also with the Milbanke family: baronets who were Isabella's close friends and her new husband's in-laws. This complex association also made both Austen and Byron distant relations-by-marriage of Annabella Milbanke, who became Lady Byron when she married the poet in early 1815. But it seems that neither Byron nor Annabella was aware of this relationship, even though they spent their honeymoon (what Byron called their 'treacle-moon') in the very place – Halnaby Hall in Yorkshire – where their relatives Isabella and William had met and fallen in love fifty-six years before.[7] A month before their wedding Byron wrote to Annabella about another link between them that had come to his attention: 'our Grandfathers were all in the same house at Westminster school', but he had nothing to say about their families' intermarriage.[8] 'So you see our coming together is quite in the course of events & vastly natural', he added – rather poignantly, given that in fact Isabella's and Sir William's marriage did not last (they separated in 1769) and that Byron's and Annabella's union was to become bitterly unhappy and scandal-ridden and barely survived a year.

By the time of her marriage, Annabella Milbanke was already an appreciative reader of Jane Austen. She described *Pride and Prejudice* in 1813 as 'a very superior work' and analysed the novel's strengths in a way that could hardly be bettered by a modern critic:

> It depends not on any of the common resources of Novel writers, no drownings, nor conflagrations, nor runaway horses, nor lap-dogs & parrots, nor chambermaids & milliners, nor rencontres and disguises. I really think it is the most probable fiction I have ever read. It is not a crying book, but the interest is very strong, especially for Mr. Darcy. The characters which are not amiable are diverting, and all of them are consistently supported.[9]

At this stage Annabella could only guess who the author was: the title page announced merely that it was 'By the Author of "Sense and Sensibility"' and *that* title page specified only that it was 'By A Lady'. But when Austen's authorship did become known later, the by-then Lady Byron never mentioned or claimed their distant cousinhood.

Such relationships were not unusual among the aristocracy, gentry and professional classes within the increasingly mobile class structure of Austen's and Byron's England, and it would perhaps have been remarkable if no links had been found between their families. But, given the celebrity status these two authors have now achieved, it is surprising that they are still often thought of as belonging to completely different worlds, different social classes and even different eras. While Austen, born in 1775, is often categorized as a middle-class eighteenth-century author, Byron, born in 1788, is generally classed as a nineteenth-century Romantic poet and a characteristic product of the Regency aristocracy. But in fact their class differences (and the age gap between them) were not dissimilar to those between their relatives Isabella and her Sir William.

Opposites and attractions

April 2024 marks the 200th anniversary of Byron's death at Missolonghi, Western Greece, where he succumbed to fever at the age of thirty-six while supporting the Greeks in their struggle for independence from the Ottoman Turks. December 2025 sees the 250th anniversary of Jane Austen's birth at Steventon Rectory, Hampshire: the seventh child and second daughter of the eight children of the Reverend George and Cassandra Austen. This book marks the near coincidence of these anniversaries by exploring the two authors' lives and writings in relation to each other at a level of detail that has not been attempted before, investigating how Austen and Byron were linked by some near-encounters and similarities of geographical location, social contact, shared interests and (particularly) by their status as authors whose writing is marked by their astute critique of their era and the coexistence of irony, humour and romance.

The agenda that presents Austen and Byron as opposites points out many contrasts: she was a country parson's daughter clinging to gentility, he a peer of the realm with large estates and an extravagant urban lifestyle; she aimed to be deliberately anonymous in her writing career, he flamboyantly famous; she chose spinsterhood and modesty, he was notoriously sexually promiscuous with both sexes; she crafted and recrafted a limited number of novels in beautifully precise but unostentatious prose, he generated volumes of verse in many different poetic forms that were sometimes marked by carelessness but often brilliant.[10] Jane had the lifelong companionship and support of loving parents and siblings, especially her sister Cassandra, while George was brought up very much as an only child, fatherless and at odds with his mother from an early age, alternately estranged from and dangerously close to his half-sister Augusta, and seeking in vain all his life for a family to belong to. All Austen's novels end with a conventional happy marriage ('Henry and Catherine were married, the bells rang, and

Figure 1 *Jane Austen*, pencil and watercolour sketch by her sister Cassandra (*c.* 1810). © National Portrait Gallery, London.

everybody smiled'), although sometimes this ending is rather perfunctorily dealt with, while Byron's 'Oriental' tales and dramas feature star-crossed lovers who cannot achieve a united happy ending, let alone marriage.[11] In the humorous *Don Juan* (which was never finished) Byron planned to present the hero's life as a series of romantic encounters: as 'a Cavalier Servente in Italy, and a cause for a divorce in England – and a Sentimental "Werther-faced man" in Germany', and intended Juan to end either 'in Hell – or in an unhappy marriage, – not knowing which would be the severest'.

While Austen described herself as 'the most unlearned, & uninformed Female who ever dared to be an Authoress', Byron was educated at Harrow, one of England's most prestigious boys' schools, and graduated from Cambridge – although in fact Austen received many educational advantages from her university-educated father and brothers, while Byron's attendance at both school and university was somewhat sporadic.[12] Austen remained an unostentatious member of the Church of England all her life, while Byron's experiences of Scottish Calvinism, institutional Anglicanism, Greek Orthodoxy, Ottoman Islam and Mediterranean Catholicism left him a theologically engaged and troubled agnostic. She was a keen and active walker and loved dancing, while his congenital lameness led him to sneer at waltzing. Above all, Austen was a woman carrying the weight of centuries of female inequality and exclusion from public life and also, in England in this period, experiencing increasing social constraint and even less freedom for

Figure 2 *Portrait of a Nobleman in the Dress of an Albanian*, by Thomas Phillips, exhibited at the Royal Academy in 1814. The 'Albanian' costume was given by Byron to his friend Margaret Mercer Elphinstone and was rediscovered in the 1960s in a dressing-up box at the home of her descendants. Government Art Collection. © Crown Copyright UK.

'ladies' than had existed in the previous decades, while Byron was a highly privileged nobleman and a peer of the realm, free to act and behave almost exactly as he wished, although nevertheless alive to issues of what he called 'their she condition' and to the ultimate fluidity of gender roles.[13]

Austen and Byron were, however, both very recognizably the products of their era and society and of the huge historical changes that characterized their lifetimes. Both lived through the French Revolution and had members of their families fighting in the Revolutionary and Napoleonic wars which engaged Britain for more than two decades between 1792 and 1815, and both were excited by the character of Napoleon. They both saw the restoration of the conservative European monarchic regimes following Waterloo and experienced the roller-coaster economic climate of the war years and after. They both observed the alterations in the landscape of England that marked the beginnings of the industrial revolution and the widespread economic, social and cultural transformations it brought about, including the increasing influence of a wealthier, bourgeois, middle-class society. They witnessed and participated in Britain's growth into the wealthiest and most ambitious country in the world, the early days of its colonial expansion and its first steps on the path to claiming the largest empire in history.[14]

'Spoken like a Tory!'

Austen's and Byron's party-political allegiances have been assumed to be very different, and the teenage Jane's marginal comments on Goldsmith's *History of England* certainly revel in their strong partiality to the Tories and the Stuart cause ('Nobly said! Spoken like a Tory!' is characteristic).[15] But critical study has shown that Austen did not always share what her nephew called 'the feeling of moderate Toryism which prevailed in her family', especially when it came to social issues, while her brother Henry's business connections were very much with members of the Whig party.[16] And Byron's radicalism, as expressed in his parliamentary speeches in favour of clemency to the industrial 'frame-breakers', on Catholic emancipation and on parliamentary reform, was constrained by his status as a patrician, though liberal, Whig.[17] In common with a great many British families of the middle and upper classes in this period, the Austens and the Byrons both had indirect connections with slavery (which are explored in Chapter 6), while both very actively welcomed the banning of the transatlantic slave trade in 1807 and supported the campaign for the abolition of slavery itself: not achieved until many years after their deaths.

Both Austen and Byron lived and consciously marked in their work what has been described as 'a peculiarly important moment in the shift of sensibility, from the formal, balanced rational views of an Augustan and Johnsonian world, to a world of sentiment, extravagance, Gothic horror, picturesque enthusiasm and romanticism', and they both loved and harked back to certain aspects of this outgoing eighteenth-century culture and literature.[18] Austen especially admired the writings of Dr Samuel Johnson and William Cowper (described by Henry Austen in his 'Biographical Note' of 1818 as her 'favourite moral writers'), while Byron aspired in particular to the wit, tone and art of Alexander Pope, whom he forcefully defended against the moral and poetic slights of the 1809 editor of Pope's works, William Lisle Bowles.[19] Both of them were voracious readers of fiction: in an age where novels were considered by the serious-minded to be conducive to frivolity and immorality, especially among young women, Jane vigorously championed them in her own voice in chapter 5 of *Northanger Abbey*, as works 'in which the greatest powers of the mind are displayed, in which the most thorough knowledge of human nature, the happiest delineation of its varieties, the liveliest effusions of wit and humour, are conveyed to the world in the best-chosen language'.[20] The Austen clergy family, too, were unusual in describing themselves as 'great Novel-readers & not ashamed of being so'.[21] At the age of nineteen Byron rather more shame-facedly claimed that he had 'read (to my regret at present) above four thousand novels'.[22] At this stage he named only male authors – 'Cervantes, Fielding, Smollet [sic], Richardson, Mackenzie, Sterne, Rabelais and Rousseau, &c. &c.' – but later he frequently mentioned the work of female novelists too, engaging passionately with Germaine de Staël's *Corinne,* seeking the acquaintance of Maria Edgeworth and sharing Austen's taste for Fanny Burney's work in particular. In requesting his publisher John Murray to send a copy of Burney's (Madame D'Arblay's) new work to Lord Holland, who was laid up with the gout, Byron confessed: 'I would almost fall sick myself to get at Me D'Arblay's writing'.[23] And we know from the *Memoir* written by Jane's nephew, that Lord Holland when 'lying on his bed . . . attacked with gout' also enjoyed being read to from 'one of Miss Austen's novels, of which he was never wearied'.[24]

Austen and Byron shared a delight in the novels of Walter Scott and a partiality for Gothic fiction, and both in their own work (Austen in *Northanger Abbey* and Byron at Norman Abbey, in cantos 15 and 16 of *Don Juan*) brilliantly used and subverted the conventions of Gothic while appreciating its potential power.[25] They both participated in the development of what has since been defined as Romanticism while combining it with laughter and the cutting edge of satire. Peter W. Graham describes them as 'the two great Romantic writers with a sense of humor', and they both became brilliant masters of comedy and irony, although Austen never saw Byron's best work in this mode, in his *ottava rima* poems *Beppo* (1818), *The Vision of Judgment* (1822) and *Don Juan* (1819–24), and Byron never had the chance to relish any of the hilarious moments in Austen's teenage writing.[26]

Stars of screen

Perhaps equally significant, in the last three decades, has been the way in which Austen and Byron have been brought together in the public imagination through the screen adaptations of Austen's novels, which from the 1990s have propelled her to super-stardom and have often used Byron and Byronic heroes as a reference point for the presentation of the Regency era in general and of Austen's leading men in particular. The Regency rage for Byron and the Byronic, which Annabella Milbanke named 'Byromania' in 1812, was, as Sarah Wootton puts it, 'reborn as Darcymania when

Austen's hero became the pin-up of the BBC's phenomenally successful series of *Pride and Prejudice,* screened in 1995'.[27] What Diego Saglia describes as Byron's 'theatricalized masculinity', complete with a sartorial elegance verging on dandyism, a manner alternately proud and detached and then warm and romantic, and a moody but beautifully chiselled profile, provided a template for screenwriters such as Andrew Davies to display Austen's heroes visually and sexually, and continues to have a marked effect on neo-Regency dramas such as *Bridgerton.*[28]

Kathryn Sutherland has pointed out how Austen's writing invites her readers to distrust the visual and does NOT generally privilege seeing over hearing; but screen presentations must find a way to overcome this, and the visual signals that indicate 'Byron' have given Austen screenwriters a powerful means of doing so.[29] Almost all the additional scenes (those not in the novel) which Davies wrote for Colin Firth's 1995 Darcy were drawn from Byron's biography: the energetic boxing and fencing which Darcy is seen using in an attempt to overcome his attraction to Elizabeth are taken straight from Byron's workouts at 'Gentleman' Jackson's premises in Bond Street, while Davies's famous 'wet-shirt' episode sees Darcy plunging Byron-like into a pool and swimming his way into Elizabeth's fascinated vision.[30] Readings of and references to Byron's works are interpolated into the Austen screenplays where in the novels Austen did not use them or

Figure 3 Chalk sketch of Byron, by George Henry Harlow (1815). Copied, re-copied and reproduced in engravings, this became one of the best-known portraits of Byron during his lifetime. Nottingham City Museums and Galleries. Photograph by Gary Hope.

quoted another poet. In Davies's 2008 *Sense and Sensibility*, for example, Willoughby woos Marianne not with William Cowper and Walter Scott (as Austen has it) but with Byron's lyric 'So, we'll go no more a-roving / So late into the night'.[31] In his 1995 screenplay for *Persuasion* Nick Dear (who also wrote a 2003 biopic about Byron) has Captain Benwick quote Byron (as Austen does in the novel) – but rather than *The Giaour* he uses the much more personal (disingenuous and controversial) poem that Byron wrote to his wife after their marital separation in 1816:

> Fare thee well! – thus disunited –
>   Torn from every nearer tie –
> Seared in heart – and lone – and blighted –
>   More than this, I scarce can die.

('Fare Thee Well' 57–60)[32]

Recent fanfiction and tribute texts, which borrow the characters of Austen's or Byron's work, and/or the characteristics of their authors, have created appealing fictions, including those in which what might be termed the avatars of Austen and Byron appear together, side by side. Narratives such as those by Georgette Heyer, Stephanie Barron, Susannah Clarke, Maya Slater, Emma Tennant, P. D. James, Reginald Hill and Thomas Ford pay homage to Austen in terms of their plots and sometimes their writing styles, and often present Austen as the canny heroine and Byron as an example of seductive but ultimately ineffectual masculinity. This 'Byron' may attract 'Austen' in spite of herself ('A diabolical figure of licence and flame, armed with a pen', as Stephanie Barron denominates 'Byron' in *Jane and the Madness of Lord Byron*) or may represent aspects of the Austenian character who wants to break out of her constricting femininity. [33]

Such fictions pride themselves on their accuracy in deploying the details of Austen's and Byron's 'real' lives, and Andrew Davies's timescale for the use of 'Fare Thee Well' in his screenplay is certainly imaginatively credible, since this poem was made public (without Byron's consent) in April 1816, and Austen did not finish writing *Persuasion* until August that year.[34] In terms of a possible relationship in Austen's mind between Mr Darcy and Byron or the Byronic hero, the case is more complex, since she initially drafted 'First Impressions' (the forerunner to *Pride and Prejudice*) in the mid-1790s, long before 'Byromania' took hold. But she was carrying out major revisions to her work just at the time of the appearance of the first famous Byronic hero, Childe Harold, and his *Pilgrimage*, in March 1812, and it is certainly possible that she responded to the craze for things Byronic when finalizing her novel for publication in January 1813.[35] She and Byron also shared knowledge of a heritage of previous 'Byronic' literary figures ranging from Shakespeare's Hamlet and Milton's Satan to Samuel Richardson's Lovelace and the antiheroes of Gothic novels such as Ann Radcliffe's Montoni.[36] As Peter W. Graham suggests, both *Pride and Prejudice* and *Childe Harold's Pilgrimage* (and in particular their male protagonists) can be described as a 'spur to fantasy', in that they both present the challenge of the potential domestication by a woman of masculine proud (or prejudiced) alienation, and Darcy can certainly be said to share the Corsair's 'lofty port', 'distant mien' and 'haughty gesture'.[37] Byron's Childe Harold and the heroes of his 'Oriental' tales, and Austen's most famous novel, all show that behind the guarded, perhaps bitter, façade of the hero is a softer and intriguingly vulnerable lover (or poet). The two are certainly connected in the biography of Annabella Milbanke who, as we have seen, recorded her 'very strong interest' in Mr Darcy and was so convinced of her own ability to reform what her cousin-by-marriage Lady Caroline Lamb described as the 'Mad – bad – and dangerous to know' Lord Byron that she was prepared to take the terrible risk of marrying him.[38]

Regency relations

Against the background of interactions such as these, this book sets out to study the near-encounters, the similarities, the coincidences and contrasts of Austen's and Byron's lives and writings in late Georgian and Regency England, centring around particular themes but also including digressions where these touch on topics relevant to both protagonists. It looks at the intersections – 'so near and yet so far' – that epitomize the way in which, although apparently never meeting or personally directly connecting, the two writers were sometimes surprisingly close to each other both in their lives and their works. The following chapters aim to show how Austen and Byron knew some of the same people, if not each other (and how they both had close links with one very strange noble family in particular); how they passionately enjoyed some of the same pastimes and places (especially London and its theatres, shows, entertainments and exhibitions); how they both collaborated and disputed with their publisher, John Murray: each negotiating complexities of class and professionalism in their dealings with him, and how both their lives and work were impacted by the complex inheritance laws (including entail) and the turbulent financial climate of Jane's final years. It demonstrates how at times their literary work shared subject matter, approach, technique, taste, tone and aspects of wit, humour, ingenuity, inventiveness and inspiration. In other words, it aims to show that Austen and Byron were related not only through (distant) family kinship but also through their interactions with and responses to the Regency world, both literally and literarily, in many important ways.

Notes

1. Brand 136–7.
2. Brand 136–7.
3. King 61, cited by Wootton (2007) 26.
4. Thomson np.
5. Thomson np.
6. Thomson np.
7. *BLJ* 4.263, to Thomas Moore, 2 February 1815.
8. *BLJ* 4.235, to Annabella Milbanke, 28 November 1814.
9. *JAFR* 196. Annabella Milbanke to her mother Lady (Judith) Milbanke, 1 May 1813.
10. Brownstein 175. Wootton (2007) 26.
11. *NA* vol. 2, chap. 16, 261. *BLJ* 8.78, to John Murray, 16 February 1821.
12. *JAL* 306, to James Stanier Clarke, 11 December 1815.
13. *Don Juan* 14.188, *LBCPW* 5.565.
14. Morrison 6.
15. Austen ed. Sabor 339.
16. Austen-Leigh ed. Sutherland 71. Clery (2017) 99.
17. Kelsall 2.
18. Drabble xiii.
19. Henry Austen in Austen-Leigh ed. Sutherland 141. Byron, 'Letter to John Murray Esqre', *LBCMP* 120–60.
20. *NA* vol. 1, chap. 5, 31.
21. *JAL* 26, to Cassandra Austen, 18–19 December 1798.
22. 'List of Historical Writers whose Works I have perused in different languages ... Novr. 30th. 1807', *LBCMP* 3–7.
23. *BLJ* 3.204, to John Murray, 27 December 1813.

24. Austen-Leigh ed. Sutherland 112.

25. Graham (2008).

26. Graham (2008) 1.

27. 'The Byromania' (1812) by Annabella Milbanke, quoted in Wilson xii. Wootton (2016) 15.

28. Saglia 25.

29. Sutherland (2011) 215–16.

30. The famous shirt starred in the 'Jane Austen Undressed' exhibition at Chawton in 2022. Jane Austen House, https://janeaustens.house/stockings-stays-a-new -display/.

31. Wootton (2016) 57.

32. *LBCPW* 3.382.

33. Barron 50. See also Hopkins.

34. Byron had this poem and 'A Sketch from Private Life' printed and circulated privately by John Murray, but they were 'leaked' by Henry Brougham and published in *The Champion*. Graham (2004) 37.

35. Wootton (2016) 77.

36. Wootton (2007) 27.

37. Graham (2013) 169–81. The phrase 'spur to fantasy' is from Patricia Meyer Spacks 6. *The Corsair* 1.541, 570, *LBCPW* 3.168–69. Wootton (2007) 35.

38. Lamb quoted in Morgan 2.200. Annabella also wrote to Lady Melbourne about *The Corsair* on 12 February 1814 that '[i]n knowledge of the human heart & its most secret workings surely he may without exaggeration be compared to Shakespeare', Airlie 162.

CHAPTER 1
READING EACH OTHER
'YOU COULD NOT SHOCK HER
MORE THAN SHE SHOCKS ME'

One major question to be considered is how well Austen and Byron knew each other's work and what they thought of it. We know that Austen read Byron, and critics have pondered over her approach to his poetry in her last completed novel, *Persuasion*; her brief comment on *The Corsair* in a letter of March 1814, and the significance of the fact that she copied out one of Byron's poems, 'Napoleon's Farewell' (1815), changing the wording in minor ways as she did so. It has often been stated that Byron did not know Austen's work, and certainly there are no references in his work or letters that would enable editors to index 'Austen, Jane'. Looking at the biographical evidence, however, it is clear that Byron knew at least some of her novels and was familiar with her style and approach.

In chapter 11 of volume 1 of *Persuasion* Scott's verse romances (*Marmion* and *The Lady of the Lake*) are paired with two of Byron's 'Oriental Tales' (*The Giaour* and *The Bride of Abydos*) as objects for discussion between Anne Elliot and Captain Benwick, who is in mourning for the recent death of his fiancée Fanny Harville. Anne and Benwick agree about 'the richness of the present age' of poetry, and that Scott and Byron are to be classed as 'the first-rate poets', although there is a touch of Austenian irony in their puzzlement about 'how the *Giaour* was to be pronounced' (Byron himself called it that 'unpronounceable name' and rhymed it with both 'power' and 'lower').[1] The irony deepens when Benwick 'show[s] himself so intimately acquainted with all the tenderest songs of the one poet, and all the impassioned descriptions of hopeless agony of the other' that Anne 'venture[s] to hope he did not always read only poetry', and recommends 'a larger allowance of prose in his daily study'. Suggesting writings 'calculated to rouse and fortify the mind by the highest precepts, and the strongest examples of moral and religious endurances', Anne is amused to find herself 'preach[ing] patience and resignation to a young man whom she had never seen before' and reflects that 'like many other great moralists and preachers, she had been eloquent on a point in which her own conduct [her continued mourning for her parting with Wentworth seven years previously] would ill bear examination'.[2]

Scott had already been admired by two other Austen protagonists before *Persuasion* was written. In *Sense and Sensibility* (1810) he is one of Marianne Dashwood's favourite authors, while in 1813 Fanny Price alludes to him approvingly in *Mansfield Park*.[3] By 1814, when Scott's first novel *Waverley* appeared, Austen herself had joined the fan-club: 'Walter Scott has no business to write novels – especially good ones', she complained to her niece Anna. 'It is not fair. – He has Fame & Profit enough as a Poet, and should not be taking the bread out of other people's mouths. – I do not like him, & do not mean to like Waverley if I can help it – but fear I must.'[4] But although Byron is coupled with Scott by Anne and Benwick as a 'first-rate poet', Austen's own opinion is not quite so clear. In *Sanditon* the sentimental Sir Edward Denham produces a set of clichéd descriptions of the sea which sounds suspiciously like an authorial parody of Romantic verse in general and the opening lines of Byron's very popular poem *The Corsair* in particular: 'the terrific Grandeur of the Ocean in a Storm, its glassy surface in a calm . . . the deep fathoms of its Abysses, its quick vicissitudes, its direful Deceptions, its Mariners tempting it in Sunshine and overwhelmed by the sudden Tempest'.[5] Margaret Kirkham has argued that in *Persuasion* Jane Austen reverses 'the burlesque stereotype of a young woman deluded by romantic reading' in her treatment of Benwick and Sir Edward, showing how these two young men are taken in by poetic sentiment while Anne – at least rationally, and with difficulty – tries to resist it.[6]

While writing *Persuasion* in the year up to August 1816, Austen would certainly have been aware of the scandalous breakdown of the Byrons' marriage, their bitter separation early in 1816, and Byron's departure in disgrace from England in April. Byron's own *Poems on his Domestic Circumstances* ('Fare Thee Well' and 'A Sketch from Private Life') were pirated, much publicized and quoted and, along with letters from Lady Byron's father, received columns of coverage in scores of London and local newspapers, including the Hampshire press.[7] 'I have read several of Burns' Poems with great delight', says the sensible Charlotte Heywood in *Sanditon*,

> but I am not poetic enough to separate a Man's Poetry entirely from his Character, – and poor Burns's known Irregularities, greatly interrupt my enjoyment of his Lines, – I have difficulty in depending on the *Truth* of his Feelings as a Lover. I have not faith in the *sincerity*

of the affections of a Man of his Description. He felt and he wrote and he forgot.[8]

Austen's attitude to Byron is unlikely to have been as clear-cut as Charlotte's is to the philandering Robert Burns, but her use of Byron's verse in *Persuasion* does highlight the mismatch between the Giaour's eternal and hopeless constancy to his lost Leila and Byron's own inability to sustain his marriage vows even for a year.[9] When Captain Benwick later forgets Fanny Harville by very quickly falling in love with Louisa Musgrove, and his own feelings of 'hopeless agony' are shown to be highly transitory, the author's critique surely extends to Byron as one of the poets whom Benwick has taken as his example.

The conversation between Anne and Benwick is continued in the following chapter with a reference to Byron's *Corsair* and its 'dark blue seas', and Peter Knox-Shaw has suggested that there may also be a Byronic influence here in the way Austen sets up a contrasting pair between the impetuous Louisa Musgrove and the patient Anne, as Byron does between the wilful, impulsive Gulnare and the faithful Medora.[10] As Knox-Shaw points out, the consequences of Louisa's accident in Austen's text are related in a manner 'that is in Byron's voice, and yet not burlesque': 'There was no wound, no blood, no visible bruise; but her eyes were closed, she breathed not, her face was like death.' This can certainly be compared with Byron's similar use of a succession of negatives to describe Conrad's reaction when he discovers the dead body of Medora: 'He turned not – spoke not – sunk not – fixed his look.'[11] And the *lack* of blood on Louisa's forehead may recall 'that spot of blood, that light but guilty streak' on Gulnare's brow after she has killed the Pasha.[12]

Did his lordship admire *Emma*?

It has often been assumed there is no evidence that Byron knew of Austen or her works. In 1986, for example, the author of an article entitled 'Jane Austen and Lord Byron: Connections' wrote that she had 'found no evidence he ever read any of her novels, or even heard of her, though her books were read and talked of by members of his social set', while in 1993 an article in the *Byron Journal* claimed that 'The sales catalogues of his books mention none of Austen's works, nor does her name occur in his correspondence, in his poems, or in his prose notes.'[13] In fact, however, we now know that

Byron owned copies of at least three of Austen's novels, including first editions of *Sense and Sensibility, Pride and Prejudice* and *Emma*.[14] The copy of *Emma* was a gift to Byron and his half-sister Augusta Leigh from his and Austen's publisher John Murray, on its publication in December 1815, and a letter from Murray of 29 December enquires, 'Tell me if Mrs Leigh & your Lordship admire Emma?'[15] Augusta was staying with Lord and Lady Byron to help at the time of the birth on 10 December of their daughter Ada (later Countess of Lovelace, of mathematical and computer-programming fame). But, since Annabella evidently admired Austen's work, it is puzzling that Murray did not mention her in his gift or ask for her response as well, so perhaps he already knew that the Byron marriage was on the rocks. In 1941 this particular copy of *Emma* came up for sale with a title page inscribed 'Augusta Leigh – 1815, the 1st copy, given by Mr. Murray'.[16]

Emma, as the first novel by an Englishwoman to be published by Murray, was, as discussed in Chapter 5, a new publishing departure for the firm, and it is not surprising that Murray was anxious to know what his most famous author thought of it.[17] Although there is no record of a written response from Byron, it is probable that he and Murray discussed it face-to-face, since they were in close contact in this period and living only a few hundred yards away from each other along Piccadilly. Murray certainly seems to have expected Byron to remember Austen and her works when in September 1817 he wrote to Byron in Italy to tell him that he was preparing to publish 'two new Novels left by Miss Austen – the ingenious Author of Pride & Prejudice – who I am sorry to say died about 6 weeks ago'.[18] *Persuasion* and *Northanger Abbey* were published together by Murray in December 1817 (dated 1818), and it seems probable that Murray sent copies of these volumes in the large parcel of books that Byron received from him in Venice in February 1818.[19] It is possible that Byron recalled *Northanger Abbey* when creating his own questionably haunted Norman Abbey in the final cantos of *Don Juan*, and Chapter 7 discusses the case that has been made that he used aspects of *Persuasion*'s conversation about women's constancy between Anne Elliot and Captain Harville when composing Julia's letter in canto 1 of *Don Juan*: 'Man's love is of his life a thing apart, / 'Tis woman's whole existence.'[20]

The first edition copies of *Sense and Sensibility* (1811) and *Pride and Prejudice* (1813) that Byron owned were published not by John Murray but by Thomas Egerton, and it seems likely that Byron had bought them himself, since he had no particular links with Egerton and these novels had already become part of his library by 1813, before he became closely connected with the Austen fan Annabella Milbanke. He may have been told, as his close friend John Cam Hobhouse was in 1814, that the novels were by Lady Boringdon, later the Countess of Morley, to whose sister Henry Austen had given drawing lessons and who later corresponded with Jane and received an author's copy of *Emma*.[21] Lady Caroline Lamb, Byron's former lover and nemesis, also owned a copy of *Pride and Prejudice*, which can now be seen at the Austen Museum in Jane's home at Chawton Cottage, Hampshire.[22] Another enthusiast for *Pride and Prejudice* whom Byron knew and admired was the playwright Richard Brinsley Sheridan, who asked his dinner-partner Miss Shirreff if she had seen it 'and advised her to buy it immediately for it was one of the cleverest things he ever read'.[23]

On 8 July 1813 Byron's copies of the two Austen novels were advertised for sale by auction along with several hundred other volumes owned by his lordship (apparently most of his library, other than the books he wanted to pass on to friends).[24] The Austen novels were part of Lot 154: a miscellaneous bundle which also included a *History of Pugilism* (1812), *Despotism, or the Fall of the Jesuits* by Isaac D'Israeli (1811, published by Murray) and an anonymous 'Volume of plays'.[25] The reason for the sale was that Byron was then planning to travel abroad for the second time and perhaps not intending to return to England. In fact, however, the travels – and the sale – never took place: initially because of reports of plague in the Levant and then perhaps because of the growing closeness between Byron and Augusta, which developed into a love affair. A sale of Byron's books eventually went ahead in 1816, when he did leave England for good, but there is no mention in this catalogue of the Austen novels, and while Byron may have taken them with him to Switzerland and Italy in his giant coach, modelled on that of Napoleon, it seems more likely that he had already passed them on to Annabella or Augusta.

John Bull does Jane Austen

'I have just read "John Bull's Letter"', Byron wrote to Murray from Ravenna in June 1821, 'it is diabolically *well* written – & full of fun and ferocity. – I must forgive the dog whoever he is.'[26] Byron's list of suspects for the author of the satirical *Letter to the Right Hon. Lord Byron by John Bull* included his close friend Hobhouse, Thomas Love Peacock ('a very clever fellow') and Isaac D'Israeli – but actually the pamphleteer was Sir Walter Scott's son-in-law, John Gibson Lockhart: harsh Tory literary critic, contributor to *Blackwood's Edinburgh Magazine* and later editor of the *Quarterly Review*.

In his letter John Bull tells Byron that although 'all the world then agree with yourself in thinking you a great poet',

> [t]he whole of your misanthropy is humbug. You do not hate men, 'no, nor woman neither,' but you thought it would be a fine, interesting thing for a handsome young Lord to depict himself as a dark-souled, melancholy, morbid being, and you have done so, it must be admitted, with exceeding cleverness. . . . Every boarding-school in the empire still contains many devout believers in the amazing misery of the black-haired, high-browed, blue-eyed, bare-throated, Lord Byron. How melancholy you look in the prints!

Lockhart's satire then morphs into a wonderful parody of *Emma*'s Highbury ladies discussing Byron's portraits, poetry and scandalous separation:

> Oh! yes, this is the true cast of face. Now, tell me, Mrs. Goddard, now tell me, Miss Price, now tell me, dear Harriet Smith, and dear, dear Mrs. Elton, do tell me, is not this just the very look, that one would have fancied for Childe Harold? Oh! what eyes and eyebrows! Oh! what a chin! – well, after all, who knows what may have happened. One can never know the truth of such stories. Perhaps her *Ladyship* was in the wrong after all. – I am sure if I had married such a man, I would have borne with all his little eccentricities – a man so evidently unhappy. – Poor Lord Byron! who can say how much he may have been to be pitied? I am sure I would; I bear with all Mr. E.'s eccentricities, and I am sure any woman of real sense would have done so to Lord Byron's: poor Lord Byron! – well, say what they will, I shall always pity him; – do you remember these dear lines of his –
>
>> 'It is that settled ceaseless gloom,
>> The fabled Hebrew wanderer bore,
>> That will not look beyond the tomb,
>> But cannot hope for rest before.'
>
> – Oh! beautiful! and how beautifully you repeat them! You always repeat Lord Byron's fine passages so beautifully. What think you of that other we were talking of on Saturday evening at Miss Bates's?
>
>> – 'Nay, smile not at my sullen brow,
>> Alas! I cannot smile again.'

I forget the rest; – but nobody has such a memory as Mrs. E. Don't you think, Captain Brown has a look of Lord Byron?[27]

In this splendid parody the narrator's, Miss Bates's, Mrs Elton's and other voices merge and diverge, giving almost the effect of Austen's famous 'free indirect discourse' and, apart from the unexpected appearance of *Mansfield Park*'s 'Miss Price' among the Highbury ladies, this might pass for a scene from Austen's own pen. If Byron could appreciate this imitation (as it seems he did, despite the satire aimed so accurately at him) he must surely have known and recognized the original and appreciated Austen's ear for the kind of apparently idle chatter that actually ruthlessly reveals character and uncovers deeper themes. Perhaps indeed he pays Austen the compliment of imitation in *Beppo* (1818), in Laura's monologue, when her lost husband suddenly reappears dressed as a Turk:

> 'Beppo! what's your pagan name?
> Bless me! your beard is of amazing growth!
> And how came you to keep away so long?
> Are you not sensible 'twas very wrong?
>
> 'And are you *really, truly,* now a Turk?
> With any other women did you wive?
> Is't true they use their fingers for a fork?
> Well, that's the prettiest shawl – as I'm alive!
> You'll give it me? They say you eat no pork.
> And how so many years did you contrive
> To – Bless me! did I ever? No, I never
> Saw a man grown so yellow! How's your liver?
>
> 'Beppo! that beard of yours becomes you not;
> It shall be shaved before you're a day older:
> Why do you wear it? Oh! I had forgot –
> Pray don't you think the weather here is colder?
> How do I look? You shan't stir from this spot
> In that queer dress, for fear that some beholder
> Should find you out, and make the story known.
> How short your hair is! Lord! how grey it's grown!'
>
> (*Beppo* 725–44)[28]

Austen too could imitate her own virtuosity, and one of the funniest moments in *Emma* is Emma herself mimicking Miss Bates:

Jane Austen and Lord Byron

How would he bear to have Miss Bates belonging to him? – To have her haunting the Abbey, and thanking him all day long for his great kindness in marrying Jane? – 'So very kind and obliging! – But he always had been such a very kind neighbour!' And then fly off, through half a sentence, to her mother's old petticoat. 'Not that it was such a very old petticoat either – for still it would last a great while – and, indeed, she must thankfully say that their petticoats were all very strong.'[29]

Austen meets *The Corsair*

Petticoats are in fact a favourite form of Austenian bathos and were the subject of a humorous reference in the last sentence of Jane's last-known letter, where she described a captain's wife and sister as 'all good humour and obligingness, and I hope (since the fashion allows it) with rather longer petticoats than last year'.[30] When her own petticoat occurs alongside *The Corsair* in a letter to Cassandra, therefore, it is unlikely to be by accident: 'Do not be angry with me for beginning another Letter to you. I have read the Corsair, mended my petticoat, & have nothing else to do.'[31] In a neat reversal of Horace Walpole's denomination of Mary Wollstonecraft as 'That hyena in petticoats', the feminine, humdrum petticoat here is nicely calculated to mock and deflate the Corsair's overwrought exoticism and strident masculinity:

But who that CHIEF? his name on every shore
Is famed and feared – they ask and know no more.
With these he mingles not but to command; . . .
'Steer to that shore!' – they sail. 'Do this!' – 'tis done.
'Now form and follow me!' – the spoil is won.
Thus prompt his accents and his actions still,
And all obey and few inquire his will;
To such, brief answer and contemptuous eye
Convey reproof, nor further deign reply.

(*The Corsair* 1.61–3, 77–82)[32]

Byron's *Corsair* was the outstanding literary success of 1814: the first edition sold 10,000 copies on the day of publication on 1 February ('a thing perfectly unprecedented', as Murray commented).[33] By 18 February it had reached its fifth edition, and there were two further issues between March and December, so it would certainly not have been difficult for the Austens to obtain a copy of it by 5 March, although they may have had to pay the hefty price of five shillings and sixpence if they bought it themselves.[34] It was also a *succès de scandale*, since the first edition also included Byron's controversial 'Lines to a Lady Weeping' (which were highly critical of the Prince Regent and had originally been printed anonymously in the *Morning Chronicle* in 1812), thus confirming that they were by Byron and causing an outcry against him in the Tory press. In response to this, Murray removed the 'Lines' from the second edition of *The Corsair* volume without consulting Byron, who reacted furiously to this 'injudicious suppression' because it looked as if he was trying to back down from his criticism of the Regent, and Murray did republish the 'Lines' in the fourth and subsequent editions.[35] Austen makes no mention of this short but notorious eight-line poem, but (if her edition of *The Corsair* volume was one which included the 'Lines') she would not have disapproved. Less than a year earlier she had depicted herself in no uncertain terms as someone who would support the Regent's estranged wife 'because she *is* a Woman, & because I hate her Husband'.[36]

In Byron's hands, not unexpectedly, the petticoat becomes sexualized as well as gendered. 'The reading or non-reading a book – will never keep down a single petticoat', he claimed, while he suspected Maria Edgeworth of writing with 'a *pencil* under her petticoat'.[37] In *Don Juan* canto 2 Juan's cross-dressing in the harem is prefigured when Haidee and Zoe give 'a petticoat apiece' to keep him warm on the beach.[38] Later '"Petticoat influence" is a great reproach', as the narrator points out in *Don Juan*, 'Which even those who obey would fain be thought / To fly from': although he too uses the garment for mock-heroic purposes:

> I for one venerate a petticoat –
> A garment of a mystical sublimity,
> No matter whether russet, silk, or dimity.

> (*Don Juan* 14. 201–3, 206–8)[39]

Perhaps, however, Byron was not aware that he too had worn a petticoat. When he described the 'Albanian' costume in which he had posed for the famous Thomas Phillips portrait in 1813–14 (Figure 2, page 5) he referred to the lower garment as a 'Camesa or *kilt*', but it was rather differently characterized by Sir Charles Eliot, a diplomat who visited the area in the 1880s:

Printed by Tho.'Stothard R.A.   Engraved by W.Finden.

Figure 4 When illustrating *The Gaiour* in 1814, Thomas Stothard dressed the protagonist in the costume shown in the 'Albanian' portrait of Byron, with its long *fustanella* or petticoat. Engraving by William Finden, 1814. The John Murray Collection, London.

> The inhabitants of the country around Janina and Preveza . . . can at once be distinguished by their costume, the *fustanella*, a voluminous white petticoat, reaching to the knees and similar to that worn by a ballet-dancer . . . but its effeminate appearance is somewhat lessened by the custom which prescribes that it must always be soiled and dusty, 'clean petticoat' being a term of reproach implying sloth and cowardice.[40]

When Byron passed on his 'Arnaout garments', including the 'petticoat', to his friend Margaret Mercer Elphinstone for her to wear at a masquerade in 1814, he was at pains to reassure her that they *were* clean and that they had been worn very little by him 'except for half an hour to Phillips'.[41]

'Napoleon's Farewell'

At some point after July 1815 Austen carefully transcribed in her best copperplate handwriting a poem by Byron about Napoleon – one of only five transcriptions of other people's verse that we know her to have made.[42] Byron's three-stanza work, 'Napoleon's Farewell', was written on 25 July: the day after HMS *Bellerophon*, with the captive former emperor aboard, entered British waters. Presented in Napoleon's voice as he faces exile for a second time, it was first published anonymously on 30 July in *The Examiner*, and both the poet and the radical editor, Leigh Hunt, made efforts to distance themselves from sharing the emperor's imagined sentiments. Byron added 'From the French' as a (spurious) subtitle, while Hunt noted: 'We need scarcely remind our readers that there are points in these spirited lines, with which our opinions do not accord; and, indeed, the author himself has told us that he rather adapted them to what he considered the speaker's feelings than his own.'[43]

Austen retitled her version 'Lines of Lord Byron, in the Character of Buonaparté', and if, as seems likely, she copied the poem from the untitled and anonymous version published in *The Examiner* on 30 July 1815, her identification of Byron's authorship seems to indicate that she could recognize his style.[44] It is perhaps surprising to find Austen reading *The Examiner*, which was a radical weekly opposed to the demonizing of Napoleon; surprisingly too, some of the changes she made present Napoleon as more sympathetic and defiant than in Byron's original.[45] Her alterations are small: for example, Byron's 'gloom of my glory' is replaced with 'bloom of my glory' in the opening line; 'name' and 'fame' are switched at the end of the second and fourth lines, and Byron's 'Yet, yet, I may baffle the hosts that surround us' becomes (with, as Sarah Wootton points out, echoes of Shakespeare's *Henry V*) 'Once more may I vanquish the foes that surround us', while the last stanza expresses the hope that 'Victory' rather than 'Liberty' may rally again in France. Taken together, these small changes intensify the sympathetic presentation of Napoleon as still a martial, charismatic and persuasive figure, at a time when his reputation was at its lowest ebb. In 1813 Austen had told Cassandra that she thought *Pride and Prejudice* was 'rather too light & bright and sparkling', and joked that it needed to be 'stretched out here & there' with 'something unconnected with the story', such as 'an Essay on Writing, a critique on Walter Scott, or the history of Buonaparté'.[46] As far as we know she never wrote such a history, although Napoleon was a crucial figure in shaping her life (and especially the careers of her naval brothers Francis and Charles) as well as providing contemporary contexts for her writing such as the militia officers in *Pride and Prejudice* and the naval background of *Persuasion*. Perhaps, however, if she *had* written such a history, it might have expressed more admiration for the Emperor than even Byron did.

Byron at other times certainly identified himself with aspects of Napoleon, describing himself as 'The grand Napoleon of the realms of rhyme' in an ironic reference to his and the emperor's parallel falls from grace in 1815–16.[47] In 1816 the cartoonist George Cruikshank, too, made comparisons between Byron and Napoleon, presenting Byron with a Napoleonic profile, knee-breeches and a pot belly as he pictured the poet going into exile by boat (like the emperor, but also with plentiful stocks of champagne and several amorous actresses to keep him company).

Napoleon did indeed become distinctly paunchy as he grew older: another circumstance that would have undermined his heroic stature in both Austen's and Byron's eyes, since the importance of body image and the inelegance of being fat were a matter on which they would have agreed, although they came to it from quite different standpoints. Byron's personal weight problems are well known, and the extent to which they had oppressed him all his life is clear from what he told Dr Julius Millingen in Cephalonia in 1823: 'I especially dread, in this world, two things, to which I have reason to believe I am equally predisposed – growing fat and growing mad; and it would be difficult for me to decide, were I forced to make a choice, which of these conditions I would choose in preference.'[48] Also well known are his struggles as a teenager and later to manage his weight through violent exercise (swimming, boxing, fencing, playing cricket with seven overcoats on), hot baths and bizarre dieting. He also chewed tobacco to keep the hunger pangs away and took vinegar and dangerous laxatives and other drugs which undermined his digestive system. There have been many studies interpreting this behaviour from the biographical, literary, medical and psychological points of view, with the suggestion that he became anorexic and/or developed bulimia nervosa, and there is no doubt that he hated being fat – and also that for much of his life he did in fact manage to keep the superfluous weight at bay.

This was not a personal problem for Austen. Her nephew James Edward Austen-Leigh described her figure as 'rather tall and slender', and a neighbour who knew her at Chawton called her 'a tall thin spare person, with very high cheek bones'. Jane's silk pelisse coat, now in the Hampshire County Archives, suggests that she was very slim and between five foot six inches and five foot eight inches (1.68 m and 1.73 m) tall: perhaps nearly as tall as Byron, who described his own height as five foot eight and a half inches.[49]

Judgements about body weight at this time would have been influenced by contemporary pseudo-scientific theories such as Johann Kaspar Lavater's 'phrenology' which claimed to be able to read character through the shape

Figure 5 George Cruikshank's 1816 cartoon made a pot-bellied Byron resemble Napoleon, going into exile by boat like the emperor (but with plentiful stocks of champagne and amorous actresses to keep him company). Engraving with watercolour (1816). © The Trustees of the British Museum, London. All rights reserved.

of facial and bodily features. The obesity of the Prince Regent was notorious, and his ever-growing corpulence certainly highlighted the issue of his self-indulgence, carelessness and laziness as a monarch. In *Don Juan* canto 8 (1823) Byron described how 'Though Ireland starve, great George weighs twenty stone', but his original draft had read 'forty stone'.[50] At a time when not only the Irish but also many people in England were far more likely to be too thin than overweight, 'fat' did not have quite the automatically pejorative meaning it has today, but nevertheless it is interesting to note how often Austen uses the adjective to imply stupidity or to register her disdain. Chapter 2 mentions how 'some Fat Woman' is her conception of a procuress or madam; while at a ball in 1800 she was disturbed by 'all the fat girls with long noses'.[51] Her most egregious use of fatness as a sign of absurdity is in *Persuasion*, where we hear of Mrs Musgrove's 'large fat sighings' over the death of her 'very troublesome, hopeless son', 'whom alive nobody had cared for'.[52] Anne's 'slender form, and pensive face' are contrasted with Mrs Musgrove's 'comfortable, substantial size, infinitely more fitted by nature to express good cheer and good humour, than tenderness and sentiment'.

Figure 6 'He went into the bath to boil off his Fat, /And when he was there, Bo'sen worried a Cat', from *The Wonderful History of Lord Byron and His Dog* (1807). Byron's attempts to lose weight and the exploits of his Newfoundland dog Boatswain (Bo'sen) were affectionately recorded by Elizabeth Pigot, his friend and neighbour in Southwell, Nottinghamshire. The Harry Ransom Humanities Research Center, The University of Texas at Austin.

'Unbecoming conjunctions'

In the next sentence the narrator seems to offer to correct her own bias: 'Personal size and mental sorrow have certainly no necessary proportions. A large bulky figure has as good a right to be in deep affliction, as the most graceful set of limbs in the world.' But then she decides to reiterate it anyway: 'But, fair or not fair, there are unbecoming conjunctions, which reason will patronize in vain – which taste cannot tolerate – which ridicule will seize.'[53] As Peter Sabor notes, the comic treatment of ugliness and physical deformity is a recurring feature of Austen's juvenilia and of her correspondence, and here it boldly enters her literary work as well. This is a long way from Henry Austen's 1817 eulogy for his sister: 'Faultless herself, as nearly as human nature can be, she always sought, in the faults of others, something to excuse, to forgive or forget. Where extenuation was impossible, she had a sure refuge in silence. She never uttered either a hasty, a silly, or a severe expression.'[54]

As no doubt Austen noticed, temperance, abstemiousness and vegetarianism are a notable source of the Corsair's image of power:

Ne'er for his lip the purpling cup they fill,
That goblet passes him untasted still –

And for his fare – the rudest of his crew
Would that, in turn, have passed untasted too;
Earth's coarsest bread, the garden's homeliest roots,
And scarce the summer luxury of fruits,
His short repast in humbleness supply
With all a hermit's board would scarce deny.
But while he shuns the grosser joys of sense,
His mind seems nourished by that abstinence.

(*The Corsair* 1.66–76)[55]

Likewise, Byron managed to present a slim and pale appearance of himself in all the portraits that were made of him during Austen's lifetime, and the first that show him looking overweight date from the early 1820s when Leigh Hunt commented, 'I hardly knew him, he was grown so fat.'[56] If, however, Austen had known about the discrepancy between the chubby poet and his glamorous appearance in frontispiece images, this might well have provided another topic for her satirical treatment of his verse.

'Letter to Lord Byron'

When W. H. Auden was packing for his visit to Iceland in 1936, he searched for reading matter to counteract the reputed humourlessness of the Icelanders and the 'unreliable and chilly' climate. 'So looking round for something light and easy,' he told Byron, 'I pounced on you as warm and civilisé.'[57] *Don Juan* therefore accompanied Auden on the trip, and Byron became the addressee of the verse 'Letter to Lord Byron' in Auden's and Louis MacNeice's *Letters from Iceland* (1937). Relishing *Don Juan*'s combination of wit, narrative and conversational style, its sharp commentary on contemporary people and politics and its dazzling use of rhyme, Auden attempted a response in similar kind, presented in 'rhyme royal' – essentially a seven-line version of Byron's *ottava rima* stanzas.

I have at the age of twenty-nine
Just read *Don Juan* and I found it fine.
I read it on the boat to Reykjavik,
Except when eating or asleep or feeling sick.

('Letter to Lord Byron' 1.18–21)[58]

There was however, competition for Byron from 'one other author in my pack', since Auden had also brought along an Austen novel (he does not tell us which) for the Iceland trip.

> For some time I debated which to write to.
> Which would least likely send my letter back?
> But I decided I'd give a fright to
> Jane Austen if I wrote when I'd no right to,
> And share in her contempt the dreadful fates
> Of Crawford, Musgrove, and of Mr. Yates. . . .
>
> She was not an unshockable blue-stocking;
> If shades remain the characters they were,
> No doubt she still considers you as shocking.
> But tell Jane Austen, that is if you dare,
> How much her novels are beloved down here.
> She wrote them for posterity, she said;
> 'Twas rash, but by posterity she's read. . . .
>
> You could not shock her more than she shocks me;
> Beside her Joyce seems innocent as grass.
> It makes me most uncomfortable to see
> An English spinster of the middle-class
> Describe the amorous effects of 'brass',
> Reveal so frankly and with such sobriety
> The economic basis of society.
>
> ('Letter to Lord Byron' 1.141–7, 1.155–61 and 1.57–63)[59]

Auden's characterization of Austen was a response to Kipling's 1920s presentation of 'The Janeites' as essentially an escapist homosocial Austen fan-club, branded 'Austenolatry' by Leslie Stephen.[60] It anticipated D. W. Harding's 1940 denunciation of this kind of reading of her in his *Regulated Hatred and Other Essays on Jane Austen*: Austen was, Harding said, 'a literary classic of the society which attitudes like hers, held widely enough, would undermine'.[61] Auden viewed both Byron and Austen as at their best in humorous rather than 'Romantic' writing, and in a 1966 critique in the *New York Review* he distinguished comedy from satire in a way that characterized both Austen and Byron as essentially comic rather than satirical:

The goal of satire is reform, the goal of comedy acceptance. . . . Satire is angry and optimistic – it believes that the evil it attacks can be abolished: Comedy is good-tempered and pessimistic – it believes that, however much we may wish we could, we cannot change human nature, and must make the best of a bad job.[62]

The Iceland 'Letter' seems to have made Auden the first literary critic to compare and contrast Austen's and Byron's writings and personalities at any length and to connect them with his own period, reflecting on how time had changed them both. Several other critics have since helped to build up this tradition, giving detailed literary and biographical consideration to aspects of Austen's and Byron's relations, including Rachel M. Brownstein, William Deresiewicz, Doucet Devin Fischer, Susan Allen Ford, Caroline Franklin, Peter W. Graham, Jonathan Gross, Robert Morrison and Sarah Wootton; and the present study is much indebted to them. Auden assumed that Austen would have found Byron 'shocking', and although that does not appear in her critique of Byron's work up to 1816, perhaps she might indeed have been 'shocked' by *Don Juan* had she lived to read it. Byron had the advantage of having read or 'looked into' perhaps all of Austen's novels other than *Mansfield Park*, and we have to assume that his silence about them meant that he did not admire them enough to single them out (as he did Burney's novels) as exceptional. By 1937 Auden had already noted that 'posterity' was reading more Austen than Byron, and he had formed the opinion that the novel was a 'higher art than poetry altogether', implying 'finer character and faculties'. Now, nearly another century later, in the year of Byron's bicentenary, it is Byron who might be 'shocked' by the still faster growth of Austen's and the novel's reputation since Auden's day, and he would surely be taken aback to find that he had so completely missed the significance of the contemporary writer, and the genre, whose fame has overtaken his own.

Notes

1. *BLJ* 3.160, to Annabella Milbanke, 10 November 1813. *The Giaour* 189–90 and 457–8, *LBCPW* 3.46 and 3.52. O'Connell 141.

2. *Persuasion* vol. 1, chap. 11, 109.

3. *S&S* vol. 1, chap. 10, 57. *MP* vol. 1, chap. 9, 100.

4. *JAL* 277, to Anna Austen, 28 September 1814.

5. *Sanditon* chapter 7, Austen ed. Todd and Bree 174. *The Corsair* 1.1: "'O'er the glad waters of the dark blue sea'", *LBCPW* 3.150.

6. Kirkham 145.

7. See *Hampshire Chronicle* 22 and 29 April and *Hampshire Telegraph* 15 and 22 April 1816. Le Faye (2002) 108 points out that 'London papers could be sent down to the country, and it was a generous kindness on the part of the subscriber to pass on his paper to the neighbours when he had finished with it. It seems that Mr Holder at Ashe Park gave his to the Austens at Steventon'.

8. *Sanditon* chapter 7, Austen ed. Todd and Bree, 175–6.

9. *LBCPW* 3.214.

10. Knox-Shaw 62–6.

11. *Persuasion* vol. 1, chap. 12, 118. There seems to be an even stronger echo here with Byron's 'Stanzas for Music' (lines 1–2) written in May 1814, although Austen cannot have known them because they were not published until 1827: 'I speak not – I trace not – I breathe not thy name;/There is grief in the sound – there were guilt in the fame', *LBCPW* 3.269.

12. *The Corsair* 3.696, *LBCPW* 3.204.

13. Barry 39, Fischer 71.

14. Murray ed. Nicholson 149–50, Cochran (2009).

15. Murray ed. Nicholson 149.

16. Gilson 69.

17. Kenyon Jones (2014) 240, 252.

18. Murray ed. Nicholson 246.

19. *BLJ* 6.11, to John Murray, 20 February 1818.

20. *DJ* 1.1545–52, *LBCPW* 5.71.

21. Hobhouse *Recollections* vol. 1, 167, October 31 [1814, at Bowood House]: 'Lord and Lady Boringdon came late at night. My lady is suspected of having written the two novels "*Pride and Prejudice*" and "*Sense and Sensibility*"'. Hobhouse later added a corrective note, 'By Miss Austen'. Morley wrote several novels, including *The Flying Burgomaster* (1832), *The Royal Intellectual Bazaar* (1832), and *The Man Without a Name* (1852). Caplan (1998) 72.

22. Viveash (1995) 32.

23. *JAFR* 196.

24. Cochran (2009) 1.

25. Cochran (2009) 21.

26. *BLJ* 8.145, to John Murray, 29 June 1821.

27. Lockhart 20–31.

28. *Beppo* 725–44, *LBCPW* 4.157–8.

29. *Emma* vol. 2, chap. 8, 243.

30. *JAL* 343, to [?]Frances Tilson, [?]28/29 May 1817.

31. *JAL* 257, to Cassandra Austen, 5–8 March 1814.

32. Walpole 4.565: letter to Hannah More, 26 January 1795. *The Corsair* 1.61–3, 77–82, *LBCPW* 3.152–3.

33. Murray to Byron, 2 February 1814, Murray ed. Nicholson 72.

34. *LBCPW* 3.444–5. Hobhouse diary, 18 February 1814.

35. O'Connell 127–8.

36. *JAL* 208, to Martha Lloyd, 16 February 1813.

37. *BLJ* 6.237, to Richard Hoppner, 29 October 1819. *BLJ* 7.217, to John Murray, 4 November 1820.

38. *LBCPW* 5.130.

39. *LBCPW* 5.566.

40. Eliot 359.

41. *BLJ* 4.113, to Miss Mercer Elphinstone, 3 May 1814.

42. Austen, Jane, University of Southampton, Special Collections.

43. Leigh Hunt, *Examiner,* 30 July 1815.

44. Southam (2000) 312.

45. Wootton (2016) 36–7.

46. *JAL* 203, to Cassandra Austen, 4 February 1813.

47. *DJ* 11.440, *LBCPW* 5.482.

48. Millingen 8.

49. Davidson 218. *BLJ* 3.251, *Journal,* 17 March 1814.

50. *DJ* 8.1008 and footnote, *LBCPW* 5.403.

51. *JAL* 63, to Cassandra Austen, 20–21 November 1800.

52. *Persuasion* vol. 1, chap. 8, 73–4.

53. *Persuasion* vol. 1, chap. 8, 74.

54. Henry Austen in Austen-Leigh ed. Sutherland 139.

55. *The Corsair* 1.66–76, *LBCPW* 3.152–3.

56. Bond and Kenyon Jones 99.

57. Auden (1937/1966, np) 40, 41–2.

58. Auden (1937/1966, np) 1.18–21.

59. Auden (1937/1966, np) 1.141–7; 1.155–61 and 1.57–63.

60. Stephen 324.

61. Harding 5–6.

62. Auden (1966).

CHAPTER 2
LONDON
'DISSIPATION & VICE'

Jane Austen and George Gordon Byron made their first appearances in London at almost the same place and time. Byron was born in London on 22 January 1788, in a five-storey townhouse at 16 Holles Street, just off Oxford Street, where the John Lewis department store now stands.[1] Jane Austen first came to the metropolis in July 1788 at the age of twelve, with her parents and her sister Cassandra, and visited her aunt Philadelphia Hancock and her cousin Eliza de Feuillide in Orchard Street, also just off Oxford Street, where Selfridges' store now presides.[2]

These locations are only a few hundred yards apart, but the geographical coincidence is not necessarily surprising, since 'polite' London in the late eighteenth and early nineteenth centuries was a small place, and the subtle social class distinctions between the Austens and the Byrons at this stage were of just the kind that Austen delighted in anatomizing in her novels. In 1788 little George Gordon Byron had no expectation of becoming Lord Byron: the title was held by his great-uncle, but there were two other lives in between. By the time he was ten years old in 1798, however, his great-uncle, his cousin and his father were all dead, and he inherited the barony of Byron of Rochdale, becoming the sixth baron Byron, owner of the ancient, former monastic, buildings and extensive though impoverished estate of Newstead Abbey in Nottinghamshire, as well as land in Lancashire and Norfolk. Byron's mother Catherine Gordon Byron was an heiress: the thirteenth laird in her own right of the Gight estate near Aberdeen, who at the time of her marriage in 1785 had been 'worth £25,000', as *Sense and Sensibility*'s John Dashwood might have put it. By the time of her son's birth, however, three years into her marriage to the handsome but spendthrift and deeply unreliable 'Mad Jack' Byron (a former Captain in the Coldstream Guards) she was already beginning to suffer severely from his extravagance. Gight Castle and estate had been sold in 1787 for £17,880, but little remained of the proceeds.[3] Although Captain Byron was in London when his son was born, he had to lie low to avoid the creditors who were pursuing him for his large debts. In September 1790 he fled to France to avoid the bailiffs, and he died there in 1791 when little George was three.[4]

Despite their already mounting debts, the Byrons had hired a doctor, a nurse and a male midwife or *accoucheur* to attend the birth of their son. The baby was born with a 'caul' (i.e. still inside the amniotic sac): a rare but generally harmless occurrence which was then believed to mean that the child was destined for greatness. Less auspicious was the baby's badly deformed right foot, also present at birth: the cause of much misery for Byron throughout his life. The famous surgeon John Hunter was called in, but (despite his large fees) could not provide a remedy. Finances and circumstances deteriorated, and eighteen months later mother and son had 'not at present a farthing nor know where to get one', and were living in very modest lodgings in Aberdeen.[5] Mrs Byron claimed that her income at this point was £150 a year: much less than the one hundred shillings a week (£260 a year) that William St Clair sets as the 'standard of gentility' for this period.[6] Their financial affairs did improve somewhat later, and they were able to move to better premises on Aberdeen's Broad Street.[7]

Here young Byron was brought up, attending Aberdeen Grammar School until the age of ten, when he became the sixth lord Byron and was transported south to Nottinghamshire. As 'an only son left with an only mother', the relationship between the young lord and his mother was difficult at the best of times, and sometimes impossible.[8] Mrs Byron was practical, determined and lively, but ill-educated, rather uncouth, often foolish, and highly irascible, alternately spoiling and raging against her son, and as Byron grew up he began to spend as much time away from her as he could. When he reached his majority at the age of twenty-one he succeeded to the rights and responsibilities of a peer of the realm, becoming part of a highly exclusive group of some 300 men entitled to take part in the government of the country as members of the House of Lords. This was a responsibility he took seriously as a teenager and a young man, before becoming disillusioned in his mid-twenties, declaring that he was 'not made for what you call a politician', and turning more decidedly to the poetry which arguably gave him a more influential liberal or radical voice than any political career is likely to have done.[9]

'Very Grand & very fine & very Large'

Byron was lucky to inherit his barony, since he began life only a little more closely connected to the nobility than Jane Austen's parents. Jane's mother,

Cassandra Austen née Leigh, had aristocratic forebears. Her grandmother was the sister of the first duke of Chandos, Handel's patron, and it was through this connection that the unusual name Cassandra came into the family.[10] Her first cousin the Reverend Thomas Leigh inherited Stoneleigh Abbey, Warwickshire, in 1806, and when she and Jane visited the ancient house they found that 'every thing is very Grand & very fine & very Large' – so large indeed that Mrs Austen suggested 'setting up directing Posts at the Angles' of the building so that visitors could find their way around.[11] The future owner of Stoneleigh, their cousin, the fifteen-year-old Chandos Leigh, was probably also present during this visit, and he provides another link between the Austens and Byron, since at that point he was one of Byron's close friends at Harrow School, and ten years later was among those who dined with Byron on the night before he left London for good on 23 April 1816. Jane's father, the Reverend George Austen, was the grandson of a baronet on his mother's side, and it was through his family that the fortunes of Jane's brother Edward, and those of his siblings too, were transformed in 1783 when Edward was adopted by his third cousin, the very wealthy Thomas Knight, and his wife Elizabeth. In 1798 the extensive Knight estates in Kent and Hampshire were transferred to Edward, including the large Palladian mansion of Godmersham and the fine Elizabethan house at Chawton, near the cottage which was to be Jane's final home. Edward's annual income from rents for land later rose to at least £8,000 a year – and overall was comparable with Darcy's 'ten thousand a year' which so excites Meryton.[12] It was thanks to this almost fairy-tale occurrence, and the prosperity it brought to the whole family, that Jane was able to settle comfortably at Chawton Cottage in 1809 with her mother, her sister and her sister-in-law's sister Martha Lloyd, and to become a writer in earnest. Edward's good fortune provided her with the opportunity to experience life not only as the daughter of a moderately circumstanced country clergyman but also as the sister of a very wealthy landowner, appreciating the contrast between the 'Elegance & Ease & Luxury' of Edward's establishment and the 'Vulgar Economy' under which (she joked) she and her mother and sister lived.[13] This ability to observe the manners of a wide range of different classes gave her an acute understanding and knowledge of wealth and status in early-nineteenth-century England and enabled her scrutinize the class structure of her world and 'to expose the economic basis of social behaviour with an ironic smile' in a way that has been described as making her 'in a sense a Marxist before Marx'.[14]

Class and respectability

Byron's inheritance of his barony in 1798 also translated him from relative poverty to the possibility of great wealth, but at the time of his birth the difference between the Byrons and the Austens was not so much one of social class as of attitude, belief, character and demeanour. The Austens had good reason to consider themselves more respectable than the Byrons, whose close relations included two separated or divorced women: Byron's great-aunt Isabella, as mentioned in the Introduction, had parted from her second husband Sir William Musgrave, while Byron's father, Captain John Byron, had eloped with the wife of the Marquess of Carmarthen, whom she divorced in 1779 in order to marry the Captain (see family tree, pages xviii–xix). Byron's great-uncle, the fifth baron Byron, was known as the 'Wicked Lord', having killed his neighbour in a duel. No such overt scandal stained the Austen family's reputation, although Jane's aunt Philadelphia was certainly suspected among the British community in India of having had an affair with the controversial Warren Hastings, later Governor-General of India, who may have been the father of her daughter, Jane's cousin Eliza.[15] The Austens would also have considered themselves the more cultivated family, since both parents came from well-educated backgrounds with close links to the University of Oxford, enabling Jane's father and two of her brothers to gain degrees there, while Byron was the first of his immediate family to graduate from Cambridge. Most significant of all, the Austens were both from respected clergy families, and although Mr Austen was Rector only of two small Hampshire country parishes, with fewer than 300 parishioners and an annual income of not more than a few hundred pounds, he and his wife raised five exceptionally successful sons, supported their disabled son (see Chapter 4), and provided the literary and cultural capital that enabled their younger daughter to express her genius.[16]

One aspect of this genius was Austen's ability to delineate the subtle and fascinating distinctions which operated within classes, ranks and families as well as between them, and one of the techniques she used to do this was a meticulous placing of her characters in precise locations, including the fashionable and not-so-fashionable streets of the cities of Bath and London. In *Pride and Prejudice* there is a yawning social divide between the Bingleys' residence with the Hursts in Grosvenor Street, in the fashionable West End district of Mayfair, and the Gracechurch Street home of Elizabeth's uncle and aunt the Gardiners, 'near Cheapside', some 3 miles to the east, in the heart of the trading and manufacturing district of the City of London, among its fumes, smells and noise.[17] The Bingley sisters indulge in much mockery of the Gardiners' location and background – overdoing the derision because they are aware, as the narrator tells us, that 'their brother's fortune and their own had been acquired by trade' in the north of England.[18]

In *Sense and Sensibility* the social shadings are more subtle, and the London residences of the various parts of the extended Jennings/Middleton/Dashwood/Ferrars family – all in the West End close to Oxford Street – are carefully selected to give readers additional information about each household. London in Austen's and Byron's time was a metropolis of over a million inhabitants, but the world of the aristocracy and the gentry formed a small and tightly knit section within this. London was rapidly expanding in every direction, but particularly north-westward, as successive generations of noble families disposed of their land for building fashionable houses around three major east-west roads.[19] The area south of Piccadilly around St James's Palace had been established since the early eighteenth century when the royal court moved there after the destruction of Whitehall Palace by fire in 1698. This was followed by the development of Mayfair, northward from Piccadilly to Oxford Street, and then again by the expansion of Marylebone further to the north, between Oxford Street and 'The New Road' (now the Euston/Marylebone Road). The New Road had been built in 1750 and was given respectability during the Regency period by the re-creation of Marylebone Park (used for pasturing cows) as Regent's Park, soon to be surrounded by John Nash's elegant white stuccoed mansions for the upper classes.

Sense, sensibility and affluence

Sense and Sensibility's Mrs Jennings owns her own house 'handsome and handsomely fitted up' and acquired 'since the death of her husband who had traded with success in a less elegant part of the town'.[20] This is north of Oxford Street in Berkeley Street (today's Fitzhardinge Street) near Portman Square, just around the corner from where the Austens visited the Hancocks in 1788. Portman Square and nearby Manchester Square were built for the nobility and the gentry between the 1760s and the 1780s, but during Austen's lifetime the mercantile, professional and commercial classes began to be affluent enough to move in.[21] Austen has the John Dashwoods rent a house a little further east in Harley Street: a newer and very fashionable area, known to Austen because Lady Burrell, a close friend of her cousin

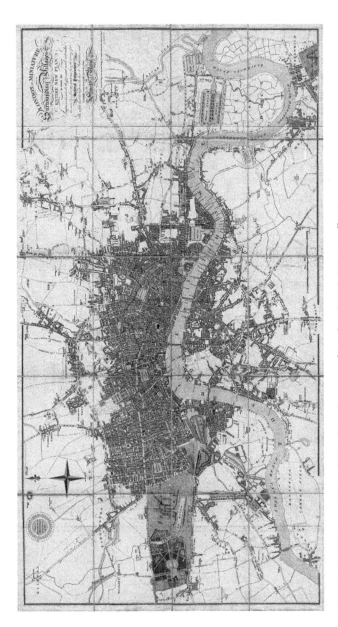

Figure 7 *London in Miniature*, Edward Mogg's pocket map of London (1806). Private collection.

Eliza, lived there.[22] The adjacent street, Wimpole Street, is *Mansfield Park*'s Mary Crawford's epitome of a desirable London address, while Lady Susan lives close by at 10 Wigmore Street.[23] The snobbish Mrs Ferrars; Mrs Jennings's daughter Mrs Palmer and son-in-law Mr Palmer (who aspires to be a Member of Parliament), and Sir John and Lady Middleton, all live in Mayfair, south of Oxford Street, with Mrs Ferrars owning her own house in Park Street (presumably at the southern end, overlooking Hyde Park). The Palmers have a rented house nearby in fashionable Hanover Square, and the Middletons rent further to the east in the older Conduit Street. Austen may have chosen this location for them because she wanted to place them near to London's most fashionable shopping thoroughfare, Bond Street, where Willoughby lives: a symbol of his expensive tastes. It was also close to Gray's, the then well-known jeweller's emporium in Sackville Street, where the egregious dandy Robert Ferrars is to be found 'giving orders for a toothpick-case for himself . . . examining and debating for a quarter of an hour over every toothpick-case in the shop'.[24]

Austen had relatively little experience of London compared with Bath, where she had lived for some five years, and she of course knew the capital far less well than Steventon and Chawton, the Hampshire villages where she spent most of her life. 'Such a spot is the delight of my life', she told her niece Anna, advising her as a would-be novelist that '3 or 4 Families in a Country Village is the very thing to work on', and later describing her own novels as 'pictures of domestic Life in Country Villages'.[25] But she was evidently also fascinated by the capital, and when she needed to understand its minutiae she could always turn to her London-dwelling brother Henry, who was based there from 1801, first as an army agent (the middleman between the government's Paymaster General and the regimental paymaster) and then a banker with a fine sense of where to locate his homes and businesses for maximum social and financial benefit. Even more useful was her cousin Eliza, who had many years' experience of living in fashionable parts of London, both before and after her marriage in France in 1781 to Jean-François Capot de Feuillide, known as the Comte de Feuillide. He was guillotined during the French Revolution in 1794, and in 1797 Eliza became Jane's sister-in-law as well as her cousin, when on 31 December she married Henry Austen in Marylebone Parish Church (where Byron had been baptized on 29 February 1788). By 1801 Mr and Mrs Henry Austen were grandly housed, with their French chef Monsieur Halavent, at 24 Upper Berkeley Street, just across Portman Square from where Austen imagined Mrs Jennings's residence. Eliza was an expert on

London locations and had the income to enable her to live in the ones that appealed to her, thanks to a gift of £10,000 from her godfather (or, possibly, her unacknowledged father) Warren Hastings. With the benefit of Eliza's sensitive social antennae and wide understanding of the capital, Austen in her novels was able to treat London almost like a village, and to deploy the nuances of the capital's geography in order to place her '3 or 4 Families' financially, socially and even morally in exactly the right location.

'A Harlot's Progress'

In 1788, Jane had been described, on her way to her first London visit, by her cousin Philadelphia (Philly) Walter in not very flattering terms: 'very like her brother Henry, not at all pretty & very prim, unlike a girl of twelve'; 'whimsical & affected'.[26] Jane had by this time, however, already started experimenting with some of her first fiction and, as in her teens she grew from an ugly duckling into something of a swan, she is likely to have made several more visits to London before the next record of her presence there when she was twenty. In August 1796 she stayed with her brothers in Cork Street, Mayfair, probably at the house of Benjamin Langlois, former MP and Under-Secretary of State, the uncle of an Austen family friend.[27] Cork Street was just east of New Bond Street and close to the jewellers frequented by Robert Ferrars. 'Here I am once more in this Scene of Dissipation & vice', Jane announced to Cassandra, joking that 'I begin already to find my morals corrupted'.[28]

The idea of London's 'Dissipation & vice' had already made a comic appearance in 'Love and Freindship' ([*sic*] dated 1790) – 'Beware of the insipid vanities and idle Dissipations of the Metropolis of England' – and it comes up in another letter to Cassandra in September 1796, when Jane jokingly calls herself a 'prodigal Daughter' and imagines what might happen to her if the people she was due to visit in Greenwich were not at home.[29] 'I should inevitably fall a Sacrifice to the arts of some Fat Woman who would make me drunk with Small Beer', she suggests.[30] She was probably thinking of the first of William Hogarth's famous series of prints, *A Harlot's Progress* (1732), in which an innocent country girl, just arrived in London on the York Wagon, is being enticed by a stout procuress (Figure 8).[31]

A similar figure appears in a caricature of Byron by Isaac Robert Cruikshank, 'Fashionables of 1816 taking the air in Hyde Park!', which imagines a confrontation between a heavily pregnant Lady Byron and her husband who is strolling by with a scantily clad beauty on each arm,

Figure 8 *A Harlot's Progress*, plate 1, by William Hogarth (1732). A country girl, Mary Hackabout, has arrived at the Bell Inn in London on the York Wagon and is accosted and examined by a stout procuress or madam, Mother Needham. © The Trustees of the British Museum, London. All rights reserved.

followed by a leering fat madam who is accepting money from Byron's accomplice (Figure 9).[32]

Austen's jokes about expecting to be morally corrupted by London refer to and satirize a very long cultural tradition (stretching back at least to Virgil, Hesiod and the 'Golden Age' Arcadian shepherds of classical literature) of representing rural life as simple, carefree, natural and unadulterated, but constantly in danger of being corrupted by the city as the location of vice, dirt, labour, modernity and exploitation. Raymond Williams, in *The Country and the City,* debunks as 'a myth functioning as a memory', every generation's imagination that, in their youth, the country really was pristine, until corrupted by the town, and highlights it as a major theme in the writings of Austen's and Byron's contemporary William Cobbett (1763–1835).[33] 'The working people of England were, when I was born, well fed, well clad, and each had his barrel of beer in his house', Cobbett declared as part of his nostalgic vision to return Britain to the rural world of his imagination while deploring in particular the rapid urbanization of London, which he referred to as the 'Great Wen'.[34]

Williams criticizes Austen for her class-based presentation of the country: 'What she sees across the land is a network of propertied houses

Figure 9 Isaac Robert Cruikshank's cartoon, *Fashionables of 1816 taking the air in Hyde Park!*, imagines a confrontation between the heavily pregnant Lady Byron and her husband, with an actress on each arm, followed by a fat madam who is accepting money from Byron's accomplice. © The Trustees of the British Museum, London. All rights reserved.

and families, and through the holes of this tightly drawn mesh most people are simply not seen.'[35] Both Austen and Byron, however, are clearly aware of the tradition that identifies the country as pristine until corrupted by the city (particularly perhaps because it was a staple of the English Restoration drama and eighteenth-century sentimental novels which they both enjoyed), and each of them explores, questions, mocks and challenges this idea in different ways. In a letter of November 1813, 'an inclination for the country' is ironically treated by Austen as only 'a venial fault' and a servant who made the choice to leave his London employment is described as having 'more of Cowper than of Johnson in him, fonder of Tame Hares & Blank verse than the full tide of human Existence at Charing Cross': with a reference to William Cowper's epitaphs on his pet hares, and Samuel Johnson's description of the streets around London's traditional centre, as well as his famous dictum that 'When a man is tired of London he is tired of life'.[36] Cowper features prominently in *Sense and Sensibility*; and Marianne's bitter experience of Willoughby's cruel behaviour to her in the city leads her to share her favourite poet's idea of London as a representation of Hell:

> Rank abundance breeds
> In gross and pampered cities sloth and lust,

And wantonness and gluttonous excess.
In cities, vice is hidden with most ease,
Or seen with least reproach; and virtue, taught
By frequent lapse, can hope no triumph there,
Beyond the achievement of successful flight. . . .
Such London is, by taste and wealth proclaimed
The fairest capital in all the world,
By riot and incontinence the worst.

(*The Task* 1.686–99)[37]

Northanger Abbey, however, presents a more nuanced idea of where evil may lie, and Catherine's announcement that 'something very shocking indeed will soon come out of London . . . uncommonly dreadful . . . murder and everything of the kind', turns out to be actually just the publication of a new Gothic novel, while Austen goes on to ironize such fears still further when she makes, not London or Bath, but the grand Gloucestershire country mansion Northanger Abbey, the location of General Tilney's real cruelty and Gothic behaviour towards Catherine and other women.

The making of a poet

In a teenage letter to his friend Elizabeth Pigot in 1807, Byron satirized, only half-ironically, the contrast between the small Nottinghamshire town of Southwell, where they had both lived, and the West End of London, which he was then beginning to explore in earnest. 'The Intelligence of London cannot be interesting to you who *have rusticated* all your life', he told Elizabeth,

> the annals of Routs, Riots, Balls & Boxing matches, Dowagers & demireps, Cards & Crim-con, Parliamentary Discussion, Political Details, Masquerades, Mechanics, Argyle Street Institution & Aquatic races, Love & Lotteries, Brookes's & Buonaparte, Exhibitions of pictures with Drapery, *& women without;* Statues with more *decent dresses* than their *originals,* Opera-singers & Orators, Wine, Women, Wax works, & Weathercocks, cannot accord with your *insulated* Ideas, of Decorum & other *silly expressions*, not inserted in our *Vocabulary* – Oh Southwell, Southwell, how I rejoice to have left thee.[38]

Byron's fellow-poet, friend and first biographer, Thomas Moore, described how at this period 'his time in London passed equally unmarked either by mental cultivation or refined amusement. Having no resources in private society, from his total want of friends and connexions, he was left to live loosely about town among the loungers in coffee-houses.' But Moore went on to point out the advantages, as well as the disadvantages, of this apparently 'squandered' time:

> By thus initiating him into a knowledge of the varieties of human character, by giving him an insight into the details of society, in their least artificial form, in short by mixing him up, thus early, with the world, its businesses and pleasures, his London life contributed its share in forming that wonderful combination, which his mind afterwards exhibited, of the imaginative and the practical – the heroic and the humorous – of the keenest and most dissecting views of real life, with the grandest and most spiritualized conceptions of ideal grandeur.[39]

Moore did not mention it specifically, but John Clubbe, quoting this passage, comments on how, in London, until his marriage, Byron 'had the possibility of retiring to his rooms whenever he pleased. A London life permitted the solitude he relished, and in that solitude he was stirred to creation.' 'London, in short', Clubbe concludes, 'enabled Byron to become the poet we know.'[40]

By March 1816, writing to the Scottish poet James Hogg, Byron was encouraging him to come to London and describing the capital as

> a damned place – to be sure – but the only one in the world – (at least in the English world) for fun – though I have seen parts of the Globe that I like better – still upon the whole it is the completest either to help one in feeling oneself alive – or in forgetting that one is so.[41]

This was written, however, only a few weeks before Byron himself was to leave London, and Britain, forever, in the aftermath of the breakdown of his marriage. And only a few months later, writing in canto 3 of *Childe Harold's Pilgrimage*, composed under the influence of the 'Wordsworth physic' with which he claimed his fellow-poet Shelley had been 'used to dose [him] . . . even to nausea', Byron was declaring in grand Romantic vein that 'High mountains are a feeling, and the hum / Of cities torture'.[42] But then a few years later still, by 1821, he had flipped again and become deeply critical of 'the Lakers' for their '"Babble of green fields" and of bare Nature in general'.[43]

The presentation of London in *Don Juan* (written between 1819 and 1824: several years after Byron himself had last been there) is equally complex and contradictory, mingling affection and satire. Seen through the enthusiastic eyes of the young Spaniard Juan in canto 11 as 'Freedom's chosen station', and filtered by the alternately jaundiced and nostalgic views of the narrator (which may or may not be those of Byron himself), London emerges as foggy, overpriced and immoral, but brimming with interest and 'life'.[44] And Byron relishes the complexities of class and London location just as much as Austen does: in *Beppo* 'suburban' is paired with 'vulgar' and 'dowdyish', while in *Don Juan* canto 11 the 'Groves' and 'Mounts' of the South London suburb of Kennington are satirized for being void of trees and having nothing to climb.[45] In canto 13 Lord Henry Amundeville has a grand mansion located in the tantalizingly anonymous 'Blank-Blank Square'.[46] Austen too could effectively deploy London anonymity when she chose to, and does so in her placement of *Pride and Prejudice*'s Lydia and Wickham somewhere in London during their scandalous cohabitation before they are married: 'They were in -- street', Mrs Gardiner reports to Elizabeth when Darcy succeeds in tracking them down.[47]

St James's

The last of *Sense and Sensibility*'s characters to be carefully placed by Austen in an appropriate part of town is Colonel Brandon, who has lodgings in St James's Street. This sites him close to the Royal Palace and Court of St James's, in a classic location for a well-off single man to live, with its hotels, smart hatters, hairdressers, famous gentlemen's and gambling clubs such as White's and Brooks's, the Cocoa Tree coffee house, print-shops, bookshops and cigar-merchants, and the wine- and spice-merchants Berry Brothers & Rudd (who are still trading, and whose records of the personal weighing service they offered to gentlemen including Byron and the Prince of Wales can still be consulted). Canny Henry Austen had his first office for his army agency (see Chapter 6) in Cleveland Court, very close to the Royal Palace, and later moved it to Albany, on Piccadilly, and it was in this area of St James's and the adjacent thoroughfare of Piccadilly that Byron too lived for nearly all his adult London years.[48]

As a boy, Byron went first to boarding school in Dulwich (some 7 miles south-east of central London, now a prosperous suburb) and afterwards to Harrow (some 14 miles north-west of London), and also stayed with his mother in lodgings in various London streets that would have been familiar to the Austens, including Sloane Terrace in Hans Town (1799–1801), Half Moon Street in Mayfair (Christmas 1801) and 23 George Street, off Portman Square (where in 1802 as a fourteen-year-old he borrowed a pony for a race in nearby Hyde Park).[49] Between 1803, when Mrs Byron moved to Burgage Manor in Southwell, and 1809 when he first went abroad, Byron lived a peripatetic, unfixed life, of the kind that he imagined (in more glamorous locations) for Childe Harold, alternating somewhat randomly between Harrow, Cambridge, Southwell, Newstead Abbey and London. When he was in 'the metropolis' he often stayed in hotels, such as Dorant's in Albemarle Street, Reddish's in St James's and Batt's in Jermyn Street, or in lodgings, including those of Mrs Elizabeth Massingberd at 16 Piccadilly. In late 1805 and early 1806 his landlady and her daughter acted as intermediaries with moneylenders and stood as guarantors for loans of at least £3,000 (some £300,000 in modern currency) for the seventeen-year-old Byron, who blithely assumed he would easily be able to repay them when he inherited his estate at the age of twenty-one. In fact, however, because of several different legal problems connected with his estates, the funds for repayment were not forthcoming, and the debts spiralled, causing problems that continued until the very end of his life in 1824.[50]

After his return from his first visit to Greece in 1811 Byron continued to use Dorant's and Batt's hotels, but then took longer-term lodgings at 8 St James's Street (where Lady Caroline Lamb stalked him at all hours) and then at 4 Bennet Street, off St James's. On 27 March 1814 he moved around the corner to the exclusive apartment A2 at Albany, on Piccadilly, which had formerly been the home of the royal Duke of York and Albany, and before that of Viscount and Viscountess Melbourne and their family. The mansion and garden had recently been converted into apartments for single gentlemen, and today Albany still provides exclusive central London quarters for the wealthy. From 1804 to 1807 Henry Austen based his business at 1, The Courtyard, Albany, and this became the address of the army agency of Austen & Maunde and the first London office of the country banks they partnered in Hampshire, Kent, Somerset and Derbyshire.[51] Their secret partner, the shadowy Major Charles James, who provided special access for their army agency to the nobility and links with the man who would turn out to be Henry's nemesis, Lord Moira (see Chapter 6), moved to live in one of the Albany chambers. Accompanying Byron to Albany from Bennet Street in 1814 were his valet William Fletcher (who provided a constant presence in Byron's life from his youth until his death fifteen years later) and the elderly housemaid Mrs Mule, 'the most ancient and withered of her kind'.[52] Another persistent young Byromaniac, Henrietta d'Ussières, tracked him down there in June 1814 and, while he was out, admired his writing-desk, his bookcase, his parrot and the crucifix hanging on his drawing-room wall.[53]

Just over a mile away at this date, in the reception rooms at Henry's house at 23 Hans Place, Jane could admire furnishings in a rather more nouveau-riche style, including a gilt-framed chimney glass, two lamps supported by pairs of bronze cupids and female figures, French curtains of superfine chintz cotton, five framed medallions of the royal family, and seven other portraits. Among these was the one painted in 1765 by Joshua (later Sir Joshua) Reynolds which has recently been identified as showing Jane's aunt Philadelphia Hancock, her husband Tysoe Saul Hancock, the Indian girl who became their maid and took the name Clarinda, and their three-year-old daughter, then known as Betsy but later to become the glamorous Eliza de Feuillide.[54] Also in the house was Reynolds's 1766–8 portrait of Warren Hastings which was to be listed for sale alongside that of the Hancocks in June 1817.[55] Sadly, the reason that the contents of this house are known in such detail is that they were part of the inventory of Henry's possessions to be sold after his bankruptcy in 1816.[56]

Figure 10 Painted by Joshua Reynolds in 1765, this family portrait shows Jane Austen's aunt Philadelphia Hancock, her husband Tysoe Saul Hancock, the Indian maid whom they called Clarinda and their three-year-old daughter, then known as Betsy but later to become the glamorous Eliza de Feuillide. Jane would often have seen it in Eliza's and Henry's home in London. Reproduced with the permission of bpk / Gemäldegalerie, Berlin, SMB / Jörg P. Anders.

Byron relished his apartment at Albany, but it had to be given up when he was married in January 1815, and his home for just over a year, during his disastrous marriage and until April 1816, was a large house rented from the Duchess of Devonshire at number 13 Piccadilly Terrace. This was much further west along Piccadilly than Albany and almost next door to Byron's *bête noire* the Duke of Wellington, whose residence (Apsley House) at Hyde Park Corner was known as Number 1 London, marking it as the place where the capital's westward boundary then stood.

Bloomsbury

As a child and before he went abroad, Byron had also often stayed with the family of the lawyer John Hanson, who was Byron's guardian or trustee during his minority and whose rising prosperity was mirrored first by his acquisition of a house in semi-rural Old Brompton as well as premises in Chancery Lane, and then a house in Bloomsbury Square, where the ill-fated marriage of Hanson's daughter to the Earl of Portsmouth, described in Chapter 4, took place. This area, east of Marylebone near the British Museum, had been developed as early as the 1660s but was now emerging as a location for well-off professionals: particularly (given its proximity to the Inns of Court) lawyers such as Hanson – and also such as John Knightley, whom, in *Emma*, Austen settles with his family in nearby Brunswick Square. Named after the Prince Regent's hated wife Caroline of Brunswick, this development was built in the former grounds of London's Foundling Hospital where abandoned babies and children were cared for, so it is a nice touch that Austen has Harriet Smith, with her unknown parentage, eventually find happiness with Robert Martin there.[57] This Square (or rather semi-circle) was built in the 1790s, so the John Knightleys' house would have been a modern one, looking onto a garden, in an area that was less fashionable than further west but well-reputed for its hygiene, good ventilation and advanced sanitation.[58] When Emma's father Mr Woodhouse complains that his elder daughter lives 'in London [where] it is always a sickly season . . . so far off – and the air so bad!' Isabella protests that the 'neighbourhood of Brunswick Square is very different' from the rest of the city: '*we* are not at all in a bad air. . . . You must not confound us with London in general, my dear sir. . . . We are so very airy!'[59]

Mr Woodhouse was right about London's very poor air quality in general, however, especially in winter, when the smoke of coal fires was thick in the air and the *haut ton* left the city altogether, often not returning until the spring.[60] As a French visitor Louis Simond described it, the city's air 'is loaded with small flakes of smoke, in sublimation – a sort of flour of soot, so light as to float without falling. This black snow sticks to clothes or linen and alights on your face.'[61] Byron presents this aspect as part of Juan's first sight of London, as the young Spaniard travels from Dover to the capital via Shooter's Hill:

A mighty mass of brick, and smoke, and shipping,
    Dirty and dusky, but as wide as eye
Could reach, with here and there a sail just skipping
    In sight, there lost amidst the forestry
Of masts; a wilderness of steeples peeping
    On tiptoe, through their sea-coal canopy;
A huge, dun cupola, like a foolscap crown
On a fool's head – and there is London Town!

(Don Juan 10.649–56)[62]

The gloominess caused by the smog was to some extent offset by the oil lamps which were introduced in London from the 1750s and were installed all along Oxford Street in 1790 – and even more so by the arrival of the brilliant gas lights, beginning in Pall Mall in 1807 and extending to large areas of Westminster by 1812. Byron celebrates them in canto 11 of *Don Juan* as having

                   a coruscation
Like gold as in comparison to dross,
    Match'd with the Continent's illumination,
Whose cities Night by no means deigns to gloss . . .

But London's so well lit, that if Diogenes
    Could recommence to hunt his *honest man*
And found him not amidst the various progenies
    Of this enormous city's spreading spawn,
'Twere not for want of lamps to aid his dodging his
Yet undiscover'd treasure.

(Don Juan 11.202–22)[63]

Austen too must have marvelled at the dramatic brightness of Westminster's gas lighting when, from 1801 onwards, she stayed with her brother Henry whenever she came to London, and these visits took her to several different parts of town. In spring 1804 Henry and Eliza moved out of Upper Berkeley Street to the much less grand address of 16 Michael's Place, part of a terrace built in the 1790s alongside the Brompton Road in Kensington, where Jane stayed from mid-May to mid-June in 1808. This bohemian area is, in fact, one of the places where she would have been most likely to encounter Byron in person, since at this point he had taken lodgings nearby in Queen Street, Brompton (now Hans Road), with 'Blue-eyed Caroline' Cameron: a sixteen-year-old girl whom he had 'rescued' for a payment of a hundred guineas from a brothel run by a Mrs Durville.[64] He described her as 'his Dalilah' (perhaps she wanted to cut his hair?) and joked that she 'has only two faults, unpardonable in a woman, – she can read and write.'[65] From early 1808, Byron and Caroline lived together in lodgings in Queen Street: an arrangement that shocked his more conventional companions, including his former schoolfellow and the future owner of Newstead Abbey, Thomas Wildman, who was invited to breakfast with Byron but became embarrassed when Caroline was called in to join them for the meal.[66]

'Ideas of Novels & Heroines'

Some eight years later, another Wildman, Thomas's first cousin James Wildman of Chilham Castle in Kent, was to be shocked – also perhaps morally – by Jane Austen, when he was paying his attentions to her favourite niece Fanny Knight of Godmersham. As a way of testing his compatibility for marriage, 23-year-old Fanny had lent him some of Jane's novels and asked him for his opinion of them, without telling him that the author was her aunt.[67] She evidently reported back to Jane that he had been disturbed by some impropriety in one or more of the heroines, for Jane replied:

> I *hope* I am not affronted & do not think the worse of him for having a Brain so very different from mine. . . . He & I should not in the least agree of course, in our ideas of Novels & Heroines; – pictures of perfection as you know make me sick & wicked – but there is some very good sense in what he says, & I particularly respect him for wishing to think well of all young Ladies; it shows an amiable & a delicate Mind. – And he deserves better treatment than to be obliged to read any more of my Works.[68]

In 1816 Fanny wisely decided not to marry her Mr Wildman, and in 1820 she selected instead the 38-year-old widower Sir Edward Knatchbull, some twelve years older than herself.

On 16 June 1808, Byron and Caroline decamped from Brompton with his less-shockable Cambridge friends John Cam Hobhouse and Scrope Berdmore Davies, to a house Byron had rented at 1 Marine Parade, Brighton. Caroline was dressed in boys' clothes (allegedly so as not to bring her to the notice of Byron's family or guardians) and passed off as Byron's brother Gordon.[69] When Lady Perceval admired the 'very pretty horse' that 'Gordon' was riding, Caroline replied, 'Yes, 'twas *gave* me by my brother.' At some point Caroline returned, pregnant, to London, and to Hobhouse's alarm Byron seems to have contemplated marrying her. Apparently, however, 'the young gentleman miscarried in a certain family hotel in Bond Street, to the inexpressible horror of the chambermaids'.[70] Oddly enough, on 14 June 1808, Jane was making her only recorded visit to a London hotel: the Bath Hotel in Arlington Street, just around the corner from Bond Street, which her brother James and family had found 'most uncomfortable quarters – very dirty, very noisy and very ill-provided'.[71]

There is no record of a meeting in the early summer of 1808 between the 32-year-old Jane Austen and the 20-year-old Lord Byron (perhaps with Blue-eyed Caroline on his arm) near where they were both staying, in Michael's Place and Queen Street respectively but, if such an encounter had taken place, it is most likely to have been in what is now Knightsbridge, close to where Harrods now stands. In summer 1809 Henry and Eliza moved from Michael's Place to 64 Sloane Street: a pleasant and spacious three-storey house in what was then called Hans Town, now part of Chelsea, developed by Henry Holland from the 1770s onwards on land owned by the Earl of Cadogan. Jane stayed with Henry and Eliza there from March to May 1811, enjoying a fashionable musical party in their house attended by more than sixty people, and in later years she returned to stay with Henry at other addresses nearby, including 23 Hans Place, where he moved in summer 1814.

Eliza died of breast cancer in April 1813, with Jane and Henry at her bedside, and thereafter Henry asked his sister to come to London even more often, both to assist him with household matters and so that he could help her in negotiations with publishers: becoming, in effect, her literary agent. Between April 1813 and the end of 1815 Jane was in London for some twenty-eight weeks – approaching a quarter of this most productive and prolific period of her life – so that perhaps the perception that she required the quietness and regularity of Chawton to be able to write should be adjusted to include the idea that her creativity was animated by the metropolis. In March 1814, during the morning after one party and before the evening of another, Byron in his *Journal* characterized the 'way half London pass what is called life' as a 'deplorable waste of time. . . . Nothing imparted – nothing acquired – talking without ideas – if anything like a *thought* in my mind, it was not on the subjects on which we were gabbling': and so, conversely, perhaps the case that he was at his best when stimulated by London society should be challenged by his evident need to be able to get *away* from society in order to write.[72] The two authors' final departures from London were, like their first arrivals, only a few months apart. Jane left London for the last time on 16 December 1815 – her fortieth birthday – and the 28-year-old Lord Byron departed five months later on 23 April 1816.

Great George Street

But although Byron never came back to London, or to Britain, during his lifetime, his body was returned to the capital after his death in Greece in April 1824, and the final London events which linked Austen and Byron took place some three months later, in July 1824. On Friday 14 May 1824 Hobhouse recorded in his diary:

> This morning at a little after eight o'clock I was roused by a loud tapping at my door, and on getting up had a packet of letters put into my hand, . . . and also a short note from Kinnaird. I anticipated some dreadful news, and on opening Kinnaird's note, found that Lord Byron was dead. In an agony of grief . . . I opened the dispatches from Corfu, and there saw the details of the fatal event.

As Byron's legal executor, Hobhouse next had the unhappy task of formally identifying his friend's body on board a ship in the Medway when it arrived from Greece, and then of making arrangements for the funeral. Eight years earlier, in 1816, Hobhouse had been an official mourner at the burial in Westminster Abbey of the dramatist Richard Brinsley Sheridan, and he evidently based his ideas about what would be appropriate for Byron on these semi-state obsequies for another notable literary figure. But when he and John Murray approached the Dean of Westminster for permission to inter Byron in the Abbey it was refused: probably because of the perceived irreligious nature of Byron's late plays *Heaven and Earth* and *Cain*, or, as *John Bull* magazine put it, because 'his mind, debased by evil associations, and the indignant brooding over imaginary ills, has been devoted to the construction of elaborate lampoons.'[73] Before Sheridan's funeral, as Hobhouse had noted, the body had lain in state at a house in Great George Street, very near the Abbey, and a 'long list of princes, dukes, earls, cabinet ministers, and other personages' had followed the coffin from there to the Abbey.[74] Although Byron could not be buried in the Abbey, Hobhouse nevertheless wanted a similar lying-in-state for the coffin at a house close by, and the one selected was number 20 Great George Street, which belonged to the Sir Edward Knatchbull, who four years earlier had become the husband of Jane Austen's niece Fanny Austen-Knight.[75]

This particular address was an odd choice for Byron's body to be honoured. Although Hobhouse and Sir Edward had become members of Parliament within a few months of each other in 1819–20, and knew each other personally, they were very much at opposite ends of the political spectrum, with Hobhouse among the radical Whigs and Sir Edward 'imbued with the principles and prejudices of a Tory country gentleman, of which he was a typical specimen'.[76] In 1829 Knatchbull became one of the 'ultra-Tories' who opposed Roman Catholic emancipation in Britain – one of the only three causes for which Byron had spoken passionately in the House of Lords. Fanny too was on the way to becoming a rather snobbish and conservative person, and some decades later she was to write a distinctly condescending comment about the aunts who had given her so much support and encouragement after her mother's death when she was fifteen, and whom Jane had described as 'the delight of my life . . . worth your weight in gold.'[77]

'[I]t is very true that Aunt Jane from various circumstances was not so *refined* as she ought to have been from her *talent*', Fanny wrote to her sister in 1869.

They were not rich & the people around with whom they chiefly mixed, were not at all high bred, or in short anything more than *mediocre* & *they* of course tho' superior in *mental powers* & *cultivation* were on the same level as far as *refinement* goes . . . Aunt Jane was too clever not to put aside all possible signs of 'common-ness' (if such an expression is allowable) & teach herself to be more refined, at least in intercourse with people in general. Both the

Aunts (Cassandra & Jane) were brought up in the most complete ignorance of the World & its ways (I mean as to fashion &c) & if it had not been for Papa's marriage which brought them into Kent, & the kindness of Mrs Knight . . . they would have been, tho' not less clever & agreeable in themselves, very much below par as to good Society & its ways.[78]

Sir Edward and Fanny would surely not have approved of their house becoming a focus for the kinds of people among whom Byron was popular, especially his followers among the leftward-leaning urban working-class. The letting was, however, probably arranged by the undertaker, Mr Woodeson, and the Knatchbulls seem to have been oblivious to the events in London that July, when they were at their country estate in Kent. On the days when Byron's body was lying in their house, Fanny's diary records little except two visits to church; that she had received 'A letter from Aunt Cass', that '20 loads of hay [were] carried from one field today', and that 'We dined at ½ past 4'.[79]

On Monday, 12 July, when Byron's funeral procession set off from Great George Street towards Nottingham, the *Courier* reported that 'The street was one mass of human beings'. 'The crowd behaved with great propriety', Hobhouse noted in his diary, 'although there was something shocking in the unavoidable noise and tumult attendant on such an assemblage of people. When the coffin was put into the hearse they pulled off their hats. . . . The streets and windows were full of people.'[80] The hearse and a separate carriage containing Byron's heart travelled from Westminster via Oxford Street (passing close to his birthplace), to Hampstead Road, followed by forty-seven carriages (empty, as was the custom – but sent as a formal mark of respect), as well as those carrying members of Byron's friends. After a second lying-in-state at Nottingham, the funeral was held on Friday 16 July at St Mary Magdalene, the Parish Church of the village of Hucknall Torkard (some 6 miles from Newstead Abbey) where Byron's coffin and the urn containing his organs were placed in the Byron family vault in the chancel of the church. Hobhouse commented that his friend was 'buried like a nobleman – since we could not bury him as a poet' (that is to say, in Westminster Abbey). Seven years earlier, after a much more low-key funeral, attended only by her brothers and nephew, it was, however, Jane Austen who had achieved the rather grander resting place, with a memorial floor-tablet in the nave of Winchester Cathedral, albeit one that makes no mention of her role as an author.[81]

Notes

1. The house was later renumbered as 24 Holles Street and was the first place to receive a blue plaque to commemorate a former occupant.
2. Le Faye (2002) 88.
3. MacCarthy 5.
4. *JAFR* 64.
5. Boyes (1991) 35.
6. Boyes (1991) 65. St Clair (1990) 4. By contrast, Jane, Cassandra and their mother had only £210 between them annually after her father died, but this was bolstered by funds from her brothers to £460 a year.
7. Letter from Catherine Gordon Byron to Frances Leigh, 21 January 1791, in Boyes (1991) 35.
8. *DJ* 1.295, *LBCPW* 5.20.
9. Medwin 228.
10. *JAFR* 7.
11. *JAFR* 156.
12. Slothouber 19. *P&P* vol. 1, chap. 3, 10.
13. *JAL* 139, to Cassandra Austen, 1–2 September 1808.
14. Daiches 289.
15. *JAFR* 30–1.
16. Slothouber 36–40. Austen-Leigh ed. Sutherland 11.
17. *P&P* vol. 1, chap. 8, 40.
18. *P&P* vol. 1, chap. 4, 16.
19. The population was nearing one million in 1801 and grew rapidly in the next decade. Austen ed. Sabor 45.
20. *S&S* vol. 2, chap. 3, 174.
21. Stabler 205. Clery (2017) 148.
22. Clery (2017) 47.
23. *MP* vol. 3, chap. 9, 456. *Lady Susan* letter 2, Austen ed. Todd and Bree 5.
24. *S&S* vol. 2, chap. 11, 250–1.
25. *JAL* 274, to Anna Austen, 9–18 September 1814. *JAL* 312, to James Stanier Clarke, 1 April 1816.
26. Le Faye (2002) 86–7.
27. *JAFR* 47.
28. *JAL* 5, to Cassandra Austen, 23 August 1796.

29. Austen ed. Sabor 105.

30. *JAL* 12, to Cassandra Austen, 8 April 1798.

31. Suggestion by Le Faye, *JAL* 359.

32. Bond and Kenyon Jones 131.

33. Williams 43.

34. Cobbett (1833) 161, and Cobbett (1853) 1.43.

35. Williams 166.

36. *JAL* 250, to Cassandra Austen, 3 November 1813. Boswell ed. Chapman 608, 859.

37. Cowper ed. Milford, 144.

38. *BLJ* 1.127, to Elizabeth Pigot, 13 July 1807.

39. Moore 1.252–3.

40. Clubbe 8, 12.

41. *BLJ* 5.38, to James Hogg, 1 March 1816.

42. Medwin 194. *CHP* 3.682–3, *LBCPW* 2.103.

43. *LBCMP* 136.

44. *DJ* 11.69, *LBCPW* 5.467.

45. *Beppo* 524, *LBCPW* 4.150. *DJ* 11.160–8, *LBCPW* 5.471.

46. *DJ* 13.200, *LBCPW* 5.532.

47. *P&P* vol. 3 chap. 10, 356.

48. Caplan (1998) 69.

49. Boyes (1991) 80.

50. MacCarthy 60.

51. Clery (2017) 100.

52. MacCarthy 218.

53. MacCarthy 220.

54. Mitchell and Mitchell 13–14.

55. Avery-Jones (21) reports that Henry's two Joshua Reynolds paintings were auctioned on 21 June 1817, 'ironically in a sale of pictures from the estate of Sir Alexander Thomson, Chief Baron of the Court of Exchequer, who "tested" the Extents against Henry and the Bank'.

56. Public Record Office document PRO E 144/77 quoted by Corley (1998) 140.

57. Kaplan np.

58. Sheppard 218.

59. *Emma* vol. 1, chap. 12, 110.

60. Mortimer 44.

61. Simond 1.37–8.
62. *DJ* 10.649–56, *LBCPW* 5.462.
63. *DJ* 11.202–22, *LBCPW* 5.472–3.
64. MacCarthy 74–5.
65. *BLJ* 1.161, to John Cam Hobhouse, 26 March 1808.
66. MacCarthy 75.
67. *JAFR* 244–5.
68. *JAL* 335, to Fanny Knight, 23–25 March 1817.
69. MacCarthy 75.
70. MacCarthy 75 quoting *Blackwood's Edinburgh Magazine*, November 1824.
71. *JAL* 125, to Cassandra Austen, 15–17 June 1808.
72. *BLJ* 3.254, *Journal,* 22 March 1814.
73. *John Bull*, 16 May 1824.
74. Sheridan lay in state at the house of Peter Moore, 7, Great Smith Street. Hobhouse *Recollections* 1.347.
75. Hobhouse *Diary* ed. Cochran, 5 July 1824. *London Courier and Evening Gazette* 7 July 1824; *Morning Post*, and *Morning Advertiser* 8 July 1824. In later decades the house was numbered differently.
76. Fisher np.
77. *JAL* 328, to Fanny Knight, 20–21 February 1817.
78. *JAFR* 279–80.
79. *Fanny Knight's Journals*, 10–12 July 1824.
80. Hobhouse *Diary* 12 July 1824.
81. Hobhouse *Diary* 12 July 1824.

CHAPTER 3
THEATRE AND OTHER ENTERTAINMENTS
'SHE WAS NOT DECEIVED IN HER OWN EXPECTATION OF PLEASURE'

Because of her portrayal of the troubled 'private theatricals' in *Mansfield Park*, Austen has often been thought of as someone who disapproved of amateur dramatics and even of theatre in general. But her biography, letters, juvenile texts – and her novels themselves – tell a different story: how adventurously she experimented with writing drama in her teenage years; how enthusiastically she took part in home theatrical 'entertainments'; how much she enjoyed attending public theatrical performances and relished good professional acting (or deplored the lack of it); how extensively drama featured in her reading, and how thoroughly she absorbed dramatic techniques and used them in her own fiction.

The idea of Austen's disapproval of theatre has been reversed by recent studies which instead demonstrate her extensive knowledge of earlier and contemporary plays and individual actors and illustrate the way in which theatrical modes and subject matter profoundly influenced her novels.[1] Many of her contemporary novelists (such as Burney, Edgeworth and Elizabeth Inchbald) also wrote and published plays, and Austen, like them, would have seen drama as a natural precursor to the novel, in terms of the extended use of dialogue, the dependence upon character in creating a scenario, the emphasis on memorable dramatic moments and the need to provide a satisfying resolution.[2] Reading her work aloud to family and friends was part of the process of composing her novels, and they were written to be 'performed' in this way. Film and television directors of the last half-century have recognized that these features help to make her novels ripe for dramatization, leading to a fame in this medium which is even greater than that in her own. As Gillian Dow remarks, 'It is no longer possible to claim that Austen disliked or disapproved of the theater because Fanny Price refused to act in *Lovers' Vows* at Mansfield Park.'[3]

Byron's love of the theatre has never been questioned, and his own dramatic works, as well as his letters, journals and verse, record both his studious knowledge of classical Greek and Latin drama and his wide reading of contemporary and earlier English plays (Thomas Sackville, co-author of the first blank-verse play *Gorboduc* (1561), gets an admiring name-check).[4] His dramatic writing was informed by his participation in private theatricals, his attendance at hundreds of performances in London and elsewhere, his personal acquaintance with actors and his thorough knowledge of theatrical conditions, onstage and off, gained as a member of the management sub-committee at Drury Lane Theatre. His interest in the power of theatrical and other costume is reflected in his commission of the 'Albanian' portrait of himself from Thomas Phillips in 1814 (see page 5) and in the Homeric helmets he had made for himself and his companions to take to Greece in 1823. Both he and Austen had experience of theatre outside London – Austen in Bath and Southampton, Byron in Aberdeen and Cheltenham, and then in Italy – but in particular they were both very keen London theatregoers, especially between 1812 and 1815. The eight plays Byron wrote himself – *Manfred* (1816), *Marino Faliero* (1820), *Sardanapalus* (1821), *The Two Foscari* (1821), *Cain* (1821), *Heaven and Earth* (1821), *Werner* (1822) and *The Deformed Transformed* (unfinished, 1822) – illustrate his intense response to good acting as well as his conflicted attempts both to accommodate and to avoid what he saw as the problems of theatrical performance in London in his own day. While Byron may never have found a satisfactory performance solution for his tragic dramas within contemporary theatrical options, he did, like Austen, adroitly deploy dramatic techniques in a non-theatrical medium – in his case, in narrative verse: presenting complex dramatic scenarios to carry the plots of the fictions in his 'Oriental' tales and creating naturalistic and fast-moving comic dialogue for *Beppo* and *Don Juan* which is completely different from the formal and rhetorical manner of his tragic plays.

Dramatic fragments

The three miniature plays among Austen's juvenilia ('The Mystery', 'The Visit' and 'The First Act of a Comedy') show not only how much she enjoyed dramatic humour and experimentation but also how early her knowledge of theatre had been acquired. 'The First Act of a Comedy', probably written in Austen's mid-teens, demonstrates a canny appreciation of the artificiality of comic theatre while satirizing the dramatist's need to convey information at the expense of verisimilitude.

> Pistoletta: Pray papa how far is it to London?
> Popgun: My Girl, my Darling, my favourite of all my Children, who art the picture of thy poor Mother who died two months ago, with whom I am going to Town to marry to Strephon, and to whom I mean to bequeath my whole Estate, it wants seven Miles.[5]

This and the other dramatic fragments Jane wrote reflect the fun she had between 1782 and 1790 and the ages of six and fourteen, when her older siblings regularly organized home theatricals at Steventon. For several years their father's tithe barn was temporarily fitted up as a theatre.[6] Many of the plays chosen for acting by the Austens had strong and outspoken roles for women (emphasized in the verse prologues and epilogues written by Jane's eldest brother James) and often they were quite risqué, such as Susannah Centlivre's *The Wonder! A Woman Keeps a Secret* (1714) and David Garrick's 1775 *Bon Ton or High Life above Stairs,* acted by the Austens in 1788. Garrick's suggestively named heroine Miss Tittup was played by their glamorous cousin Eliza, who had performed with *éclat* in court theatricals at Versailles; and watching her brothers James and Henry both flirting with Eliza during rehearsals may well have given Austen ideas for the disastrous amorous dramas that play out in *Mansfield Park.*

Byron was proud of his schoolboy 'declamations' given on public Speech Days at Harrow, when he performed to a distinguished audience of parents and patrons: first in 1804 as King Latinus in a passage from Virgil's *Aeneid* (in Latin); and then in 1805 when he delivered a speech by Zanga the Moor, the villain of Edward Young's play *The Revenge* (1721), and recited Lear's impassioned address to the storm from act three of Shakespeare's play.[7] Outside school, however, not all his performances were so serious or so classical, and in 1806, when he was eighteen, Byron led some 'private theatricals' in Southwell, the small Nottinghamshire town where his mother lived, starring himself in two highly contrasting contemporary roles. For three nights running he performed both as the embittered misanthropist Roderick Penruddock in Richard Cumberland's *The Wheel of Fortune* (1795) – one of the plays considered for production but rejected in *Mansfield Park* – and (as a complete contrast) Tristram Fickle in John Till Allingham's 1805 farce *The Weathercock.*[8]

Mary Ann Bristoe – an older girl from Southwell who played opposite Byron in both plays – left a vivid account which is strongly reminiscent of the world of Austen's novels, particularly *Mansfield Park*.

In the autumn of the year 1806, Lord Byron consulted with some of his friends on the possibility of getting up some private theatricals; . . . many obstacles came in the way; some who possessed superior abilities, declined taking a part and also others from the fear of not acting well, required great powers of persuasion to make them act at all. The characters were at length finally cast, though not entirely to the satisfaction of the noble manager. . . . It now remained to determine 'the scene of action'. A public room [probably in the new Assembly Rooms attached to the Saracen's Head Inn in Southwell] was proposed but the females of the company immediately put in their negative, for . . . it is not only necessary to *act* with propriety, but also to keep up the appearance of it in the eyes of the world, which is always more ready to condemn than to approve. . . . Mr Leacroft then kindly consented to allow his dining parlour to be fitted up for the theatre; no place could have been better calculated for such a purpose . . .

Affairs being put *en train*, Lord Byron left us to learn our lessons and set out for Harrogate. . . . Our rehearsals were always sanctioned by the presence of Mrs Holmes, a maiden lady, the daughter of a deceased clergyman, who had not only trained her up in the practice of every religious and moral duty but had also stored her mind with both useful and ornamental literature . . .

The next arrangement to be considered was the fitting up of the theatre. About this there was some difficulty, as the artificers of Southwell had no great idea of setting about any work of this kind. In this dilemma, application was made to my Father, who was known to be a great mechanic, with a request that he would give all the proper orders, and also overlook the men . . . to prevent them doing the least damage to the walls and floor of the room. This, he agreed to do with pleasure, he even took upon himself the office of prompter on the nights of our performing, for, although a clergy-man in every sense of the word, he was always ready to give his assistance to promote any innocent amusement for the gratification of youth.

At the end of three weeks, during which period we had rehearsed twelve times, our little theatre was finished, and tickets, with Lord Byron's name and seal affixed, were distributed to our acquaintance.[9]

In *Mansfield Park* Tom Bertram is happy to take on 'the rhyming Butler . . . if nobody else wants it; a trifling part, but the sort of thing I should not dislike, and, as I said before, I am determined to take anything and do my best', while in Southwell there was a 'Mr G. Wylde' who declared that 'sooner than the party shall be disappointed he will take any part – sing – dance – in short anything to oblige', and who ended up reciting the Prologue composed by Byron, as well as playing Weazle in *The Wheel of Fortune* and the Barber in *The Weathercock*.[10]

Backstage drama

Then on the first night there was the classic backstage drama when one of the actors turned up 'inebriated'. Captain Lightfoot,

> feeling himself as time drew near, very nervous, had, in order to 'screw his courage to the sticking place' gone beyond his usual very moderate bounds and taken a few glasses of wine extra, in quick succession . . . the greatest consternation prevailed, with Lord Byron exclaiming, 'It's all over, we cannot possibly act this evening. Lightfoot is quite tipsy.'

'[R]estoratives were administered', however, 'which in a short time had the desired effect, and he was able to walk and stand steadily, but he still looked perfectly stupefied.' In the end, however, Lightfoot 'acted the character remarkably well, and nothing of what had occurred was in the least suspected by the audience'. Byron's friend John Pigot got the biggest laugh of the evening by wearing his grandfather's embroidered suit stuffed out with a pillow for an extensive stomach.[11]

Byron's own acting was evidently highly impressive in both parts. '[M]y pen could not do justice to Lord Byron's delineation of this arduous character', Mary Ann Bristoe wrote of his performance of Penruddock. 'The interview between Penruddock and Mrs Woodville, Lord Byron requested to rehearse with me alone, for what reason I never knew', she continued rather archly, but 'I had cause to rejoice at his having made this request, as it prepared me for what I might expect on the stage'. Byron's extraordinary ability to fuse himself with a fictional world and a dramatic character – what would later be part of the 'mobility' he shared with *Don Juan*'s Lady Adeline Amundeville – appears in the way Mary Ann describes how 'He' (meaning Penruddock, or Byron, or both?)

> was struggling to appear a philosopher, but, when he spoke the melting tone of voice in which he pronounced his first words, shewed that the struggle was in vain, and the latent tenderness of 'twenty years' burst forth in spite of his efforts to conceal it. I was perfectly unnerved and could almost imagine that we were the very characters we then represented.[12]

Byron's Southwell friend Elizabeth Pigot agreed, writing many years later how 'when Byron said, "Ah, Madam, you see what a philosopher I am – " it was the perfection of acting – the Pathos, the peculiar kind of tone in which he uttered it . . . the tenderness and sweetness of his voice was beyond any expression to convey an idea of'.[13] Byron was by his own representation at this stage a 'stout' teenager, but it is perhaps not surprising that Miss Bristoe believed he might be in love with her and, according to one of his contemporary poems, she lay in wait for him in the churchyard at night with amorous intentions.[14] In the 'whimsical character' of Tristram Fickle too, Elizabeth Pigot found '[t]here was an elegance in Lord Byron's acting which was never lost sight of, and threw a peculiar charm over his *comic* scenes, a charm which is very rarely to be met with even in the greatest comic performer on our public stage. The curtain fell amidst thundering applause.'[15]

Flirtation, and perhaps more serious amorous activity, was certainly part of the scenario: Byron's poems of this time reflect his encounters with several other Southwell 'belles' whose competition to catch the attention of the young Lord during rehearsals recalls that of the Bertram sisters for Henry Crawford; and the brother of Julia Leacroft (whose father lent the performance room) wrote a formal letter of remonstration to Byron about his flirtation with his sister.[16]

'The best gifts of the comic muse'

Austen, too, evidently had strong gifts as an actor. Even her brother Henry (by then becoming the increasingly evangelical Reverend Henry) in his

'Biographical Notice' of 1817 acknowledged that her works 'were never heard to so much advantage as from her own mouth; for she partook largely in all the best gifts of the comic muse', while her niece Caroline reported how her aunt took up 'a volume of Evelina and read a few pages of Mr Smith and the Brangtons and I thought it was like a play. She had a very good *speaking* voice'.[17] At Godmersham in summer 1805, while still in mourning for her father (which indicates that she cannot have believed that home theatricals were wrong in principle), Jane and Cassandra, as reported by their niece Fanny, 'acted a play called *Virtue Rewarded*. Anna was the Duchess St. Albans, I was the Fairy Serena and Fanny Cage a shepherdess "Mona"'.[18] And a few weeks later they gave a private performance of a play called 'The Spoilt Child', which may have been drawn from the 1792 London hit ascribed to Isaac Bickerstaffe, or could, as Gillian Dow suggests, have been an English version of 'L'Enfant Gatée' from Stéphanie-Félicité de Genlis's *Théatre à l'usage des jeunes personnes* (1779).[19] They also performed a piece called *Pride Published; or Innocence Rewarded*, possibly written by the children's governess and Jane's friend, Anne Sharp.[20] In a more public setting, Austen was remembered by Sir William Heathcote, son of her Hampshire friend Elizabeth Bigg, at a Twelfth Day (6 January) party, probably in 1808, where she 'drew the character of Mrs Candour' from Sheridan's *The School for Scandal* (1777) 'and assumed the part with great spirit'.[21] In Pisa in 1821, Byron, the Shelleys, Thomas Medwin and others planned a performance of *Othello*, with Byron as Iago, which only got as far as the first run-through but greatly impressed Medwin. 'Perhaps Lord Byron would have made the finest actor in the world', Medwin thought. 'His voice had a flexibility, a variety in its tone, a power and a pathos beyond any I ever heard; and his countenance was capable of expressing the tenderness as well as the strongest emotions.'[22]

Byron's dramatic abilities were evidently in danger of breaching the dividing line that Edmund Bertram, in *Mansfield Park*, carefully draws between 'the raw efforts of those who have not been bred to the trade: a set of gentlemen and ladies, who have all the disadvantages of education and decorum to struggle through', and 'real acting, good hardened real acting'.[23] There is a complicated resonance here with Austen's presentation of the sexual allure of Henry Crawford, whose reading of scenes from Shakespeare's *Henry VIII* impresses Fanny Price as 'a variety of excellence beyond what she had ever met with . . . whether it were dignity or pride, or tenderness or remorse, or whatever was to be expressed, he could do it with equal beauty. – It was truly dramatic'.[24] Austen's picture of Crawford cannot of course be actually related to Byron's private performances, and neither (tantalizingly) does it seem to be connected with the acting of the new London star player of 1814, Edmund Kean, whom Austen first saw in his electrifying role as Shylock on 5 March, several months after *Mansfield Park* had been handed over to the publisher (but before its actual publication in May 1814). Samuel Taylor Coleridge memorably remarked of Kean that 'to see him act is like reading Shakespeare by flashes of lightning'.[25] Byron saw Kean as Shylock and as Richard III in February 1814, describing him as 'Life – nature – truth – without exaggeration or diminution', and over the next two years he attended probably all of Kean's performances (which included Macbeth, Hamlet, Iago, Othello and King Lear), sometimes seeing him several times in the same role.[26] He first met Kean personally in October 1814 and subsequently came to know the actor well, enjoying – as well as occasionally becoming the butt of – the actor's conspicuously subversive and anti-establishment status and attitudes.[27] After Kean's performance as Sir Giles Overreach in Philip Massinger's *A New Way to Pay Old Debts* (*c.* 1625) in January 1816 (which reduced Byron to 'the agony of reluctant tears') Byron presented him with a magnificent Turkish sword and gave £50 for his benefit.[28]

'I cannot imagine better acting', Jane wrote to Cassandra about Kean in a letter written between 5 and 8 March 1814, and it seems clear that

Figure 11 *Edmund Kean as Sir Giles Overreach in 'A New Way to Pay Old Debts'*, by George Clint (1820). Kean's performance in this role reduced Byron to 'the agony of reluctant tears' in 1816. © Victoria and Albert Museum, London.

she herself did link Kean and Henry Crawford at this stage.[29] When she reverted to Kean later in the same letter, it was immediately after a sentence about Henry Austen's opinions on the character of Crawford, whom he was reading about for the first time.[30]

> Henry has this moment said that he likes my M.P. better and better . . . he said yesterday at least that he defied anybody to say whether H.C. would be reformed, or would forget Fanny in a fortnight. – I shall like to see Kean again excessively, & to see him with You too; – it appeared to me that there was no fault in him anywhere; & in his scene with Tubal there was exquisite acting.[31]

Austen's own association of Henry Crawford with Kean seems particularly apt because she presents Crawford as being, like Kean, not physically impressive.[32] The Bertram sisters initially see him as 'absolutely plain, black and plain', and the jealous Mr Rushworth calls him 'an undersized, little, mean-looking man, set up for a fine actor', while Kean, who was short and swarthy, was described as 'a horrid little man' by Mrs Siddons, who considered that 'there was too little of him to make a great actor'.[33] Byron, too, described Kean's acting as 'the triumph of mind over matter for he has nothing but countenance & expression – his figure is very little & even mean'.[34] Byron's own later performance of Iago in Pisa was, however, certainly influenced by Kean's portrayal, which, he told Thomas Moore, was 'perfection . . . particularly the last look . . . I never saw an English countenance half so expressive.' 'I am acquainted with no *im*material sensuality so delightful as good acting', he added.[35]

Longer-standing stars

Austen must have been delighted by the way Kean's explosive London debut made the subject of the theatre and acting headline news just at the time *Mansfield Park* was published, but she also admired longer-standing stars too, such as the great comic actress Dorothy Jordan. Bickerstaffe's *The Spoilt Child*, which may have been acted by Jane with her niece and nephews in 1805, had been made famous in the 1790s by Jordan in the 'breeches' role of 'Little Pickle' – the naughty child of the title whose exploits include sewing together the clothes of clandestine lovers so that they cannot part. Described by William Hazlitt as 'all gaiety, openness, and good nature . . . noted for her fine animal spirits' and for having 'the great spirit of enjoyment in herself,' (not to mention 'the best legs in London'), it has been suggested that Jordan may have provided a model for Elizabeth Bennet.[36] By 1812 Jordan was in her fifties and coming to the end of her career, as well as to the close of her twenty-one-year relationship with the Duke of Clarence, third son of George III, with whom she had produced a family of ten 'FitzClarences'. In fact she had recently moved into a house in Cadogan Street, just around the corner from the Henry Austens.[37] Byron certainly shared this admiration, and he and Austen almost coincided at Covent Garden in seeing Jordan: on 7 March 1814 (the day of the disastrous Hanson-Portsmouth wedding described in Chapter 4) Jane saw her as Nell in the 'operatical farce' *The Devil to Pay* (1731) by Charles Coffey and John Mottley, and three days later on 10 March Byron saw her as Miss Hoyden in Sheridan's *A Trip to Scarborough* (1777), describing her as 'superlative'.[38] A more recent actress about whom Austen and Byron shared ambivalent feelings was the Irish star Eliza O'Neill, who succeeded to some of Siddons's roles and acclaim between 1814 and 1819 (when she retired from the stage to become Lady Becher). Byron seems deliberately to have avoided seeing her – perhaps because she was in the company of the 'opposing side' to Byron's Drury Lane, at Covent Garden.[39] Austen, however, saw her as Isabella in Garrick's 1776 play of that name on 28 November 1814 and pronounced her not 'quite equal to my expectation. I fancy I want something more than can be. Acting seldom satisfies me. I took two Pocket handkerchiefs, but had very little occasion for either. She is an elegant creature however & hugs Mr Younge delightfully'.[40]

A third actor much admired by both Austen and Byron was the popular and handsome Robert William Elliston, whose career in Bath and London Austen followed avidly. 'Elliston . . . has just succeeded to a considerable fortune on the death of an Uncle. I would not have it enough to take *him* from the Stage', she wrote anxiously in 1807.[41] Some of Elliston's most noted roles were in plays adapted from works by August von Kotzebue, famous (and notorious) for his dramas exploring subjects such as illegitimacy and adultery, including the controversial Elizabeth Inchbald adaptation of his *Das Kind der Liebe (The Love Child)* as *Lovers' Vows* (1798). By the time Austen featured this drama in *Mansfield Park* in 1813 it was very well known and had been performed hundreds of times at Covent Garden, Drury Lane and the Theatre Royal Haymarket, as well as seventeen times during Austen's years in Bath between May 1801 and July 1806, with Elliston often playing the (Henry Crawford)

Figure 12 *Robert William Elliston as Frank Heartall,* by Thomas Charles Wageman (*c.* 1808). Elliston was one of Austen's favourite actors and he delivered the controversial 'Address' Byron wrote for the gala reopening of Drury Lane Theatre in 1812. © National Portrait Gallery, London.

part of Frederick.[42] Elliston had also played Rolla in Sheridan's adaptation of Kotzebue's *Pizarro,* and Austen liked him in both comic and tragic or heroic parts.[43] She was, however, disappointed by his lead performance in the melodrama *Illusion; or, The Trances of Nourjahad* which she saw at Drury Lane on the same evening in 1814 as Kean playing Shylock. 'There is a great deal of finery & dancing in it, but I think little merit', she concluded. 'Elliston was Nourjahad, but it is a solemn sort of part, not at all calculated for his powers. There was nothing of the *best Elliston* about him. I might not have known him, except for his voice'.[44]

Byron agreed both about Elliston ('I can conceive nothing better than Elliston in *gentleman's* comedy and in some parts of tragedy') and about the disappointing *Nourjahad* melodrama (first played on 23 November 1813 and seen by Byron on 27 November): 'The dialogue is drowsy – the action heavy – the scenery fine – the actors tolerable', he wrote.[45] He had lent some drawings of oriental figures to help create costumes for *Nourjahad* but was then mortified to find that two newspapers – the *Morning Post* and the *Satirist* – were claiming that he had actually written the script of the play, as he commented wryly in the doggerel verse of 'The Devil's Drive' in December 1813:

The Devil . . . had been vastly glad
To see the new Drury Lane,
And yet he might have been rather mad
To see it rebuilt in vain,
And had he beheld their Nourjahad,
Would never have gone again;
And Satan had taken it much amiss
They should fasten such a piece on a friend of his.
Though he knew that his works were somewhat sad,
He never had deemed them quite so bad.

('The Devil's Drive' 225–34)[46]

The play had in fact been adapted by Samuel Arnold and the tenor Michael Kelly from a 1767 romance by Frances Sheridan, although Byron did not know this. 'The *Orientalism* . . . is very splendid', he told his publisher John Murray, suggesting that it would serve as 'an Advertisement for your Eastern stories [including his own forthcoming *Bride of Abydos*] – by filling their heads with glitter'.[47]

Elliston and 'The Address'

Elliston became closely linked with Byron in 1812 when Byron requested that he should deliver the 'Address' Byron had written for the gala opening of Drury Lane Theatre, rebuilt after the disastrous fire of 1809.[48] This Address was highly controversial, since there had been a competition to write it, and many other hopeful verses had been submitted and rejected before Byron was invited by the Whig party leader Lord Holland to write one. When James and Horace Smith published their satirical collection of *Rejected Addresses* (which Austen loved, and for which she declared she was 'in love' with them), Byron was rightly concerned about how his own effort would be received.[49] It was 'certainly too long in the reading', he told Lord Holland, 'but if E[lliston] exerts himself – such a favourite with the public will not be thought tedious. – *I* should think it so – if *he* were not to speak it'.[50] Byron stayed away from the grand opening on 10 October, but John Murray reported to him that, although his address had been received with 'applauding satisfaction', Elliston's delivery had been 'exceedingly bad – indeed his acting exhibits nothing but conceit'.[51]

One of the reasons for Elliston's variable performances at this time may have been that he was succumbing to alcoholism, although he did go on to become the owner of ten different theatres and to be the Manager of Drury Lane from 1819. But another real difficulty for him as an actor would have been the cavernous proportions of the new, as of the old, Drury Lane Theatre (and of Covent Garden, which had also recently been rebuilt after a fire).[52] As the dramatist Richard Cumberland commented: 'the stages of Drury Lane and Covent Garden have been so enlarged in their dimensions as to be henceforward theatres for spectators rather than playhouses for hearers.'[53] And it was not only the stages but also the vast auditoriums, capable of holding audiences of more than 3,000, which must have severely tried the throats, energies and nerves of the actors. The house 'lights' (candles or gas) were left alight during performances and, as Walter Scott complained, there were scores of pimps plying their trade, with 'prostitutes and their admirers . . . forming the principal part of the audience.'[54] A quiet audience was a great rarity, and when Byron's friend Hobhouse visited Berlin in 1814 he was particularly surprised to find that 'During the action the utmost silence prevails – the least noise is corrected with a hiss.'[55] In London theatres at half-time an additional audience was admitted of people who could not afford the full prices. Those who *could* afford them (including the Austens and Byron) scrambled for the best seats in the boxes nearest to the stage so that they could hear as well as see the actors: in 1815 Byron had a private box for alternate weeks at Drury Lane and offered the use of it in June to Leigh Hunt 'in case you should like to see him [Kean] quietly.'[56] The public boxes were also in great demand: 'so great is the rage for seeing Keen [*sic*] that only a third & fourth row could be got', Austen wrote in March 1814. 'As it is in the front box, however, I hope we shall do pretty well.'[57]

The effect of these changes on serious dramatic performances, and on writing for the theatre, was not favourable. 'The persons of the performers are, in these huge circles, so much diminished that nothing short of the mask and buskin could render them distinctly visible to the audience', Scott lamented in 1819 (with a reference to the special boots worn by actors in classical times).

> Show and machinery have therefore usurped the place of tragic poetry; and the author is compelled to address himself to the eyes, not to the understandings or the feelings of the spectator . . . we have enlarged our theatres, so as to destroy the effect of acting, without carrying to a perfection that of pantomime and dumb show.[58]

'I beleive [*sic*] the Theatres are thought at a low ebb at present', Jane commented to Cassandra on 25 September 1813, less than a year after the opening of the new Drury Lane Theatre, while Byron, as he explained in the draft preface to *Marino Faliero* (1820), was deterred from writing 'performable' plays rather than what he described as 'mental theatre' and has since been called 'closet drama': plays to be read in one's study or closet, rather than performed in a real theatre.

> I have had no view to the stage; in its present state it is, perhaps, not a very exalted object of ambition. . . . I cannot conceive any man of irritable feeling putting himself at the mercies of an audience. . . . Were I capable of writing a play which could be deemed stageworthy, success would give me no pleasure, and failure great pain.[59]

Marino Faliero was, ironically, the only one of Byron's plays to be performed during his lifetime, unauthorized by him, in 1821, and was not a success. Byron did have extensive experience of judging 'play[s] which could be deemed stageworthy' (or not), since as chief literary advisor for Drury Lane in 1815 he had been asked to look through some 500 scripts sent in to the theatre by hopeful (but generally hopeless) authors, including one, Byron wrote, 'in which the unities could not fail to be observed, for the protagonist was chained by the leg to a pillar during the chief part of the performance'.[60] His own plays illustrate his intense response to good acting, especially that of Edmund Kean, and his appreciation of effective staging, but his claim for *Manfred* (which he subtitled 'a Dramatic Poem') was that it was an attempt to turn away from 'the Old English dramatists' (including Shakespeare, whom he admired, but felt was too dominant a presence in the theatre of his own time). Instead, as he wrote to Murray, he wanted to create 'quite another field . . . nothing to do with theirs', making 'a *regular* English drama – no matter whether for the Stage or not – which is not my object – but a *mental theatre*'.[61]

Manfred (written in 1816 and 1817) was, however, as James Armstrong has demonstrated, heavily indebted to Charles Maturin's play *Bertram,* starring Kean, which Byron had been largely responsible for bringing to the stage of Drury Lane in 1816.[62] Byron supported Maturin financially (along with Walter Scott) and engineered a new ending for his play, written by George Lamb rather than Maturin, which abolished the appearance of a ghostly 'dark Knight' imagined by Maturin. It was in fact in *Manfred*, written under the immediate influence of Drury Lane's conditions, that Byron seems to have experimented most deliberately with trying to combine tragic drama with the onstage spectacle demanded by the audiences in the huge London theatres he knew.

Manfred and the Witch of the Torrent.

Figure 13 'Manfred and the Witch of the Torrent' from *Forty Illustrations of Lord Byron*, by George Cruikshank (1824–5). Private collection.

The opportunities for an impressive cast of spirits, destinies, witches and phantoms, for aerial and other displays, for vast Alpine panoramas and for tableaux such as the 'globe of fire' on which Arimanes' throne is placed in act 2, scene 4, all seem intended by Byron to provide ample scope for the 'effects' department of Drury Lane while at the same time attempting to ensure that they are firmly anchored to the serious theme and powerful verse of the play. Manfred himself shows a notably contemptuous attitude towards the spirits he summons, reminding them that

> the power which brought ye here
> Hath made you mine. Slaves – scoff not at my will! . . .
> Answer, or I will teach you what I am.

> *(Manfred, 1.1.152–8)*

and perhaps this defiance towards the spirits and the special effects associated with them expresses something of Byron's own hostility towards the 'Show and machinery' which, as Scott said, had 'usurped the place of tragic poetry' in the theatre of the period.[63] When Byron's plays were performed later in the nineteenth century, they underwent major cutting and livening up to meet the expectations of audiences, and early productions of *Sardanapalus*, for example, featured a catchy 'Assyrian Cymbal Dance' and spectacular fire effects that all but literally brought down the house in the final scene.[64]

However, as Peter Cochran (professional actor, theatre director and Byron expert) has recently demonstrated by staging them, Byron's poems, especially those that have a comic aspect and are based on Italian models, can work better as performances than his designated dramas may do. Laura's 'soliloquy' from Byron's 1818 comic poem *Beppo*, quoted in the Introduction, and the scene in Julia's bedroom where Juan is hidden under the bedclothes when her husband Alfonso arrives unexpectedly (*Don Juan* 1.1073–1496), show how Byron could write with equal (or more) dramatic appeal when he turned from the declamatory mode and solemn scenarios he generally used in his dramas, to a comic style more like that of the Restoration comedies or Goldsmith's and Sheridan's plays, with speech imitating ordinary language and a variety of different idioms. Julia and her maid, Antonia, have especially vocal parts:

'For God's sake, Madam – Madam – here's my master,
    With more than half the city at his back –
Was ever heard of such a curst disaster!
    'Tis not my fault – I kept good watch –Alack!' ...

Poor Donna Julia! starting as from sleep,
    (Mind – that I do not say – she had not slept)
Began at once to scream, and yawn, and weep;
    Her maid Antonia, who was an adept,
Contrived to fling the bed-clothes in a heap,
    As if she had just now from out them crept: ...

Now Julia found at length a voice, and cried,
    'In heaven's name, Don Alfonso, what d'ye mean?
Has madness seized you? would that I had died
    Ere such a monster's victim I had been!
What may this midnight violence betide,
    A sudden fit of drunkenness or spleen?
Dare you suspect me, whom the thought would kill?

Search, then, the room!' – Alfonso said, 'I will.'

He search'd, *they* search'd, and rummaged every where,
      Closet and clothes'-press, chest and window-seat,
And found much linen, lace, and several pair
      Of stockings, slippers, brushes, combs, complete,
With other articles of ladies fair,
      To keep them beautiful, or leave them neat:
Arras they prick'd and curtains with their swords,
And wounded several shutters, and some boards. . . .

During this inquisition, Julia's tongue
      Was not asleep – 'Yes, search and search,' she cried,
'Insult on insult heap, and wrong on wrong! . . .

'Was it for this you took your sudden journey,
      Under pretence of business indispensable
With that sublime of rascals your attorney,
      Whom I see standing there, and looking sensible
Of having play'd the fool? . . .

'If he comes here to take a deposition,
      By all means let the gentleman proceed; . . .
Let every thing be noted with precision,
      I would not you for nothing should be fee'd –
But, as my maid's undrest, pray turn your spies out.'
'Oh!' sobb'd Antonia, 'I could tear their eyes out.' . . .

The Senhor Don Alfonso stood confused;
      Antonia bustled round the ransack'd room,
And, turning up her nose, with looks abused
      Her master and his myrmidons, of whom
Not one, except the attorney, was amused.

                    (*Don Juan* 1.1088–1269)[65]

One dramatic work which may be partially by Austen is a theatrical version of Samuel Richardson's 1753 novel *The History of Sir Charles Grandison*, which knowingly reduces the thousands of pages of Richardson's novel to a compact collection of scenes in 'five acts' and reproduces parts of his dialogue while adding a few new, humorous elements, such as constant references to mealtimes.[66] If this *is* by Austen it must be a deliberate and affectionate joke, since Jane had loved *Grandison* and its heroine Harriet (or Harriot) Byron since childhood: a circumstance which may have given her a special interest in her contemporary author of the same surname.[67] Since, however, Austen's fine sense of the dramatic, her canny timing and her mastery of the possibilities of different kinds of dialogue are shown to such advantage in her chosen form the novel, perhaps we do not miss any longer play written by her. Indeed, as John Mullan has shown, in Austen's mature novels almost half the words are allocated to dialogue: in *Emma* 49.8 per cent of the text and in *Pride and Prejudice* 46.7 per cent.[68] And, as Mullan has also vividly demonstrated, Austen is second to none in her mastery of another theatrical technique: the individual 'idiolect' or the special word- and voice-pattern given to each of her characters.[69]

Patent theatres

As Covent Garden and Drury Lane turned more to the kinds of spectacle that could work well in large spaces with poor acoustics, the new developments also undermined the special status of these two theatres as London's exclusive 'patent' theatres. Under the Licensing Act of 1737, these were the only London venues (along with the Theatre Royal Haymarket, or 'Little Theatre', during the summer months) that were permitted to produce plays with spoken dialogue for 'hire, gain or reward'. The Licensing Act also gave the Lord Chamberlain the power to award and remove licences for places of entertainment and to examine plays for content deemed to be seditious or immoral.[70] There were many ingenious attempts to get around this legislation, particularly by setting words to music, so that it could be claimed that the audience watching a 'melodrama' or a 'burletta' were paying for the music and getting the words free. In other cases the playwright's original words were 'adapted' for semi-musical presentation:

> Horatio: To see dad's funeral I popp'd my head in.
> Hamlet: No quizzing – 'twas to see my mother's wedding.
> Horatio: Indeed, my lord, one follow'd hard on t'other. –
> I never should have thought it of your mother.
> Hamlet: Thrift, thrift, Horatio! Denmark's cooks were able
> With funeral meats to cheer the marriage-table.[71]

By Austen's and Byron's time there were numerous recognized 'minor' theatres in London, outside the patent houses, providing various kinds of entertainment including melodrama and musical theatre. Particularly well-known among these was the Pantheon in Oxford Street, which was visited by both Byron and the Austens in 1808. On 5 February Byron invited his Harrow school friend Edward Noel Long to accompany him and a 'large party', including the famous clown Joseph Grimaldi, to attend a masquerade at the Pantheon. In May and June that year Jane was in London staying with Henry and Eliza and, since they owned a private box at the Pantheon, she is sure to have visited it at least once.[72] The building – which was huge and had a dome reminiscent of that of the original Pantheon in Rome – was used at this time mainly for exhibitions, masquerades, ballets and short comic operas, although between 1809 and 1812, while Drury Lane was being rebuilt after the fire, it was licensed as a replacement patent theatre.

Both Byron and Austen were fascinated by the juxtaposition between real life, masquerade and drama, and in 1823 Byron wrote delightedly of how, during the Carnival in Venice, 'Life becomes for the moment a drama without the fiction', while in 1821 he recalled vividly how

> In the Pantomime of 1815–16, there was a Representation of the Masquerade of 1814, given by 'us Youth' of Watier's Club to Wellington and Co. Douglas Kinnaird, and one or two others with myself, put on Masques, and went *on* the Stage with the 'όι πολλοι,' to see the effect of a theatre from the Stage. It is very grand. Douglas danced among the figuranti too, and they were puzzled to find out who we were, as being more than their number. It was odd enough that D.K. and I should have been both at the *real* Masquerade, and afterwards in the Mimic one of the same on the stage of D[rury] L[ane] Theatre.[73]

In *Mansfield Park*, Austen steps adroitly backward and forward across the footlights between performance and 'real life'; and *Northanger Abbey* and *Emma* both use scenes set in the theatre for important plot developments. Particularly crucial is *Northanger Abbey*'s scene at the theatre in Bath where, as Paula Byrne points out, 'Henry Tilney, in the audience, is as much part of the spectacle for Catherine as the actors on stage.'[74]

> She was not deceived in her own expectation of pleasure; the comedy so well suspended her care that no one, observing her during the first four acts, would have supposed she had any wretchedness about her. On the beginning of the fifth, however, the sudden view of Mr. Henry

Tilney and his father, joining a party in the opposite box, recalled her to anxiety and distress. The stage could no longer excite genuine merriment – no longer keep her whole attention. Every other look upon an average was directed towards the opposite box; and, for the space of two entire scenes, did she thus watch Henry Tilney, without being once able to catch his eye. No longer could he be suspected of indifference for a play; his notice was never withdrawn from the stage during two whole scenes. At length, however, he did look towards her, and he bowed – but such a bow! No smile, no continued observance attended it; his eyes were immediately returned to their former direction. Catherine was restlessly miserable; she could almost have run round to the box in which he sat and forced him to hear her explanation.[75]

Because there was no dimming of the house lights, Catherine would have been able to see Henry almost as well as she could see the actors, and – given that Austen originally drafted this novel in the 1790s – the Bath theatre described here is evidently the old, Orchard Street, Theatre Royal, which was in use until 1805 and was particularly small and intimate. Its boxes were very close indeed to the dramatic space, and the forestage was within the enclosure of the auditorium, making the audience almost as much participants as consumers.[76]

'At Astley's tonight'

Another famous London venue where such juxtapositions between performance and reality could be explored was Astley's Amphitheatre, founded by Philip Astley in 1770 originally as a performance ring for equestrian displays but later expanding to take in many other kinds of acts.[77] When Austen looked forward to visiting Astley's on 23 August 1796 it was located near the south end of Westminster Bridge: 'We are to be at Astley's tonight, which I am glad of', she told Cassandra.[78] In 1806 Astley moved north of the river and opened his new 'Pavilion' in Wych Street, off the Strand. Built like a playhouse with a stage, orchestra, boxes and galleries, but with a sawdust-covered ring, it could accommodate some three thousand people.[79] It continued to specialize in equestrian displays, but by 1814 (when it had been sold by Astley to the actor Robert Elliston for £2,800) it also offered acrobats, harlequinades, puppet-shows, jugglers, music, comedians and clowns.[80]Astley's was in fact the origin of the nineteenth-century and modern idea of the circus – a term which, although Astley himself did not use it, was deployed by Byron in 1818 when facetiously rhyming about William Upton, who 'For Astley's Circus ... writes / And also for the Surr[e]y' (the Surrey being variously a theatre and a circus, located on the south – or 'Surrey' – side of the Thames.[81] Astley's was very popular with children – and with both the genteel and the working classes and all those in between – and this is reflected in Austen's choice of it as the place where in *Emma* the parentless Harriet Smith and the yeoman farmer Robert Martin resume their courtship.[82] As the guest of Mr and Mrs John Knightley, Robert accompanies them and their two little boys, and Harriet, to Astley's, where they 'were all extremely amused' and, after escorting Harriet through the crowds on the way out, the next day Robert takes the opportunity to ask her to marry him, and is accepted.[83]

As we have seen, Byron knew and liked the famous clown Joseph Grimaldi, and Grimaldi later recounted an elaborate anecdote of 1812 in which Byron tried and failed to persuade him to eat soy sauce with his apple tart.[84] Byron would certainly have seen Grimaldi perform at one of the other 'minor' theatres, the Lyceum on the Strand, in one of his most famous roles as Scaramouch in *Don Juan, or, The Libertine Destroyed*. It is with this pantomime, based on Thomas Shadwell's comedy of 1675, that Byron introduced readers to his hero in the opening stanza of his own epic:

I want a hero: an uncommon want,
    When every year and month sends forth a new one,
Till, after cloying the gazettes with cant,
    The age discovers he is not the true one;
Of such as these, I should not care to vaunt,
    I'll therefore take our ancient friend Don Juan,
We all have seen him, in the pantomime,
Sent to the devil somewhat ere his time.

(Don Juan 1.1–8)[85]

On 14 September 1813 Austen and her nieces also saw and enjoyed 'Don Juan, whom we left in Hell at ½ past 11'. Subtitled *The Libertine Destroyed*, this piece was a mixture of drama and pantomime, enlivened with generous helpings of music, which concluded with a spectacular representation of the infernal regions.[86] Although, as Byron undoubtedly did, Austen appreciated the wily comic *commedia dell'arte* role of Scaramouch (not played by Grimaldi on this occasion, although 'we had Scaremouch & a Ghost – and were delighted'), it was the powerful figure of Don Juan himself that particularly intrigued her. 'I must say that I have seen nobody on the stage that has been a more interesting Character than that compound of Cruelty & Lust', she wrote.[87] The Austens were in a private box 'directly on the Stage', and this gave them the opportunity to appreciate the young and handsome actor James Wallack in the role of Don Juan. Wallack was then at the beginning of a career which went on to include the role of Anhalt in *Lovers' Vows*, Laertes to Kean's Hamlet (he was a particularly good fencer), Jack Absolute in *The Rivals* and Bertuccio in Byron's drama *Marino Faliero*, and which eventually led him to become an admired and respected actor-manager in New York, with his own theatre, 'Wallack's', on Broadway.[88] At the time Byron and the Austens saw him in *Don Juan,* however, he was only eighteen, with 'sparkling' eyes, 'dark, curly and luxuriant' hair, a 'rich sweet and clear' voice and 'finely chiselled' facial features – 'a remarkable specimen of manly beauty', and altogether much more like the sixteen-year-old, 'curly-headed' and 'Tall, handsome, slender, but well-knit' youth that Byron introduces as *his* Don Juan, than the world-weary libertine usually associated with this role.[89] Again, Byron came to know Wallack personally, at Drury Lane, and his attractiveness – and the contrast between this and

Figure 14 *Mr Wallack of Drury Lane*, by Thomas Charles Wageman (1818). In 1813 Austen and Byron both saw the eighteen-year-old James William Wallack playing Don Juan. He later became a respected actor-manager in New York with his own theatre, Wallack's, on Broadway. Private collection.

the 'Cruelty & Lust' portrayed by the Don Juan character – seems to have made the actor and his role particularly 'interesting' both to him and to Austen.

Exeter 'Change

The Lyceum was only a few hundred yards from Henry Austen's home near Covent Garden, where Jane often stayed.[90] Even closer to Henry's home in Henrietta Street was the Exeter 'Change, or Exchange: an arcade on the north side of the Strand lined with individual shops for milliners, sempstresses, hosiers and other traders. Upstairs on the first and second floors was an extensive menagerie that was one of the famous sights of London. Known successively as Pidcock's, Polito's and Cross's, after the names of its proprietors, from the mid-1770s until 1829 it displayed a wide range of exotic wild animals in cages. *Sense and Sensibility*'s John Dashwood uses a trip to the menagerie with his spoilt little son Harry as an excuse for not visiting his sisters in London: 'we were obliged to take Harry to see the wild beasts at Exeter Exchange . . . Harry was vastly pleased', he reports smugly. The Dashwoods would have seen not only lions, tigers and other ferocious animals, but also monkeys, a hippopotamus, a large elephant called Chunee (who performed at some of the theatres nearby) and – apparently – a whale.[91] Cages were stacked one on top of another to save space and to make the show a more dramatic experience for visitors, while the decorative murals showing jungles and forests belied the actual cramped and grim conditions in which the animals were kept.

This must have been where Cassandra saw the 'Elephants & Kangaroons' that Jane mentioned in a letter in February 1811, and it is these captive creatures that she referred to in May 1813 when she described herself as a 'wild Beast' when faced with meeting someone who admired her work.[92] 'I should like to see Miss Burdett very well', she wrote, 'but that I am rather frightened by hearing that she wishes to be introduced to *me*. If I *am* a wild Beast, I cannot help it. It is not my own fault.' The context here – and Austen's other references to animals, such as her comparison of her pregnant niece Anna Lefroy to a 'Poor animal' who 'will be worn out before she is thirty' – makes it clear that it is the threat of being confined and passively 'exhibited' as an author, like the caged wild animals at Exeter 'Change, rather than some more active and exciting 'wild Beast' role for herself, that she is thinking of.[93]

Figure 15 Polito's Royal Menagerie, at the Exeter 'Change on the Strand, London, as pictured in *Ackermann's Repository* in July 1812. Cassandra Austen saw elephants and 'Kangaroons' there in 1811 and Byron described a visit in 1814 when he saw tigers, panthers, antelopes, an elephant, a hyaena, a hippopotamus and an 'ursine sloth'. Private collection.

Byron had an exceptionally strong bond with animals, particularly dogs, and it was when the university authorities would not allow his large Newfoundland dog Boatswain to accompany him to Cambridge that he turned the tables by arriving with a rescued performing bear instead.[94] He came to deplore hunting, shooting and even fishing; voted in the House of Lords for the first attempt at British Parliamentary legislation to limit cruelty to domestic animals, and kept a collection of animals and birds in Ravenna which were allowed to wander freely (and somewhat dangerously) around the house.[95] Shelley on one visit spotted 'eight enormous dogs, three monkeys, five cats, an eagle, a crow and a falcon' and described the resulting scene as a 'Circean palace', characterizing Byron as Homer's sorceress who had turned her former lovers into animals.[96] Byron's journal for 12 November 1814 gives a detailed description of a visit to the London menagerie:

> Two nights ago I saw the tigers sup at Exeter 'Change . . . the fondness of the hyaena for her keeper amused me most. Such a conversazione!
> – There was a 'hippopotamus,' like Lord L[iverpoo]l in the face; and

the 'Ursine Sloth' hath the very voice and manner of my valet – but the tiger talked too much. The elephant took and gave me my money again – took off my hat – opened a door – *trunked* a whip – and behaved so well, that I wish he was my butler. The handsomest animal on earth is one of the panthers; but the poor antelopes are dead. I should hate to see one *here*.[97]

The fact that Jane's eldest brother James and several of her nephews were keen huntsmen does not seem to have conflicted with their affection for pet animals, and James wrote a touching poem addressed to his eleven-year-old son on the death of the boy's first pony, as well as verses reprimanding his daughter's cat Tyger for stealing a mutton steak, and other verses in Tyger's own voice.[98] Jane and her mother and sister, on the other hand, appear never to have kept animals as domestic pets at Chawton or elsewhere, and no pets are named in Jane's letters. Her references to Newfoundlands in her work are somewhat offhand: in her teenage piece 'The Generous Curate' she satirizes the vogue for these huge dogs when she mentions a young sailor posted to Newfoundland: 'from whence he regularly sent home a large Newfoundland Dog every month to his family'.[99] And when, in *Northanger Abbey*, she gives Henry Tilney 'a large Newfoundland puppy and two or three terriers', the indefinite number of the dogs makes them seem little more than stage props to emphasize the hero's masculine 'solitude' at Woodston Parsonage.[100]

Social and political animals

Austen and Byron, however, both deployed animals in their writing to make social and political points. Byron's 1808 'Inscription on the Monument of a Newfoundland Dog', for instance, contrasts the loyalty of the dog with 'man' who is 'Debas'd by slavery, or corrupt by power', and in the bullfight described in *Childe Harold* canto 1 it is the bull and the horses, rather than the matadors or the inhumane audience, that are cast as the heroes.[101] Fanny Price's bond with the 'old grey pony' she rides in *Mansfield Park* is presented as part of her sensitive nature, while Lady Bertram's Pug has been characterized by Stephanie Howard-Smith as part of the slavery context of the same novel, through its association with the then-notoriously spoiled pugs (dressed in little scarlet bonnets and cloaks, and each with its own liveried servant) that were kept by Lady Penrhyn, the wife of the well-known Liverpool MP, slave-owner and anti-abolitionist.[102]

Austen was in London in November 1814, but not until the 25th, and it does not seem likely that she and Byron could have encountered each other at the Exeter 'Change then. A moment when they may, however, have been at the same place at the same time was in May 1813, at an exhibition of Sir Joshua Reynolds's paintings displayed at the British Institution in Pall Mall. Both Austen and Byron had an ulterior motive in visiting this show, and both were looking for a particular portrait. Jane in fact searched three different London exhibitions, and at the one in Spring Gardens (off St James's) was particularly pleased with 'a small portrait of Mrs. Bingley, excessively like her. I went in hopes of seeing one of her Sister, but there was no Mrs. Darcy.'[103] What might be called Austen's 'ekphrastic' literary game continued at the Royal Academy Summer Exhibition at Somerset House and at the Reynolds exhibition (apparently visited by the Austens on 24 May); but at both she was disappointed, 'for there was nothing like Mrs. D. at either. – I can only imagine that Mr. D. prizes any Picture of her too much to like it should be exposed to the public eye. – I can imagine he wd have that sort [of] feeling – that mixture of Love, Pride & Delicacy.' But 'setting aside this disappointment, I had great amusement among the Pictures', she reported.[104]

Byron probably visited the Reynolds exhibition in the second or third week of May. The show included Sir Joshua's 1770–1 portrait of the then

Figure 16 *Elizabeth Lamb, Viscountess Melbourne, with her son Peniston*, by Sir Joshua Reynolds (1770–71). This painting was seen by both Austen and Byron in the British Institution's exhibition in London in 1813. © National Portrait Gallery, London.

seventeen-year-old Lady Melbourne (Lady Caroline Lamb's mother-in-law and aunt of Byron's future wife), and this became the opportunity for a flirtatious exchange between the 25-year-old poet and his 61-year-old mentor and confidante.[105] 'I *must* see you at Sir *Joshua's* – though I don't much like venturing on the sight of *seventeen* – it is bad enough *now* – it must have been *worse then* – the painter was not so much to blame as you seem to imagine by adding a few years – he foresaw you would lose nothing by them', he wrote mischievously to Lady Melbourne on 7 May. In *Don Juan* canto 16 the musings upon family portraits – 'the pale smile of Beauties in the grave, / The charms of other days' – are decidedly melancholy, and the poet reflects that 'A picture is the past; even ere its frame / Be gilt, who sate hath ceased to be the same.'[106] But in 1813 both Byron and Austen were gaily and playfully fantasizing that a portrait might have a life and a back-story of its own, to be called into being by the power of their imaginations: imaginations which had been richly fed not only by the paintings, but also by the plays, pantomimes, exhibitions, shows, performances and other entertainment which had brought the two authors into such a close and rewarding area of shared experience in Regency London.

Notes

1. See in particular Byrne and Gay (both 2002).

2. Dow (2021) 119.

3. Dow (2021) 120.

4. 'To the Duke of D[orset]' 66–9, *LBCPW* 1.68.

5. 'The First Act of a Comedy', Austen ed. Sabor 219.

6. Gay 4.

7. Elledge 57, 120–34, 156–64.

8. Boyes (1988) 27–38.

9. Mary Ann Bristoe quoted in Boyes (1988) 28–9.

10. *MP* vol. 1, chap. 14, 155. Elizabeth Pigot quoted in Boyes (1988) 30.

11. Boyes (1988) 34–5.

12. *DJ* 16.820, *LBCPW* 5.649. Mary Ann Bristoe quoted in Boyes (1988) 33–8.

13. Pigot quoted in Boyes (1988) 34.

14. 'His form it was stout, and his shoulders were broad': 'A parody upon "The Little Grey Man" in Lewis' *Tales of Wonder*', 37, *LBCPW* 1.14.

15. Boyes (1988) 36.

16. MacCarthy 49.

17. Henry Austen in Austen-Leigh ed. Sutherland 140. Caroline Austen in Austen-Leigh ed. Sutherland 174.

18. Byrne 25, quoting Knight (*Fanny Knight's Journals*). 'Virtue Rewarded' is the subtitle of Samuel Richardson's novel *Pamela* (1740).

19. Dow (2021) 122.

20. Byrne 25, quoting Knight (*Fanny Knight's Journals*).

21. Byrne 27, quoting Charlotte M. Yonge.

22. MacCarthy 409. Medwin 132.

23. *MP* vol. 1, chap. 13, 146.

24. *MP* vol. 3, chap. 3, 390.

25. Henry Nelson Coleridge 13.

26. *BLJ* 3.244, *Journal,* 19 February 1814.

27. *BLJ* 4.212, to Lady Melbourne, 17 October 1814. Armstrong (155) cites Thomas Moore's account of how Kean made Byron furious by leaving early a dinner arranged in his honour, in order to take the chair at a pugilistic supper.

28. MacCarthy 219. *BLJ* 6.206, to John Murray, 12 August 1819.

29. *JAL* 257–60, to Cassandra Austen, 5–8 March 1814.

30. Byrne 53.

31. *JAL* 257–8, to Cassandra Austen, 5–8 March 1814.

32. *JAL* 257–8, to Cassandra Austen, 5–8 March 1814.

33. *MP* vol. 1, chap. 5, 51. *MP* vol. 1, chap. 18, 194. Hawkins 1.70.

34. *BLJ* 4.216, to Annabella Milbanke, 19 October 1814.

35. *BLJ* 4.216, to Annabella Milbanke, 19 October 1814. *BLJ* 4.115, to Thomas Moore, 8[?] May 1814.

36. Gay 91, 174.

37. Tomalin 227.

38. *BLJ* 3.249, *Journal,* 10 March 1814.

39. *BLJ* 4.235, to Annabella Milbanke, 28 November 1814.

40. *JAL* 283, to Anna Lefroy, 29 November 1814.

41. *JAL* 122, to Cassandra Austen, 20–22 February 1807.

42. Johnson and Tuite 109.

43. Byrne 39.

44. *JAL* 257–8, to Cassandra Austen, 5–8 March 1814.

45. 'Addendum' to the Preface to *Marino Faliero*, Byron ed. Cochran, 25. *BLJ* 3. 226, *Journal,* 28–30 November 1813.

46. *LBCPW* 3.103. *BLJ* 324, *Journal,* 27 November 1813.

47. *BLJ* 3.175, to John Murray, 27 November 1813.

48. *BLJ* 2.204, to Lord Holland, 23 September 1812. 'I think Elliston should be the man'.

49. *JAL* 198, to Cassandra Austen, 24 January 1813.

50. *BLJ* 2.214, to Lord Holland, 28 September 1812.

51. MacCarthy 185.

52. The 1794 Drury Lane Theatre accommodated more than 3,600 spectators and the 1812 theatre seated 3,060. Its capacity today is 1,996.

53. Gay 13.

54. Scott quoted in Viveash (2005) 423.

55. Cochran and Allen 7.

56. *BLJ* 4.294, to Leigh Hunt, [?] May–1 June 1815.

57. *JAL* 256, to Cassandra Austen, 3 March 1814.

58. Scott, *Encyclopaedia Britannica,* cited by Gay 15.

59. 'Preface to Marino Faliero' 165–78, *LBCPW* 4.305.

60. *BLJ* 9.36–7, 'Detached Thoughts' 70, 1821–2.

61. *BLJ* 8.186–7, to John Murray, 23 August 1821. Erdman 219.

62. Armstrong, 145–50. *BLJ* 4.336, to the Reverend Charles Robert Maturin, 21 December 1815.

63. Armstrong, who argues strongly that the role of Manfred was written with Kean in mind, associates this mockery of 'aristocratic' spirits with Byron's perception of the 'proletarian masculinity he saw and admired in Kean' (155).

64. Richardson 136.

65. *LBCPW* 5.52–9.

66. Austen ed. Todd and Bree 558. Todd and Bree (cxvi) conclude that Jane's niece Anna 'composed the piece with her aunt writing out her words'.

67. Austen-Leigh ed. Sutherland 71.

68. Mullan 73.

69. Mullan 73.

70. Byrne 30–2.

71. John Poole, *Hamlet Travestie in Three Acts* (1811) 5, quoted by Cochran, *Byron in London* 115.

72. Byrne 45.

73. *LBCMP* 192–3. *BLJ* 9.36–7, 'Detached Thoughts' 70, 1821–2.

74. Byrne 16.

75. *NA* vol. 1, chap. 2, 91–2.

76. Byrne 16.

77. Byrne 30.

78. *JAL* 5, to Cassandra Austen, 23 August 1796.

79. Byrne 32.

80. Elliston became the manager of the Theatre Royal, Drury Lane, in 1819. Christopher Murray (np).

81. *BLJ* 6.27. The Royal Surrey Theatre was in St George's Fields, north of Hyde Park.

82. Byrne 34.

83. *Emma* vol. 3, chap. 18, 515.

84. Grimaldi 2.181.

85. *LBCPW* 5.9.

86. Lucas 255.

87. Viveash (2002) 128. *JAL* 221, to Cassandra Austen, 15–16 September 1813.

88. Lucas 257.

89. Lucas 257 quoting James Hackett in Bordman (no page reference given). *DJ* 1.426, *LBCPW* 5.25.

90. *JAL* 218, to Cassandra Austen, 15–16 September 1813.

91. Adam-Wolfgang Töppfer (letter of 1816) quoted in Agasse 96.

92. *JAL* 80, to Cassandra Austen, 5–6 May 1801. *BLJ* 212–13, to Cassandra Austen, 24 May 1813.

93. *JAL* 336, to Fanny Knight, 25 March 1817.

94. The bear was kept in the stables of a coaching inn, not in Byron's rooms at Trinity College.

95. Kenyon Jones (2001) 79–94.

96. Shelley 2.331.

97. *BLJ* 3.206, *Journal,* 14 November 1813.

98. James Austen ed. Selwyn 35, 51 and 52.

99. Austen ed. Sabor 94.

100. *NA* vol. 2, chap. 11, 219.

101. *CHP* 1.765–87, *LBCPW* 2.36–7.

102. Howard-Smith 193–4.

103. *JAL* 211–13, to Cassandra Austen, 24 May 1813.

104. See Wootton 33.

105. Reynolds's 'Lady Melbourne and child' was included in the British Institution's exhibition of 1813. *BLJ* 3.46, letter to Lady Melbourne, 7 May 1813, and footnote 1.

106. *DJ* 16.145–52, *LBCPW* 5.624.

CHAPTER 4
PORTSMOUTHS AND HANSONS
'LUNATIZING' THE EARL

On Wednesday 9 March 1814 Jane Austen was suffering from a cold. It had 'been very heavy in my head', she wrote to Cassandra, and she thought she might stay in bed late the next day. The cold was a nuisance, because she was relishing her stay in London with her brother Henry, who was then living in Henrietta Street, Covent Garden: going to the theatre, shopping and dining out with her brother Edward and her niece Fanny. But the weather was bad, too – 'nothing but Thickness & Sleet', she reported. 'What cruel weather this is! And here is Lord Portsmouth married too to Miss Hanson!'[1]

Half a mile away, at his lodgings in Bennet Street, St James's, Lord Byron was also thinking about the weather and the Portsmouth-Hanson marriage. It had been a 'misty morning' two days earlier when, after attending two balls the night before, he 'rose at seven – ready by half-past eight – went to Mr. Hanson's, Bloomsbury Square – went to church with his eldest daughter, Mary Anne (a good girl), and gave her away to the Earl of Portsmouth'.[2] On Thursday 10 March he was pleased to receive 'many, and the kindest, thanks from Lady Portsmouth, *père* and *mère*, for my matchmaking'.[3]

'I don't regret it', Byron confided to his journal, with as much complacency as Austen's Emma might have expressed if she had succeeded in making a match between Harriet Smith and Mr Elton. Mary Ann Hanson was the 23-year-old eldest daughter of John Hanson, who had been Byron's guardian and trustee during his minority and had continued as his lawyer when he reached adulthood. Mary Ann's husband the Earl was forty-six: but, although the match was distinctly unequal in age and class terms, Byron thought 'she looks the countess well. . . . It is odd how well she carries her new honours. She looks a different woman, and high-bred, too.'[4] It was, however, Austen's guarded tone about the marriage – the implication that it was somehow as 'cruel' as the weather – that proved to be correct. Far worse than anything that might have happened if Harriet *had* wed Mr Elton, the Portsmouth marriage ended – and even began – in deceit, cruelty, violence, madness and notoriety.

John Charles Wallop, third Earl of Portsmouth, is the only person, apart from their publisher John Murray, whose first-hand interactions with both Austen and Byron are recorded. His life touched both theirs in various strange ways, and their contact with this troubling figure – who was eventually declared a lunatic at the age of fifty-five – revealed aspects of their respective worlds which were much darker than the bright lights of Regency London that they were both enjoying in March 1814. The Austen family's relationship with him had begun in 1773, two years before Jane's birth, when, as the five-year-old Lord Lymington, heir to the earldom, he came to live with them for six months. The placement probably arose out of the friendship between Jane's father and another local clergyman, the splendidly named Honourable and Reverend Dr Barton Wallop, Rector of the nearby Hampshire village of Upper Wallop, who was Lymington's uncle and godfather. The child was placed with the Austens as a boarder at their vicarage in Steventon, some 10 miles from the grand Hurstbourne Park which was his home, and he was one of the earliest of a series of boy pupils who helped to increase the Austen family's modest income as paying guests to be educated by the Reverend George Austen, former proctor of St John's College, Oxford. Many of these boys remained lifelong friends of the Austen family, and one of them, Tom Fowle, became the fiancé of Jane's sister Cassandra (but tragically died before they could marry).

Mrs Austen's succinct analysis of Lymington's character is typically sharply observed: he was, she reported, 'Very backward for his Age, but good-temper'd and orderly'.[5] Portsmouth's recent biographer hesitates to categorize his condition or diagnose his disabilities in modern terms, but it is probable that he would now be identified as a person with autism. He had a combination of abilities and disabilities which made normal life impossible, and later provoked long and profound debates about whether he was, in contemporary terms, an 'idiot', a 'lunatic' or, as Byron described him, 'no . . . more insane than any other person going to be married'.[6] He grew up to be a large and well-built man, but his appearance was marred by his eyes, which were abnormally shaped and had a squint.[7] Possibly thanks to the Austens' early efforts, his handwriting was neat and legible; as an adult he could speak French well, and he was particularly good at arithmetic and accounting. During his very strict upbringing by his forceful mother Urania, Countess of Portsmouth, who was determined to present him as being as good an earl as possible, he learned manners and social graces enough to pass in society without undue comment. But this near-normal public appearance hid a private and emotional life that was stunted, strange and became deeply disturbing as time went on.

James, George, Edward, Henry and Cassandra

The boy also had a stammer. Mrs Austen described how the 'hesitation in his speech' was growing worse during the time he spent with her family, and this and his poor learning skills must have contrasted particularly sharply with the exceptional articulacy, sprightliness and intelligence of her own children who were his playmates at the vicarage. Eight-year-old James Austen, a future clergyman, was perhaps already experimenting with the verse-writing that he later perfected in prologues and epilogues for the family's private theatricals and for his Oxford magazine *The Loiterer*, and Edward Austen, who was almost exactly the same age as Lymington, grew up to own and successfully run two large estates, with a status comparable to Mr Darcy's.[8] Toddler Henry Austen – later a soldier, army agent, banker and clergyman – was also in the house, but Cassandra, Jane's beloved older sister, then only a few months old, had been sent to live with a foster family in the village, as was the custom for all the Austen children. They would remain with the village family from the time they were weaned until they were toddlers – visiting their parents regularly but not living at home with them again until they had learned to run about and talk.[9]

There was also another Austen brother who was probably not at home with the family in 1773, since at some stage he was sent away permanently to live elsewhere. This was little George Austen, the second son, born in 1766, who suffered from fits and failed to develop normally. It has been suggested that, since Jane Austen mentions 'talking on her fingers' in a letter of 1808, she might have used sign language to communicate with him.[10] He was evidently severely disabled: when he was six his godfather commented that he 'must be provided for without the least hopes of his being able to assist himself', and it was with Christian resignation that his father wrote: 'We have this comfort, he cannot be a bad or a wicked child.'[11] Although he was still at home in November 1772, the Austens seem to have felt it was better in the long-term for him not to live with them, and perhaps it was the arrival of little Lord Lymington in 1773 that spurred them into the decision to send George away from home. It is ironic that at the same time that they were welcoming one boy with learning difficulties into their family on a paying basis, they were planning to send their own disabled son away and paying for him to be cared for by others.[12] George was placed with the Cullum (or Culham) family who were thatchers in the nearby village of Monk Sherborne, and he remained with them until his death in 1838.[13] There are records of payments from his brother Edward Austen (later Knight) for his care, his clothes, and his medical and funeral expenses, but no mention of him in Jane's surviving letters.[14] By the time James Edward Austen-Leigh was writing his *Memoir* of his Aunt Jane in 1869, George had been brushed out of the record completely, and Edward, Jane's third brother, was presented as the second.[15]

George was, moreover, not the first member of the family to be 'put away' like this. Also living with the Cullum family until his death in 1821 was Thomas Leigh, George and Jane's uncle, described as the 'imbecile brother' of Mrs Austen.[16] It must have been especially hard for Mrs Austen to see one of her own children develop similar problems to those of her own disabled brother and, given that George was only her second child, she must have been anxious every time a new baby was born that they might share his handicap. Scanning the Austen and Leigh family trees does indeed show a distressing number of members suffering from mental or developmental disabilities. In 1774 an inquisition of insanity consulted the 'mad-doctors' who later attended King George III and found that Mrs Austen's distant cousin Edward Leigh, fifth Baron Leigh was 'a Lunatick of unsound mind', while Elizabeth Broadnax-May-Knight, sister of Thomas Knight II who adopted Edward Austen, was described as 'feeble-minded' and was looked after by attendants at her own establishment near Godmersham.[17] Jane's aunt on her father's side, his sister Leonora Austen, was described by her brother-in-law as 'poor Leonora', and research suggests that she may have been brain-damaged from birth.[18] She lived with the Linton and Cumberlege families in London, never worked or married, and had to be supported financially by her siblings all her life until her death in 1783. Leonora's great-nephew Hastings (the son of Jane's cousin and later sister-in-law, Eliza de Feuillide) also did not develop normally. He was born in June 1786, and two years later his cousin Philly Walters wrote:

> Poor little Hastings has had another fit; we all fear very much his faculties are hurt; many people say he has the appearance of a weak head: that his eyes are particular is very certain: our fears are of his being like poor George Austen. He has every symptom of good health, but cannot yet use his feet in the least, nor yet talk, tho' he makes a great noise continually.[19]

Hastings died in 1801 at the age of fifteen.[20] Unlike his other disabled relatives, however, he did live with his mother, grandmother and stepfather and was very affectionately cared for by his family: an arrangement which was possible because Eliza was rich enough to be able to hire a devoted servant to help look after him. Jane knew Hastings well, and she must also have been acutely aware of her other close, disabled relatives living in the shadows, out of sight of her own immediate family.

Melancholy

There was, as far as is known, no incidence of learning or developmental disability in Byron's family; but mental illness and in particular a tendency to 'melancholy' was certainly characteristic of his mother's family, the Gordons of Gight. Byron's maternal great-grandfather, Alexander Gordon, drowned himself in the river Ythan in Aberdeenshire in 1760, and Byron told John Murray that his grandfather, George Gordon, was also

> strongly suspected of suicide – (he was found drowned in the Avon in Bath [in 1779]) – there was no apparent cause – as he was rich, respected – and of considerable intellectual resources – hardly forty years of age – and not at all addicted to any unhinging vice – It was however but a strong suspicion – owing to the manner of his death – and his melancholy temper.[21]

Byron had been informed by his mother that 'in temper I more resembled my maternal Grandfather than any of my father's family', and in January 1816 he himself came close being declared insane on his wife's testimony about his bizarre behaviour during their marriage (see Chapter 5).[22] From *Childe Harold* onwards, his works became famous (and sought after) for their exploration and expression of 'melancholy', and occasionally he was chided by reviewers for not being melancholy *enough*: 'Sometimes the Childe forgets (accidentally, we believe,) the heart-struck melancholy of his temper, and deviates into a species of pleasantry, which, to say the truth, appears to us very flippant, and very unworthy of the person to whom it is attributed', demurred the *Eclectic Review*.[23] It was, indeed, the disturbing incongruity of 'flippant' and melancholy passages side by side, rather than the fashionably melancholy mode itself, that suggested to Byron's contemporaries possible signs of mental instability in the author of

Childe Harold.[24] Other Byronic heroes, such as the Giaour and the Corsair, manifest their perhaps less complicated melancholy through personal bitterness, unsociability, scorn and disdain, but they seem to have no lack of will to action – especially where that action is concerned with revenge – and this sets them apart from modern definitions of depression which generally include loss of interest in activity, low self-esteem and anxiety. Perhaps closer to modern interpretations is the contrast Byron draws, in 'The Dream' (1816), between the overt 'sickness of the soul' which 'the world calls phrenzy', and the 'deeper madness', 'melancholy', which he believes is inevitable for 'the wise' who see life as it really is:

> The lady of his love; – Oh! She was changed
> As by the sickness of the soul; her mind
> Had wandered from its dwelling, . . .
> She was become
> The queen of a fantastic realm; her thoughts
> Were combinations of disjointed things;
> And forms impalpable and unperceived
> Of others' sight familiar were to hers.
> And this the world calls phrenzy; but the wise
> Have a far deeper madness, and the glance
> Of melancholy is a fearful gift;
> What is it but the telescope of truth?
> Which strips the distance of its fantasies,
> And brings life near in utter nakedness,
> Making the cold reality too real!
>
> ('The Dream', 168–83)[25]

Most of Austen's female characters who undergo the kind of adverse circumstances that might be expected to make them melancholic or depressed (including Jane and Elizabeth Bennet, Fanny Price and Emma Woodhouse) are shown to be able to overcome or repress their grief, sorrow, anxiety or frustration so that it is rarely noticed by their families. In *Sense and Sensibility* Elinor's heroically repressive behaviour is positively contrasted with the implied selfishness of Marianne's very overt suffering, brought about partly by her own misjudgement, and in *Persuasion* what might be termed the 'false' or 'over-acted' (and possibly 'Byronic') melancholy of Captain Benwick is, as we saw in Chapter 2, compared unfavourably with Anne Elliot's self-analysed and movingly described private misery after her parting with Wentworth. A less sympathetic character who might be thought of as suffering from depression is Lady Bertram, if we assume that she was not always the dull, indolent and disengaged figure that she appears in the novel (and which makes her the obvious reason for the need for Fanny at Mansfield Park). Also cognitively impaired, but devotedly cared for, is Emma's father the 'valetudinarian' Mr Woodhouse, and it has been suggested that his condition may be the result of a physical illness such as an underactive thyroid gland, which would cause shiveriness, mental nervousness, weakness and difficulty in swallowing.[26]

'Beware of fainting-fits', the dying Sophia advises Laura in the fourteen-year-old Austen's comic novel, 'Love and Freindship'. 'Run mad as often as you choose, but do not faint.'[27] The somewhat uncomfortable humour here lies in the idea that young ladies of sensibility can choose whether or not to indulge in faints or frenzies as an aspect of their assumed, fashionably romantic, behaviour. Laura allows herself a two-hour 'phrenzy' (in which she hallucinates a leg of mutton and is convinced that her dead husband has been taken for a cucumber), but she can swiftly snap out of it once she realizes that night is approaching and she needs to find shelter. The insouciant assumption that fainting and madness are both voluntary is at the playful end of a continuum that leads to the idea that self-control, perseverance, stoicism and secrecy are admirable ways of dealing with mental suffering, however painful it may be. And although the effect of melancholy is differently gendered by Austen and Byron, this belief in the need for suppression seems to be common to them both.

'Attentive recollection'

The Portsmouth family may have chosen the Austens as carers for little Lord Lymington specifically because of George Austen's disability, and certainly Mrs Austen was particularly well-placed to understand and meet her boarder's needs.[28] Although the future Earl was no longer at the vicarage by the time Jane was born in December 1775, the Austens remained in social contact with him: the Portsmouths were one of the richest and most powerful families in Hampshire, active in the patronage and social life of the area and sponsors of many of the balls and assemblies that Jane attended. She met the Earl frequently and was evidently well aware of his character and the developments in his life and circumstances. On 1 November 1800, for example, she described to Cassandra 'a pleasant Ball' at Basingstoke Town Hall, with 'the Portsmouths, Dorchesters, Boltons, Portals & Clerks' in attendance. 'Lord Portsmouth surpassed the rest in his attentive recollection of you', she told her sister. He 'enquired more into the length of your absence, & concluded by desiring to be "remembered to you when I wrote next"'.[29] Jane also noticed that the Earl's new wife, Lady Portsmouth, 'had got a different dress on', which implies that she was used to seeing the Countess quite frequently; and less than three weeks later she attended another ball held by the couple at Hurstbourne Park itself to mark the first anniversary of their marriage.[30] In subsequent years this anniversary ball became a regular and popular annual event for the Austens and their friends.[31]

This first, 1799, marriage, however, like Portsmouth's second one in 1814, was not quite all it seemed. The Earl's family had deemed that it would be impossible (or unwise) for him to father children, and they had created a legal settlement that made the Honourable Newton Wallop (Portsmouth's next brother, later known as Newton Fellowes) heir to the estates, which were worth some £17,000 or £18,000 a year. There was therefore a strong impetus for Newton to prevent his brother from being put in a situation where he might have a son – or where a fertile and unfaithful wife might produce a child who was not in fact his but could claim to inherit the title and the property. Keeping the Earl unwed had therefore at first seemed like the best course for his family, but in the summer of 1799 another problem had arisen, requiring Portsmouth's respectability to be reinforced through marriage. This was when he either ran away with, or was abducted by, his Swiss valet, Jean Seilaz, and at Yarmouth spent time locked in an inn bedroom with Seilaz and signed papers drawn up by a rascally Hampshire attorney named Gabriel Tahourdin, making over to Tahourdin all authority to manage his estates. Some nine years later the same Tahourdin was involved with Henry Austen's bank in other dubious transactions concerning the illegal sale of positions in the East India Company.[32] At Yarmouth the Earl came very close to being taken onto a boat bound for Hamburg, and this move was only prevented at the last moment by the arrival of a rescue party comprising Newton, the Reverend Dr John Garnett (an old family friend) and the Portsmouth's family lawyer, John Hanson.[33] The Earl was quickly extricated and returned to the family seat at Hurstbourne Park, but because of worries about his safety – or about his sexuality – the family decided that wedlock was now the best solution in the circumstances.

The Honourable Grace Norton, who married the Earl in November 1799, was a member of the wealthy and aristocratic Grantley family from Surrey, but she was forty-seven at the time of her marriage, while her husband was thirty-two. The marriage was one of convenience and was arranged by the families on both sides, providing a home and the title of Countess for Grace, and for the Earl a wife who was expected to be able to 'manage' him: and who did so, on the whole successfully, for many years, with the help of a burly manservant, Charley Coombes. The other expectation, of course, was that at her age Grace would NOT bear children. In the legal settlement signed the day before the marriage on 23 November 1799, Portsmouth handed over his estates to four trustees: his brother Newton, Grace's brother Lord Grantley, Dr Garnett and the lawyer John Hanson (who had drawn up the settlement).[34]

Increasing homophobia

News of the Earl's abduction by Seilaz is likely to have reached the Austens through various routes. Their close friends and relatives-by-marriage, the Lloyds, lived at Ibthorpe, just down the road from Hurstbourne, and the Austens also maintained friendly relations with the widow and daughter of Portsmouth's uncle Dr Barton Wallop.[35] They would certainly have heard about the next stage of the saga when reports of Seilaz's attempts to blackmail Portsmouth on the grounds of sodomy were widely reported in the press in 1802. The Portsmouths' response to Seilaz's blackmail attempt was to take their former servant to court for attempting to extort money dishonestly: a very brave move because, if Seilaz's defence that the Earl had indeed had sex with him had been believed, the Earl would have been guilty of a felony that was punishable by death. This was an era of increasing homophobia in Britain, and sixty men were hanged for sodomy in England between 1800 and 1830.[36] Others who were convicted of same-sex offences faced being attacked by angry crowds in the pillory, and at least one man was stoned to death in this way. Women (especially prostitutes) were expected to be particularly outraged by this crime, and they were given special access to pelt the men at close range with stones, mud, offal and excrement.[37] The newspapers did not, of course, print Seilaz's accusation in so many words, resorting to long dashes to replace the words 'sodomy' and 'sodomitical' and referring to 'a nameless crime'. The coverage was extensive, however, and the *Hampshire Chronicle* on 13 December 1802 devoted more than a column to a report of the case in the Court of the King's Bench on 7 December. It quoted the words of the lawyer acting for the prosecution of Seilaz, Thomas Erskine (later a Whig associate of Byron's), to the effect that 'God, in his infinite wisdom' had 'implant[ed] in the mind of man, an abhorrence of this crime, the tendency of which was to disappoint the works of the Creator, by diminishing those joys which Divine Providence intended for the continuation of our species.'

Usually in such cases, as Erskine explained to the jury, the blackmailer took care to disguise or distance himself from any personal involvement in the alleged sodomy, but in this case, as Erskine pointed out, Seilaz had 'directly and plainly avowed his own guilt' when, in his letter to Portsmouth of 18 April 1801, he threatened to 'expose to the world the repeated –– attempts you have made on me'. The letter was, Erskine said, 'the most daring profligacy that ever was exhibited in a Court of Justice', and he praised the Earl for pursuing the prosecution, mentioning particularly that he 'was married, and stood in a circle of high connections, where he was esteemed and honoured'. Portsmouth was cross-examined and spoke of Seilaz as 'a faithful servant' and admitted that the valet had been owed about £200 by him when they parted.[38] The jury returned a unanimous verdict of Seilaz's guilt in his attempt to extort money dishonestly but, since he had been deported in 1800 to Hamburg, no punishment could be meted out to him. Seilaz did in fact have an opportunity to tell his side of the story through written testimony to the Court of Chancery in 1803, when the Portsmouths brought in a bill to declare that the legal documents the Earl had signed for Seilaz were false; but Seilaz's account of events 'fell on deaf ears' and there appear to have been no newspaper reports at this stage.[39]

How closely might Austen have followed this case? In early December 1802 she was staying with her friends Catherine and Alethea Bigg at Manydown House, within a few miles of the Earl at Hurstbourne Park. But she was also distracted by personal concerns, since she had just accepted – and then after a night of reflection refused – a marriage proposal from her friends' younger brother, Harris. If it had gone ahead, the marriage would eventually have made her the mistress of a large and prosperous estate and, at the age of nearly twenty-seven, perhaps she was tempted to avoid the prospect of spinsterhood. But Harris, who was twenty-one, was 'very plain in person – awkward & even uncouth in manner – nothing but his size to recommend him', according to Jane's niece Caroline (who might almost have been describing Lord Portsmouth), while another niece believed that Jane had accepted him 'in a momentary fit of self-delusion'.[40] Harris also had a particularly unattractive hyphenated surname, and we can only speculate on the effects on Austen's reputation and the sales of her future novels (had she still been able to write them) if the work that was first presented as 'By A Lady' had then been revealed to be by 'Mrs Harris Bigg-Wither'. Perhaps these events distracted her from reading the details of the Portsmouth case, but it is impossible to believe that she remained unaware of it altogether.

Sexual knowingness

And, when she did hear about it, would Jane have grasped the full implications of Seilaz's accusations against the Earl? Literary commentators are markedly divided in their opinions about the extent of sexual knowingness and deliberate risqué allusion in Austen's novels and other work. On the one hand, critics such as Jill Heydt-Stevenson have suggested that there is a good deal of 'bawdy humor and body politics' in Austen's writing and that she does indeed mean a *double-entendre* when, for instance, in chapter 10 of *Pride and Prejudice*, she has Miss Bingley say to Mr Darcy, 'I am afraid you do not like your pen. Let me mend it for you. I mend pens remarkably well', while Darcy's answer 'thank you – but I always mend my own', might, as Heydt-Stevenson claims, 'playfully invoke [. . .] auto eroticism'.[41] And is Lydia's letter home from Brighton in chapter 5 of volume 3 ('I wish you would tell Sally to mend a great slit in my worked muslin gown') intended to signal the loss of her virginity to Wickham?[42] And then there is the heavily allusive scene in chapter 10 of volume 1 of *Mansfield Park*, where Maria Bertram escapes around the side of a locked iron gate to join her future lover Henry Crawford while Fanny, watching helplessly, warns: 'you will certainly hurt yourself against those spikes – you will tear your gown – you will be in danger of slipping into the ha-ha', which does indeed seem to indicate that Austen (if not Fanny) was deliberately using sexually suggestive and what we would now call Freudian language.

On the other hand, some of these supposed bawdy references may seem to rely too much on modern (especially American) slang usage. Does John Thorpe, in chapter 7 of volume 1 of *Northanger Abbey*, really 'congratulate . . . himself on his masculine prowess by displacing it on to his carriage' when he describes his horse-drawn gig as 'Well hung; town built'?[43] Is Captain Wentworth actually being alluded to in the same metaphor in *Persuasion,* when in chapter 19 Lady Russell comments on some curtains as being 'the handsomest and best hung of any in Bath'?[44] And when Wentworth himself compares his first warship, the *Asp*, to an 'old pelisse' or cloak, and describes it to Louisa Musgrove as 'a dear old Asp to me. She did all that I wanted. I knew she would. I knew that we should [...] go to the bottom together' is he in fact making a 'scatological double pun on an "old ASS" and a "bottom"', and 'suggesting, in modern sexual slang, that Anne Elliot is in effect a worn-out old "piece of ass", one that Wentworth, in code, is telling Louisa he would like to exchange for a new, unused, fresh "pelisse" like Louisa'?[45]

In 1991 Eve Kosofsky Sedgwick gained notoriety for suggesting that Jane herself enjoyed a sexual relationship with her sister Cassandra, and as Peter Sabor, editor of Austen's *Juvenilia*, notes, the teenage Austen's awareness of masculine same-sex attraction is clearly evident in her juvenile work.[46] In *The History of England* (written when she was only fifteen) Lambert Simnel is described as 'the widow' of Richard III and, at the court of King James I, Henry Percy's 'Attentions' are 'entirely Confined to Lord Mounteagle' while Sir Robert Carr is described as the King's 'pet'. What is referred to as James's 'keener penetration' in his close friendships with young men is, Sabor thinks, 'probably a risqué double entendre'.[47] Austen's most apparent use of risqué and knowing language about homosexuality is surely that in chapter 6 of volume 1 of *Mansfield Park*, where she has Mary Crawford declare to Edmund and Fanny: 'Certainly, my home at my uncle's brought me acquainted with a circle of admirals. Of *Rears* and *Vices*, I saw enough.'[48] And she adds provocatively: 'Now do not be suspecting me of a pun, I entreat.' Austen seems to signal the sexual allusion not only by Mary's explicit reference to making a pun but also by the way in which Edmund (the future clergyman) feels 'grave' about the tone of her remarks. And surely this is what Edmund is thinking of when he anxiously asks his young cousin: '[W]as there nothing in her conversation that struck you Fanny, as not quite right?' (The innocent Fanny responds that Mary ought not to have been so 'ungrateful' to her uncle for his kindness to her brother.)

Cultural conventions

Even in this case, however, respected Austen scholars such as John Wiltshire have insisted that 'it is inconceivable, given the proprieties of the period' that Austen would consciously introduce the subject of sodomy in the navy into her text, while Brian Southam, author of *Jane Austen and the Navy*, maintains that 'Mary Crawford's "pun" means nothing of the sort', and argues that Mary is not making a reference to sodomy but only to the large bottoms and generally bad morals of her uncle's friends.[49] The 'cultural conventions' of 'polite society' in Austen's time 'allowed no place for joking about sodomy', Southam insists, contending that 'a novel announced as the work of "A LADY" could be counted on to be ladylike in its freedom from indecent humour'. He cites the change from free eighteenth-century manners to the 'March of Modesty' in the early nineteenth century and quotes in support of his argument Byron's lines from *Hints from Horace* (1811):

> In such an age, when all aspire to Taste;
> The dirty language, and the noisome jest,
> Which pleased in Swift of yore, we now detest.

> (*Hints from Horace* 392–94)[50]

These literary debates may remain unresolved, but in support of the argument that Austen would indeed have understood about Seilaz's accusations of Portsmouth, we can cite the experience of her two sailor brothers, both of whom rose to the rank of admiral and were involved in several naval courts trying sodomy cases. With more than half a million men in the armed forces and the merchant navy during the Napoleonic wars, Britain showed a particular anxiety about same-sex sexual contact in this period, and between 1795 and 1837 the Navy held over 180 trials of this kind, giving rise to thousands of reports in the press about naval sodomy.[51] Between them, Frank and Charles Austen served on at least ten naval trials trying homosexual crimes before 1840 and were involved in sentencing at least five men to death on these grounds.[52] Although it is unlikely that Frank and Charles would have discussed their experiences in any detail with their sister, the prominence of the topic in this period makes it likely that Jane did know about it, and could apply her knowledge to the Portsmouth case.

Byron was a fourteen-year-old schoolboy at the time of the case in December 1802 and, in the highly sexualized atmosphere of Harrow, he and his schoolmates may well have noticed and joked about the press reports – especially since one of these schoolmates was Hargreaves Hanson, eldest son of the John Hanson who was both Byron's and Portsmouth's lawyer. Later, Byron himself was to be at real risk from punishment under the anti-sodomy laws, because of the overtness of his own homoerotic interests and activities in the years before his departure to Greece in 1809 and his frankness in his letters while he was there, which made it clear that he was enjoying same-sex romantic encounters and relationships. In France, sodomy had been decriminalized in 1791, and this stance was preserved in the Napoleonic code of 1810, with most of Catholic Europe following suit, but in England, as noted above, while Byron was abroad between 1809 and 1811, measures against homosexual men became even harsher. A letter to Byron from his Cambridge friend Charles Skinner Matthews told him about a police raid on the White Swan Inn in London's Vere Street in July 1810. 'Your Lordship's delicacy wd I know be shocked by the pillorification (in the Hay M[arket]) . . . & how the said gents were bemired and beordured.'[53] Matthews and another Cambridge friend, Scrope Berdmore Davies, also went to Newgate prison to visit Ensign John Newball Hepburn (aged forty-two) and drummer Thomas White (sixteen), who were hanged before a huge crowd on 14 March.[54] Not surprisingly, Byron's friend John Cam Hobhouse, who had been in Greece with him, advised him to burn all compromising manuscripts; to keep his Greek experiences 'entirely to yourself' and to destroy any evidence that might bring his actions to the attention of the authorities.[55] In England in 1816 Byron maintained that he had 'never done an act that would bring me under the Law – at least on this side of the Water' and later described his undergraduate love for the Cambridge chorister John Edleston (the subject of the intense series of poems addressed to 'Thyrza' in 1811–12) as a 'violent, though pure love and passion'.[56]

> Ours too the glance none saw beside;
> The smile none else might understand;
> The whisper'd thought of hearts allied,
> The pressure of the thrilling hand;
>
> The kiss, so guiltless and refined,
> That Love each warmer wish forbore;
> Those eyes proclaim'd so pure a mind,
> Even Passion blush'd to plead for more.
>
> ('To Thyrza' 29–36)[57]

But, despite his numerous affairs with women, Byron's attraction to boys in their mid- and late-teens remained a crucial part of his emotional life right up to his death in Greece at the age of thirty-six, when his unrequited love for Loukas Chalandritsanos cast a deep shadow over his final months.

The Byrons and the Hansons

As the Portsmouths' lawyer, John Hanson was in constant contact with the Earl and his family, and his presence was equally evident in terms of his role in Byron's life. The link between them had in fact begun before Byron was born in January 1788, when Mrs Byron was introduced to Hanson by James Farquhar, a London lawyer whom she had consulted, and it was Mrs Hanson who recommended the *accoucheur* who attended Byron's birth.[58] In 1798, when the ten-year-old sixth Lord Byron and his mother arrived at Newstead Abbey to claim his inheritance, Hanson and his wife came to meet and greet them. By this date, in fact, Hanson already knew a great deal about Newstead and its legal situation, having also advised the fifth Lord about his legal position after his grandson died in 1794. Byron was a ward of Chancery until he was twenty-one, with Hanson as one of his three official guardians or trustees, and it was the lawyer who made most of the key decisions about the young lord's childhood and education. In 1799 Hanson had intervened to protect Byron against the physical and sexual abuse he had suffered at the hands of his nurse, May Gray, and to secure her dismissal.[59] These events and Hanson's recognition of the boy's abilities and intelligence had led to an affectionate and quasi-parental relationship between Byron and the Hansons. Mrs Hanson 'has often been a mother to me', Byron wrote wistfully to Hanson from Athens in 1811, reflecting on his difficult relationship with his own mother, and adding 'as you have always been a friend'.[60]

The Hanson family offered Byron a London home during many of his school holidays, and it was not long before the lawyer's two most important clients met each other there. In November 1799, when Portsmouth was visiting the lawyer at his home at Earls Court House, Old Brompton, to sign papers connected with his forthcoming first marriage, there was a confrontation between him and the eleven-year-old Lord Byron in the conservatory.[61] As was the Earl's unpleasant habit with servants and children, he pinched Byron's ear, and Byron in retaliation picked up a conch shell which was lying on the ground and hurled it at Lord Portsmouth's head, missing it by a hair's breadth and smashing the glass window behind. In vain Mrs Hanson tried to make peace by saying that Byron did not mean the missile for Lord Portsmouth. 'But I *did* mean it!' the boy reiterated, insisting that 'he would teach a fool of an Earl to pull another noble's lugs'.[62] Some fifteen years later (oddly enough, on the day before he was involved in the second Portsmouth marriage) Byron recorded how the 'youngest brat' of his lover Lady Oxford had done the same thing to him, when the boy 'cut my eye and cheek open with a misdirected pebble'.[63]

Byron and Portsmouth continued to be linked through Hanson in the following years. In late September 1805, just before he went up to Trinity College, Cambridge, Byron stayed for a while at the Hansons' country home, Farleigh House in Farleigh Wallop, Hampshire: a very substantial property near Hurstbourne, which belonged to the Portsmouths and had been used as the dower house before it was let or loaned to their lawyer in 1804. Farleigh was within 5 or 6 miles of the rectory at Steventon where Jane's brother James Austen still lived, although at the time Byron visited the area Jane herself was based in Worthing, Sussex.[64] Byron did, however, meet the Terrys who were close friends of the Austens: an old-established family with a manor house in the nearby village of Dummer. Thirteen Terry children were born there between the 1770s and 1790s, and many of them figure in Jane's letters. One of them, Michael, was later engaged to her niece Anna, although she broke off the engagement.[65] Which of the Terrys became the subject of a joke between Byron and Hargreaves Hanson is difficult to tell: 'Beware of *Mr Terry*', Byron wrote to Hargreaves in October 1805, and signed off another letter in November, 'Believe me *Mr Terry* yours truly'.[66] Perhaps the most likely candidate was the eldest son, Stephen Terry, a year older than Jane Austen, who was a Fellow of King's College, Cambridge and may perhaps have bored Byron and Hargreaves with advice about the university where Byron was about to study.[67] Jane danced with this Mr Terry several times at the ball at Basingstoke in 1800 when the Portsmouths were present and, when she reported to Cassandra that she had seen him in April 1805 in Bath with his future wife Maria Seymer, she added a comment which may imply that she found him boring or over-talkative: 'her dress was not even smart, & her appearance very quiet. Miss Irvine says she is never speaking a word. Poor Wretch, I am afraid she is *en Penitence*.'[68]

It was also this Mr Terry who recorded a humorous verse written by Austen in 1813 about the marriage of her friend Urania Catharine Camilla Wallop (the Earl's cousin, daughter of Dr Barton Wallop) to an elderly curate, the Reverend Henry Wake:

Camilla, good humoured, & merry, & small
For a Husband was at her last stake;
And having in vain danced at many a Ball
Is now very happy to Jump at a Wake.[69]

The Austens and the Hansons

Whichever Mr Terry it was that Byron joked about, he has the distinction of being a member of the select group of people recorded to have been personally acquainted with both Byron and Jane Austen. Perhaps, however, this group can be extended to include Mr and Mrs John Hanson and their family as well. Although Jane, Cassandra and their parents had left Steventon to live in Bath by the time the Hansons arrived at Farleigh House in 1804, Cassandra visited the Lloyds near Farleigh in September 1804 and in early 1805, James Austen continued to live, dine and socialize in the area, and Jane returned to the Steventon Rectory to stay with her brother for several weeks in early 1806. When she spotted the announcement of the Portsmouth-Hanson marriage in the press on 8 March 1814 ('MARRIED. Monday, at St George's, Bloomsbury, the Earl of Portsmouth, to Miss Hanson, eldest daughter of John Hanson, Esq. of Bloomsbury-square') she clearly recognized the identity of 'Miss Hanson' as well as that of 'Lord Portsmouth', and expected Cassandra to do likewise – and, judging from her exclamation mark, to share her surprise that they should be marrying each other.[70] It is likely that the Hansons, as well as the Austens, were invited to the Earl and Countess's anniversary balls, and that sometime after 1804 they might both have been at Hurstbourne together, before Grace's death in 1813 brought the annual event to a close.

Byron continued to be close to the Hansons in both professional and personal terms, and in March 1814 he seems not to have been unduly surprised when John Hanson invited him to be present at the wedding of his daughter to the recently widowed Lord Portsmouth, or even when he was asked to give the bride away at the altar (Hanson and his wife did not attend the ceremony).[71] Hanson had told him, Byron recalled,

> that Portsmouth's brother wanted him to marry *another old* woman – that he might have no children, but that Lord P[ortsmouth] wished to marry a *young* woman – and seemed inclined to one of Hanson's daughters. – I saw nothing very unnatural in this – nor lunatical . . . I thought that if Ld. P. got a good plain homekeeping wife – *young* too – instead of the tough morsel prepared for his brother – it was no bad bargain for either party.[72]

Later he commented to Hobhouse, 'It struck me so little as entrapment for Ld. P. that I used to wonder whether the *Girl* would have him – and not whether *he* would take the Girl.'[73] Byron was not the only one to be optimistic about the benefits of a cross-class marriage, however, or to imagine that a woman of lower social status might turn down the proposal of an aristocratic man – as of course Lizzie Bennet does when she refuses

Mr Darcy. The cross-class marriage is indeed a major theme of most of Austen's fiction, playing a critical part in *Northanger Abbey* and *Mansfield Park* as well as *Pride and Prejudice*, and also (with an interesting reversal of the heroine's and hero's social status) in *Persuasion*. And the 1797 marriage between Austen's own brother Henry, son of a minor country clergyman, to the widowed comtesse Eliza de Feuillide could perhaps be presented in similar terms, although Eliza's first husband seems actually not to have had a firm claim to his title as 'Comte', and she and Henry were, after all, first cousins.[74]

In the run-up to the second Portsmouth marriage, Hanson presented the union to Byron as being very much the bridegroom's own choice, but he evidently used other means to actually 'persuade' the Earl, who later told a gardener at Hurstbourne that Hanson had said he must marry his daughter 'otherwise I never should have a wife, and my brother would take me into Devonshire and shut me up'.[75] Hanson also seems to have deliberately misled Portsmouth as to which of his daughters he would be marrying, and the Earl believed it would be Laura, 'the pretty one', rather than her elder sister Mary Ann who was described as a 'well-informed person', but 'not of a good figure; very genteel in her manners, and of uniform decorum'.[76] 'She was not pretty', Byron later declared, offended that a French newspaper had claimed that he had had an affair with her. 'I beg leave to decline the liaison, which is quite untrue.'[77]

Blunder

Hanson also asked Byron to sign the special licence for the wedding and to witness the financial marriage settlement, and it was later alleged in court that this provided Mary Ann, John Hanson and Byron himself with payments of a thousand pounds a year each, up to a total of thirty thousand pounds.[78] The actual settlement document was, however, never made public at the Lunacy Commissions, and it is highly unlikely that Byron (who was then still squeamish in class terms about being paid for anything, even by his publisher) would have accepted this or any other payment from his lawyer – and even more so that he would have remained silent about it, addicted as he was to sharing his personal details with others. 'I was told that Lord P's property was in trust, well secured – and that Lady P could only have a jointure of a thousand a year', Byron recalled; and, he pointed out, 'my liaison was with the father, in the unsentimental shape of long lawyers' bills, through the medium of which I have had to pay him ten or twelve thousand pounds within these few years'.[79] On the day of the wedding itself, 7 March 1814, Byron walked to the church with the bridegroom, and in his diary he noted his own part in the ceremony:

> made one blunder, when I joined the hands of the happy – rammed their left hands, by mistake, into one another. Corrected it – bustled back to the altar-rail, and said "Amen." Portsmouth responded as if he had got the whole by heart; and, if anything, was rather before the priest.[80]

Perhaps the Earl's eagerness to speak the responses was in fact a sign of having been carefully coached in them rather than really understanding them; and the ominous symbolism of the left-handed marriage proved to be entirely portentous.

Hobhouse added further details in his own journal, written the next day, together with an altogether cannier analysis of Hanson's motives:

> Byron came and sat with me from half-past seven till eleven. . . . Lord Portsmouth is a fool, and was before married by his brother, Newton Fellowes, to Lord Grantley's sister, who was past childbearing but had £12,000. . . . Hanson had certainly some scruples about the honesty of the transaction, and therefore asked Byron, and therefore got him to give his daughter away in order to involve him.[81]

Hobhouse was always (rightly) suspicious of Hanson's influence over Byron and saw clearly the dubious procedures and financial motives in the connection that Byron seemed (perhaps because of their long personal connection) to want to ignore. The rather insouciant air with which Byron presented his own part in the marriage soon came back to haunt him, however, and by the end of 1814 he was facing the fact that he might be subpoenaed to give evidence about it in court. This was when Newton Fellowes petitioned the Chancellor for a Commission of Lunacy to judge whether the Earl was insane, using the marriage as evidence of this. One of Fellowes's motives for, as Byron put it, wanting to 'lunatize' his brother was certainly to forestall the possibility of the birth of an heir, but he was also spurred into action by the way in which the trust under which the Earl's finances had been governed during his first marriage had been promptly dissolved by the Hanson family following the second marriage, leaving

Fellowes without any say in this brother's affairs.[82] This was, of course, exactly what Hanson intended, and why he wanted to get the Earl wedded to his daughter quickly and in secret, before any of the other trustees got wind of the matter. They and the Austens would have learnt about the marriage at the same moment: through the announcements in the newspapers the following day.

The Chancellor, Lord Eldon, began to hear the legal arguments for a Commission of Lunacy in January 1815. The hearings were held in private, but the case was widely reported in the press, and both Byron and Austen could have read dozens of reports about it in the London and provincial newspapers. The Austens' neighbour passed on his London newspapers to them, and Jane mentions consulting the papers in early 1815.[83] The *Hampshire Chronicle*, for instance, reported on 23 January:

> The Brother and presumptive Heir of the Earl of Portsmouth has preferred a private Petition to the Court of Chancery, for a Commission of Lunacy against the Nobel Personage in question, grounded on charges of acts of irrationality and improvident conduct, denoting mental derangement and incompetency to manage his own affairs. His Lordship was, during the life of his first wife, under a certain trusteeship. He married again a year ago, with the eldest daughter of one of the Trustees, and the trust was dissolved soon after by the new family.

The *Bristol Mirror* on 28 January further noted that 'the father of the new married Lady has filed eighty-seven affidavits to rebut the charge of incompetency on the part of the Noble Lord'. One of these must have been the legal statement that Byron wrote in autumn 1814 about his impression of the Earl's sanity on the day of the wedding. 'I could not foresee *Lunacy* in a man who had been allowed to walk about the world five and forty years as Compos – of voting – franking – marrying – convicting thieves on his own evidence – and similar pastimes which are the privileges of Sanity', Byron protested later.[84] Finally, on 22 April 1815 the Chancellor announced that he had decided not to call a Commission of Lunacy. The result was reported in the press later that week, and Byron's evidence at the time is said to have been crucial in the Chancellor's decision. Although Byron had by now become a celebrity poet, no word of his part in the case was reported in the press.[85]

Fairlawn Grove

The Hansons and the Earl made a triumphal return to Hurstbourne and promptly sacked any servants who had spoken in favour of the Commission. Mary Ann was confirmed in her role as Countess of Portsmouth and took over the reins at Hurstbourne and at the couple's new house, 'Fairlawn Grove' in Acton Green, west of London.[86] With its twelve bedrooms, billiard room and conservatory, and eight acres of pleasure grounds, Fairlawn Grove sounds very like the deliciously vulgar Bristol establishment of Mrs Elton's brother-in-law Mr Suckling, 'Maple Grove', in *Emma*. Mary Ann, like Mrs Elton, even had a sister called Selina who sometimes resided there, although whether the Portsmouths were lucky enough, like the Sucklings, to own a 'barouche-landau' is not known.

From this point there are no more extant references to the Portsmouth story in Austen's letters. Cassandra and Jane, with their mother and Martha Lloyd, were by now well settled in Chawton Cottage, on their brother Edward's Hampshire estate, and Jane's writing career had taken off. In late 1815 she was busy in London checking the proofs of *Emma* and looking after her brother Henry, who became suddenly and seriously ill that autumn. Probably her last close connection with the Earl's family, his cousin Camilla who had married the Reverend Henry Wake, died in January 1815, and, if Jane did have any idea how badly things were going with the Portsmouth marriage before her death in July 1817, no comments on it by her are recorded. Byron's marriage – in January 1815 to Annabella Milbanke – also proved ill-fated and broke down within a year, amid allegations of his highly erratic behaviour towards his wife, heavy drinking and rumours of incest and sodomy. Like Portsmouth a year earlier, these allegations placed Byron at some risk of being categorized as insane, when Lady Byron called in the eminent physician Dr Matthew Baillie (of whom more in Chapter 5) on the grounds that her husband had delusions of being 'a fallen angel', and proposing that 'restraint' should be applied to his intentions to travel abroad.[87] Lord and Lady Byron separated permanently soon after the birth of their daughter Augusta Ada in December 1815, and Byron left England in disgrace (although perhaps not entirely unwillingly) for the last time in April 1816.

The horrors of the Portsmouth marriage were on a completely different scale, but they did not become fully public until the Fellowes family called for a second Commission of Lunacy in 1822. This time the Chancellor gave permission for the Commission to go ahead, giving rise to sensational reports in the press in 1823 as the proceedings revealed Mary Ann's blatant adultery and her physical abuse of her husband, and also exposed Portsmouth's alarming violence towards his servants and his own bizarre sexual behaviour. It emerged that the new Countess had taken a lover soon after her marriage: one William Rowland Alder, a Northumberland gentleman about the same age as her father, said to have been trained as a barrister, who had been the other signatory of the Portsmouth marriage contract, along with Byron.[88] Mary Ann had several miscarriages, but it was not until she gave birth to a daughter in 1822 that the Portsmouth family took action. The Countess, her lover and her brothers and sisters had by then for years been humiliating the Earl and treating him with malicious cruelty, including whipping him and locking him in and out of the house, threatening to send him to a mad-house and, as he complained, treating him like a dog.[89]

The sadistic behaviour was not all on one side, however. Revelations about Lord Portsmouth's conduct came from scores of witnesses, mostly his servants and tenants, who appeared before the Commission at the Freemasons' Hall in London. These included accounts of his enjoyment of inflicting pain on both animals and people: more Gothic than any of the 'dreadful suspicions' that *Northanger Abbey*'s Catherine Morland could have imagined or Henry Tilney could have repudiated on the grounds that such things did not happen in the 'country and the age in which we live'.[90] The Earl was alleged to have flogged his horses unmercifully and showed an unnatural interest in the slaughter of cattle, visiting the slaughterhouse and striking them on the head with his own axe, shouting, 'serves you right you vicious Devil'.[91] He apparently liked to knock about his servants too: pulling and pinching their ears, whipping them and pushing them into ditches – and on one occasion he deliberately re-broke the leg of a workman who was recovering in bed from an earlier break.[92] He had an obsession with funerals, which he called 'black jobs', and eagerly sought out and disrupted funeral services by trying to officiate himself, ringing the church bells and demanding to carry the coffin. 'Anything cruel and death of any kind delighted him', reported the carpenter William Litchfield, whose own child's death and funeral were devastated in this way.[93] Most sensational was his macabre mania for surgical blood-letting, which seems to have had a sexual appeal for him, according to the testimony of several of the wives and daughters of his tenants.[94]

Great emergency

When Byron heard about this in 1823, he responded with a joke about this rarefied form of sexual gratification:

> We owe to him however the greatest discovery about the blood since Dr Harvey's; – I wonder if it really hath such an effect – I never was bled in my life – but by leeches – and I thought the leeches d––d bad pieces – but perhaps the tape and lancet may be better. – I shall try them on some great emergency.[95]

The next 'great emergency' in Byron's life, however, was his final illness, just over a year later, in Missolonghi, Western Greece, where he was supporting the Greeks' armed struggle against the Ottoman Turks. When his fever first became serious the doctors wanted to bleed him, but Byron resisted fiercely, declaring that 'he knew very well that the lancet killed more people than the lance'.[96] The doctors then warned him that if he did not allow himself to be bled the disease 'might so act on his cerebral and nervous system as entirely to deprive him of his reason'. 'Then casting at us both the fiercest glance of vexation he threw out his arm and said, in the most angry tone, "Come, you are, I see, a damned set of butchers. Take as much blood as you will, but have done with it."'[97] Using leeches, the doctors drew a full pound of blood and another pound two hours later plus a further ten ounces the following day. By this time Byron was delirious and having convulsions, but the doctors continued to administer dangerous treatments and drugs until he died two days later, on 19 April 1824, at the age of thirty-six.

The Austens, like most families in those days, were no strangers to bleeding by leeches. Mrs Austen had her blood drawn this way to treat headaches in 1813; in June 1814 Jane matter-of-factly reported to Cassandra that 'we had handsome presents from the Gt House yesterday – a Ham & the 4 Leeches', and when Henry Austen was dangerously ill in 1815 he had had 40 ounces of blood taken over two days.[98] Perhaps Jane was sceptical about the benefits, however: in *Sanditon* the hypochondriac Parker sisters go in for the use of leeches to a typically excessive degree, and Diana reports that Susan

> has been suffering much from the headache and six leeches a day for ten days together relieved her so little that we thought it right to change our measures – and being convinced on examination that

much of the evil lay in her gum, I persuaded her to attack the disorder there. She has accordingly had three teeth drawn, and is decidedly better, but her nerves are a good deal deranged.[99]

There is no mention of Jane herself being subjected to bleeding during her final illness in 1817, and she seems to have been spared this ordeal – as well as the possibility of having to think about Lord Portsmouth while enduring it.

The Lunacy Commission gave its verdict through a jury consisting of twenty-three distinguished men, including the banker Sir Thomas Baring and the architect Sir John Soane.[100] The Earl was judged to have been insane since 1809.[101] His marriage to Mary Ann was annulled in 1828, by which time she had had another child with Alder (whom she married later that year). A judgement for the £40,000 costs of the trial was issued against her, and she later fled abroad, living at one time in Canada. Her father John Hanson was disgraced and ended his life in debt in 1841. The third Earl of Portsmouth died in 1853, and Newton Fellowes succeeded him as the fourth Earl but outlived his brother by less than six months.

Notes

1. *JAL* 257–62, to Cassandra Austen: 5–8 March 1814 and 9 March 1814.

2. *BLJ* 10.129, to Lady Hardy, 28 March 1823. *BLJ* 3.248, *Journal*, 7 March 1814.

3. *BLJ* 3.249, *Journal*, 10 March 1814.

4. *BLJ* 3.249, *Journal*, 10 March 1814.

5. *JAFR* 26.

6. *BLJ* 10.129, to Lady Hardy, 28 March 1823.

7. Foyster xxvi.

8. Slothuber 19–20.

9. Austen-Leigh ed. Sutherland 39.

10. Tomalin 7–8.

11. Tomalin 8, 22.

12. Mrs Austen wrote that she had 'all four' of her children at home in November 1772. *JAFR* 25.

13. Hurst 348–51.

14. Hurst 348–9.

15. Austen-Leigh ed. Sutherland xxxiii and 16.

16. Hurst 348.

17. *JAL* 550, 542: biographical notes by Le Faye.

18. Le Faye (1998) 'Leonora Austen' 182–4.

19. Austen-Leigh (1942) 130.

20. Walton 77. Tomalin 55, 130, 188.

21. Boyes 2. *BLJ* 8.217, to John Murray, 20 September 1821.

22. MacCarthy 262.

23. Anonymous, *Eclectic Review* 8.2 (1812) 632.

24. See Stabler (2002) 18–23.

25. 'The Dream' 168–83, *LBCPW* 4.28.

26. Gullette np, Bader np.

27. Austen ed. Sabor 130–3.

28. Foyster 22.

29. *JAL* 53, to Cassandra Austen, 1 November 1800.

30. On 12 November 1800 (*JAL* 59) Austen described the invitations for the ball as 'very curiously . . . worded', in a letter to Martha Lloyd who, because she lived near Hurstbourne, would have known the Earl and his peculiarities well. James Edward Austen-Leigh described him in 1870 as 'the Lord Portsmouth whose eccentricities afterwards became notorious', Austen-Leigh ed. Sutherland 54.

31. Foyster 110.

32. Caplan (2010) 106.

33. Foyster 70.

34. Foyster 99.

35. Jane was socializing with the Wallops in Southampton in 1809 and later: see *JAL* 168, to Cassandra Austen, 17–18 January 1809.

36. Crompton 18.

37. Gilbert 106–7.

38. *Hampshire Chronicle*, 13 December 1802, 1.

39. Foyster 66, 73.

40. *JAFR* 137–8.

41. Heydt-Stevenson (2000) 309–39.

42. *P&P* vol. 3, chap. 5, 321.

43. Heydt-Stevenson (2005) 1. *NA* vol. 1, chap. 7, 40.

44. Heydt-Stevenson (2000) 333.

45. Perlstein np.

46. Kosofsky Sedgwick (1991). Austen ed. Sabor lxii.

47. Austen ed. Sabor 467.

48. *MP* vol. 1, chap. 6, 71.

49. Austen ed. Wiltshire 657.

50. Southam 25, 27, quoting Byron's 'Hints from Horace' 392–4, *LBCPW* 1.303.

51. LeJacq np.

52. LeJacq np.

53. Crompton 161.

54. Crompton 18.

55. MacCarthy 105. Hobhouse ed. Graham 67, to Byron, 15 July 1811.

56. MacCarthy 261, quoting Lady Byron, March 1816, Lovelace-Byron Archive. *BLJ* 8.24, *Ravenna Journal,* 12 January 1821.

57. 'To Thyrza', 29–36, *LBCPW* 1.347.

58. Boyes 27.

59. MacCarthy 22–3.

60. *BLJ* 2.25, to John Hanson, 11 November 1811.

61. Langley Moore 98.

62. Langley Moore 460.

63. *BLJ* 3.247, *Journal,* 6 March 1814.

64. *JAFR* 151.

65. *JAFR* 181–2.

66. *BLJ* 1.78, to Hargreaves Hanson, 25 October 1805. *BLJ* 1.81, to Hargreaves Hanson, 12 November 1805.

67. *JAL* 577, biographical note by Le Faye.

68. *JAL* 53, to Cassandra Austen, 1 November 1800, and *JAL* 99, to Cassandra Austen, 8–11 April 1805.

69. 'Camilla, good humoured, & merry, & small', Austen ed. Todd and Bree 255.

70. The announcement appeared in the *Morning Chronicle,* the *Star,* the *Saint James's Chronicle* and *The Sun* on 8 March 1814.

71. *BLJ* 4.236–7, 'Statement concerning Lord Portsmouth'.

72. *BLJ* 10.124–5, to Hobhouse, 19 March 1823.

73. Foyster 183.

74. In 1781 Eliza Hancock married Jean-François Capot de Feuillide, an officer in the Queen's Regiment of Dragoons and owner of an estate in Guyenne (*JAFR* 37, 40). He was executed for conspiring against the French Republic in February 1794 (*JAFR* 77).

75. Foyster 184.

76. Foyster 182.

77. *BLJ* 10.129, to Lady Hardy, 28 March 1823.

78. Foyster 181.

79. *BLJ* 10.129, to Lady Hardy, 28 March 1823.

80. *BLJ* 3.248, *Journal*, 7 March 1814.

81. Hobhouse ed. Cochran (*Diary* 13, 'Early 1814') 183, 7 March 1814.

82. *BLJ* 4.235, to Annabella Milbanke, 25 November 1814.

83. *JAL* 289, to Anna Lefroy, 'late February–early March 1815'.

84. *BLJ* 10.125, to Hobhouse, 19 March 1823.

85. Foyster 173.

86. Foyster 200.

87. MacCarthy 262.

88. Foyster 200.

89. Foyster 219, 211–23.

90. *NA* vol. 2, chap. 9, 203.

91. Foyster 142.

92. Foyster 151.

93. Foyster 142.

94. Foyster 125.

95. *BLJ* 10.25–6, to Hobhouse, 19 March 1823.

96. Mills 76.

97. Mills quoting Julius Millingen, one of the doctors present at Byron's deathbed.

98. *JAL* 222, to Cassandra Austen, 16 September 1813. *JAL* 264, to Cassandra Austen, 23 June 1814. *JAL* 292, to Cassandra Austen, 17–18 October 1815.

99. *Sanditon* chap. 5, Austen ed. Todd and Bree 164.

100. Foyster xxiv.

101. Foyster xxiv.

CHAPTER 5
PUBLISHING WITH JOHN MURRAY
'HE IS A ROGUE OF COURSE, BUT A CIVIL ONE'

Between 1815 and 1817 Austen and Byron were published simultaneously by what was in effect the world's first modern publishing house, John Murray's, which issued four of Austen's six major novels and produced nearly all of Byron's works between 1812 and 1822.[1] Murray knew both 'his' authors personally and made a major contribution to the way in which their work appeared in public.

John Samuel Murray was born in London in 1778 and was the second in a long line of John Murray publishers which continues today. He had inherited the publishing business from his Scottish father (John McMurray) at the age of fifteen. Despite losing the sight of one eye in a boyhood accident, he was highly active and energetic, and by 1815 he had built up the firm over two decades to unprecedented levels of success, sophistication and influence: first in Fleet Street, on the borders of the City of London, and then from 1812 in fashionable Albemarle Street, just off Piccadilly and across the road from Byron's lodgings in St James's. Murray's drawing room on the first floor of 50 Albemarle Street became the centre of London's publishing world and a meeting place for literary Londoners, including Byron – Murray's most famous author. Walter Scott and Byron first met in Murray's drawing room in April 1815, as the result of a reconciliation brokered by Murray after Byron had berated Scott, in *English Bards and Scotch Reviewers* (1809) for his 'conceit' in trying to 'foist [his] stale romance', *Marmion*, on public taste.[2] Murray's son John Murray III remembered how as a boy he had seen 'the two greatest poets of the age – both lame – stumping downstairs side by side'.[3] Jane Austen may also have visited the famous Albemarle Street premises, perhaps with her brother Henry, in the autumn of 1815.

It was in this drawing room fireplace, just after Byron's death in 1824, that the manuscript of his autobiographical *Memoirs* was burnt by a group including Murray, Hobhouse, Thomas Moore and representatives of Lady Byron and Augusta Leigh. The participants (most of whom had not seen or read the document) feared that it might be scandalous and unpublishable,

Figure 17 *John Samuel Murray,* by Henry Pickersgill (1833). Murray was the second generation of the John Murray publishing dynasty and worked closely with both Austen and Byron. Private collection.

and it appears that no copies had been made, so that once burnt it could not be recovered. The green notebook from which the pages were torn out for burning is still at 50 Albemarle Street.[4] Perhaps as an act of penance, Murray later paid nearly £5,000 to Moore (one of the very few who *had* read the *Memoirs*) to write a biography of Byron and make a collection of his letters.

Murray's brilliance as a publisher lay not only in his shrewdness in business, his inspired use of advertising and publicity, his savvy dealings with printers, illustrators and suppliers, and his skill in finding profitable writers, but also in his ability to develop personal relationships with his authors, to treat them as individual colleagues and friends, to supply them with publications and resources and generally to assist them in producing good work. Austen understood his methods: 'He is a Rogue of course, but a civil one', she commented wryly to Cassandra when she received her first (much lower than expected) publishing offer from him for *Emma*, in October 1815.[5] Nevertheless, her relationship with Murray developed from a mixture of mistrust about his financial dealings and gratification at his 'praise' for her writing, to the point a few months later where, as her nephew noted, 'the increasing cordiality of her letters shows that the author felt that her interests were duly cared for, and was glad to find herself in the hands of a publisher whom she could consider as a friend'.[6] Byron's much longer and more complex relationship and correspondence with Murray is well known: lasting over a decade of tumultuous poetic and personal events in Byron's life, and ranging from warm friendship, satisfaction and trust to acrimonious detachment.

Murray's influence as a publisher was increased by his key role in the powerful new literary magazines of this period, which were the first to employ professional and (importantly) anonymous critics to review new publications. Initially, he was the London agent for the Whig-supporting *Edinburgh Review*, but in February 1809 he took the ambitious step of launching his own journal, the *Quarterly Review:* a Tory counterblast to the *Edinburgh*, with a circulation of around 13,000 and contributors including Walter Scott, George Canning, John Hookham Frere, Robert Southey and the ferocious John Wilson Croker. Croker savaged Hobhouse's account of Napoleon's Hundred Days, *The Substance of Some Letters written by an Englishman resident at Paris* (1816), and it was also he whose 1818 *Quarterly* review of *Endymion* castigated Keats as a failed apothecary and (following Lockhart) a member of the 'Cockney School' of poetry, giving rise to Byron's jingle:

> Who killed John Keats?
>   I, says the Quarterly
> So savage & Tartarly,
>   'Twas one of my feats.[7]

In this context of powerful critical and political rivalry, Byron himself was in a very lucky place in 1812. After receiving a scathing review from Henry Brougham in the *Edinburgh* for his first published work, *Hours of Idleness* (1808) he had made the Whig Scottish journal a major target of his 1809 satire *English Bards and Scotch Reviewers,* and this had brought him to Murray's favourable notice even before the arrival of *Childe Harold* on the publisher's doorstep in 1811. As a well-known and controversial Whig, Byron was extremely fortunate to have had Murray on side as his publisher from so early on in his career, since Murray provided him and his work with very effective protection against the attacks of the intimidating Tory reviewers. This was particularly true during the savage press commentary on the breakdown of the Byron marriage in 1816. 'Murray has long prevented "The Quarterly" from abusing me', Byron commented to Thomas Medwin in 1821.[8]

Politics and publishing

The first editor of the *Quarterly* was the formidable William Gifford (1756–1826), previously editor of the *Anti-Jacobin Review* whose purpose was to ridicule any British literary attempts to sympathize with French revolutionary ideas.

Gifford had risen from a very poor background to become the respected translator of Juvenal and had himself written admired verse satires. As Murray's trusted professional reader and literary advisor he had a crucial role in selecting Austen's work as well as Byron's for publication and, here again, Byron was extremely lucky, since, despite their very different politics, he had been a genuine fan of Gifford's from an early age and had praised him (almost uniquely) in *English Bards* as a 'Bard in virtue strong', capable of raising the low poetic standards of the time.[9] Byron described Gifford as 'my *literary* father' and himself as 'his *prodigal* Son', writing to Gifford in 1813, for instance of 'the veneration with which I have ever regarded you, long before I had the most distant prospect of becoming your acquaintance, literary or personal.'[10] This deferential friendship was perhaps strengthened by a shared bond of physical disability, since Gifford was very small, hunchbacked and infirm, and reminded Byron of his hero Alexander Pope.[11] In 1816 it was on Gifford's advice that Byron extensively revised

Figure 18 *William Gifford*, by John Hoppner (*c.* 1790). Gifford rose from poverty and overcame disability to become John Murray's chief editorial consultant and editor of the powerful *Quarterly Review*. By permission of Llyfrgell Genedlaethol Cymru / The National Library of Wales.

his first draft of the third act of *Manfred*, although he was furious when Gifford and Murray then removed the crucial line at the end of the play: 'Old man! 'tis not so difficult to die.'[12] Overall, however, Murray's tactic of using Byron's admiration for Gifford as a way of persuading him to make changes was, as Peter W. Graham says, a 'brilliant strategy' for keeping 'a poet with anti-commercial prejudices, "tempestuous passions", and liberal Whig sentiments suitable for the list of a conservative publishing house and an elite readership'.[13]

Neither Gifford nor Murray, nor any of the contemporary reviewers, ever expressed concerns about the political content of Austen's work or her personal politics, although perhaps they might have responded differently if they had seen some of her unpublished work and her letters. 'She was always very careful not to meddle with matters which she did not thoroughly understand', pronounced her nephew James Austen-Leigh, adding rather sweepingly: 'She never touched upon politics, law, or medicine, subjects which some novel writers have ventured on rather too boldly, and have treated, perhaps, with more brilliancy than accuracy.'[14] Richard Whately (later the Whig-appointed Archbishop of Dublin), in an influential review of *Northanger Abbey* and *Persuasion* in the *Quarterly* in 1821, characterized Austen as having 'the merit (in our judgement most essential) of being evidently a Christian writer: a merit which is much enhanced, both on the score of good taste, and of practical utility, by her religion being not at all obtrusive'.[15] He described how the 'moral lessons' of the novels 'though clearly and impressively conveyed, are not offensively put forward, but spring incidentally from the circumstances of the story'.[16] Continuing with a general critique of 'novels in the first person', Whately rather surprisingly appears to quote a Byronic phrase from the first line of *Don Juan*. 'I want a hero: an uncommon want, / When every year and month sends forth a new one', Byron had written in 1819, while in 1821 Whately opined: 'It is objected to them, not without reason, that they want a *hero*: the person intended to occupy that post being the narrator himself, who of course cannot so describe his own conduct and character as to make the reader thoroughly acquainted with him.'[17] Praising Austen's third-person narrative in contrast, Whately concluded rather patronizingly that 'Miss Austin's [*sic*] works may safely be recommended, not only as among the most unexceptionable of their class, but as combining, in an eminent degree, instruction with amusement'.[18]

Murray must have viewed Austen and Byron as highly contrasting clients. Nevertheless, there were some similarities in his relationships with them, and in both cases he deployed his charm and friendliness while sometimes being rather less than open in his financial dealings with them. Issues of class also affected both associations, with Byron's rather precariously achieved nobility and Austen's hard-held gentility playing off against Murray's status as tradesman, professional and aspiring gentleman; adviser, expert and business partner; servant, colleague and friend. Neither Byron nor Austen was a 'typical' Murray author, if such a thing existed. Byron was a unique – and uniquely profitable – publishing phenomenon, described by Gifford as 'a wonderful creature' who should be 'shew[n] . . . only on high days and holydays'.[19] But in 1815 Austen too, as a female novelist, was a highly unusual 'creature' for the Murray stable. Although by this period women in Great Britain were publishing nearly twice as many novels as men, Murray seems to have been rather behind the curve in this respect, and *Emma* (1815) was in fact the first-ever novel by an Englishwoman to be published by him.[20]

Before 1815, Murray had published only a handful of works by female authors, and these were almost entirely non-fictional. They included Maria Rundell's *A New System of Domestic Cookery . . . Adapted to the Use of Private Families* (1806), the world's first mass-market cookery book, which sold up to 10,000 copies a year and rivalled Byron's work as a source of high earnings for its publisher.[21] Germaine de Staël's *De l'Allemagne* and its translation *Germany*, published by Murray in 1813 and 1814, respectively, were an indication of the company's future success as a publisher of literary travel-guides.[22] In 1815, the year in which he was preparing to publish *Emma*, Murray added more works by women authors to his list than in any of his previous twenty years as a publisher. These included Helen Maria Williams's *Narrative of the Events Which Have Taken Place in France, from the Landing of Napoleon Bonaparte . . . till the Restoration of Louis XVIII*; Eleanor Porden's ten-canto poem *The Veils; or The Triumph of Constancy,* and Barbarina Wilmot's tragedy *Ina*, which Byron saw being 'damned' at Drury Lane in April 1815.[23] Meanwhile, many male poets were turned away by Murray, and Wordsworth later persuaded himself that Murray was 'too great a personage for anyone but a Court, and Aristocratic or most fashionable Author to deal with'.[24]

Childe Harold was brought to Murray in the summer of 1811 by Byron's distant relative (and in effect literary agent), Robert Charles Dallas, having been turned down by Longman's and by Murray's predecessor at Albemarle Street, William Miller.[25] Murray was already beginning to specialize in travel literature, and it may have been the loco-descriptive aspect of the *Pilgrimage* that particularly appealed to him.[26] We do not know how Austen's work first came to Murray's attention. There had been various problems with the publication of her previous novels, including Thomas Cadell and William Davies's rejection of 'First Impressions' (forerunner to *Pride and Prejudice*) in 1797; Benjamin Crosby's failure to fulfil his promise to publish 'Susan' (forerunner to *Northanger Abbey*) in 1803, and the sale of the copyright of *Pride and Prejudice* to Thomas Egerton for only £110, which turned out to be far too small a sum for a novel that sold very well and made the publisher a profit of £450.[27] Egerton had been prepared to publish, but not to buy the copyright for, *Mansfield Park*, and he had also refused to issue a second edition of this novel (which would have given Austen the opportunity to correct the printer's errors in the first edition). By 1815 Austen was looking for a better and more appreciative publisher. Murray's editor Gifford was certainly appreciative, and he was recommending Austen to Murray's attention as early as November 1814. 'I have for the first time looked into "Pride & Prejudice"', he told the publisher then, '& it is really a very pretty thing. No dark passages – no secret chambers, no wind howling in long galleries, no drops of blood upon a misty dagger – things that should rather be left to lady's maids and sentimental washer-women', he wrote, with much of the same emphasis as Annabella Milbanke's critique (quoted in the Introduction).[28] 'I have read Pride and Prejudice again', he wrote later, ''tis very good – wretchedly printed, and so pointed [i.e punctuated] as to be almost unintelligible'.[29]

'Your banker's sister'

It may have been Henry Austen who recommended an approach to Murray, as he shared some business contacts with Murray's printers. As Kathryn Sutherland has pointed out, in 1817 Gifford wrote to Murray in terms which might appear to link Austen with Henry, describing an unknown novel as 'com[ing] nearest your bankers sisters Novels – more business and incident, & freedom of obsert [? observation]; but less penetration and nature'.[30] Henry was not, however, literally Murray's banker, and if in fact it was Henry who actually made the publishing approach on behalf of his sister, perhaps it was Jane herself who selected Murray, as she evidently already knew a good deal about him.[31] Murray's journal the *Quarterly* is mentioned in *Mansfield Park*, and the plot of *Persuasion* (which Austen began in August 1815) does, as Janine Barchas has pointed out, revolve around a 'battle of the books' between 'The Baronetage' (favourite reading of Sir Walter Elliot) and 'The Navy List', pored over by the Miss Musgroves (and by Anne in secret) as a chronicle of Captain Wentworth's career.[32] It looks as if Austen, in researching Murray's publications before approaching him as her own potential publisher, had seen that he was both part of the consortium selling the new, 'considerably enlarged' third edition of John Debrett's *Baronetage of England* (March 1815) and also the publisher of the new and 'official' *Navy List*, issued on a monthly basis from 1814 with an imprint that announced Murray as 'Bookseller to the Admiralty and the Board of Longitude'.[33]

> Tours, Travels, Essays, too, I wist,
> And Sermons, to thy mill bring grist;
> And then thou hast the 'Navy List,'
> My Murray.
>
> And Heaven forbid I should conclude
> Without 'the Board of Longitude',

Byron quipped in a letter to Murray in March 1818.[34]

Whichever Austen it was who decided to make an approach to Murray, by 29 September 1815 Gifford had read the manuscript of *Emma* and was reporting back to the publisher:

> Of Emma I have nothing but good to say. I was sure of the writer before you mentioned her. The m.s. though plainly written has yet some ^ indeed, many little ^ omissions, & an expression may now & then be mended in passing through the press. If you print it which I think you will do (though I can say nothing as to its price) I will readily undertake the revision.[35]

This and Gifford's earlier notes highlight the essential role he played in Murray's enterprise. They show not only the knowledge of the literary scene that enabled him to recognize Austen's anonymous authorship, and his willingness to act as a copy editor, adding punctuation, rectifying 'omissions' and 'mend[ing]' 'expression[s]' in the text, but also demonstrate his willingness to encourage Murray to add a good new author to his stable, although not typical of the publisher's existing list. Gifford's wide-ranging literary taste is also evident, of course, in his ability to appreciate the very different merits of Austen's and Byron's writing.

In November 1815 Austen received a surprising invitation to dedicate her next work to the Prince Regent. Although a most unexpected honour, it had in fact been cheekily anticipated by Jane's nephew James Edward Austen, whose poem about the publication of *Pride and Prejudice* in 1813 envisaged that the Prince would enjoy it so much that he would make her a countess or even his second wife.[36] The 1815 connection between the Prince and the Austens seems to have come about through Dr Matthew Baillie, who is most likely to be 'the Prince Regent's physician' mentioned by James Edward as having been called in to treat Henry in October 1815 when Jane was staying with him in London and he became dangerously ill.[37] Dr Baillie had successfully treated Henry for a chest complaint in 1801.[38] If so, Baillie was another of the small group of people to have known both Byron and Austen, since as an anatomist (and nephew of the famous John Hunter who had been called in at Byron's birth) by 1799 Baillie had become the specialist in charge of the treatment of the boy's lame foot. Some of the most detailed descriptions of Byron's disability come from Baillie, who noted how the foot was 'inverted and contracted as it were in a heap and of course did not go fully and flatly to the ground'.[39] If Byron had received treatment when he was a baby, Baillie believed, it might have corrected the deformity, but by the time he was called in when Byron was eleven he considered it was too late to do much good. Nevertheless, over the next four years he continued to see Byron and had various 'instruments' made to try and straighten the foot, and by around 1803 Byron's condition had improved enough for him to be able to wear an ordinary boot. Two surgical boots which would help to correct and disguise the shape of the foot – one for a boy of about eleven, and the other for a youth of about eighteen – can be seen in the John Murray Collection at Albemarle Street. Designed to be worn under an ordinary boot, the soles were built up to counteract the tendency for the foot to bend inwards, and the larger boot includes a steel plate to provide a rigid platform (Figure 19).[40]

'Could not pronounce a positive opinion'

Dr Baillie came very close to meeting Byron again on 8 January 1816 when, in the last days of her marriage, Lady Byron called the doctor to their house while Byron was out to discuss whether her husband was suffering from temporary mental derangement: a diagnosis on which Baillie (not having seen Byron) declared he 'could not pronounce a positive opinion'. He suggested that Byron should be put under the discreet surveillance of Annabella's own physician, Francis Le Mann.[41] Byron learnt only later that his wife had, as he put it, intended him for 'a strait waistcoat'.[42]

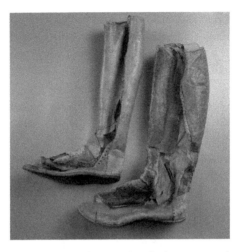

Figure 19 Corrective boots, both for Byron's right foot. Designed to be worn under an ordinary boot, there was padding in the calf and the sole contained a steel plate to counteract the tendency of the foot to bend inwards. The John Murray Collection, London. Photograph by Nasser Al Tell LRPS.

As the Austens would have been aware, Dr Baillie was the brother of the then renowned dramatist Joanna Baillie, who was a friend of Lady Byron's. She was best known for her *Plays on the Passions*, including *De Monfort* (produced in 1800 at Drury Lane with John Kemble and Sarah Siddons in the leading roles) and *The Family Legend*, given at Drury Lane in May 1815 when Byron escorted Baillie and her sister to a performance alongside Lady Byron and Walter and Mrs Scott.[43] While the *Edinburgh* attacked Baillie's plays as 'poor in incident and character and sluggish in their pace', Byron was intrigued by her ability to portray what he considered 'masculine' passions.[44] In 1817 he reflected on the prejudice of his culture by quoting Voltaire: 'When Voltaire was asked why no woman has ever written even a tolerable tragedy? "Ah (said the Patriarch) the composition of a tragedy requires testicles". – If this be true, the Lord knows what Joanna Baillie does – I suppose she borrows them.'[45]

Dr Baillie's employer, the Prince Regent, was notably gracious to both Austen and Byron, although they both thoroughly disapproved of him. Byron despised his politics and (as discussed in the Introduction) he reacted angrily – when in March 1812 he heard that the Prince's open abuse of the Whigs had reduced his daughter Princess Charlotte to tears – in his 'Lines to a Lady Weeping' which described 'a Sire's disgrace, a realm's decay'.[46] In July 1812 (after the 'Lines', but before Byron's authorship of them was known) Byron reported to Walter Scott:

He ordered me to be presented to him at a ball, & after some sayings
peculiarly pleasing from royal lips, as to my own attempts, he talked
to me of you & your immortalities; he preferred you to every bard
past & present. . . . He spoke alternately of Homer & yourself &
seemed well acquainted with both . . . with a tone & taste which gave
me a very high idea of his abilities & accomplishments, which I had
hitherto considered as confined to *manners*.[47]

Byron went on to say, however, that he had not attended a royal levee or
reception, because 'my politics being as perverse as my rhymes, I had in fact
"no business there"'.

In autumn 1815 Austen was told by Dr Baillie 'that the Prince was a
great admirer of her Novels; that he often read them, and had a set in
each of his residences': a compliment which must have caused her some
embarrassment, given her emphatic statement a couple of years earlier
(discussed in the Introduction) that she 'hate[d]' him.[48] The Prince may have
been introduced to Austen's work by his close friend Lord Moira who was a
customer and patron of Henry Austen, and an invoice for a pre-publication
copy of *Sense and Sensibility* has recently been found in the Royal Archives
at Windsor.[49] When the Regent heard Austen was in London he asked his
Librarian (who was also his Domestic Chaplain) to call on her, to invite her
to visit Carlton House and to show her the library. On 13 November 1815
Austen was duly conducted around the Prince's sumptuous new residence
by the Reverend Dr James Stanier Clarke, and in the course of the visit
she was invited by Dr Clarke to dedicate her forthcoming novel to the
Prince: an honour which she apparently intended to disregard until told by
her 'friends' that she should consider it as a command.[50] Later she would
suggest to Murray that perhaps 'the Printers will be influenced to greater
Dispatch & Punctuality by knowing that the Work is to be dedicated, by
Permission, to the Prince Regent'.[51]

This attention from the Prince must have considerably raised Murray's
assessment of his new author's social as well as literary capital. He seems to
have been quite straightforwardly snobbish about his own connections with
the royal family, as Byron teased him: 'I have a great respect for your good
& gentlemanly qualities – & return your personal friendship towards me . . .
although I think you a little spoilt by "villainous company" . . . together with
your "I am just going to call at Carlton House[;] are you walking that way?"'[52]
But whereas Murray would have regarded the Regent's endorsement of *Emma*
as a very welcome marketing bonus, Austen must have had some concern

that her respectability might be compromised by the Prince's unsavoury sexual and moral reputation. She was also annoyed to find that she had to pay twenty-four shillings for a special binding in 'red morocco gilt' for the copy of *Emma* that was presented to him. 'It strikes me that I have no business to give the P.R. a Binding', she commented to Cassandra.[53]

Incumbent

It was, however, in this context of royal etiquette that Austen had most cause to be grateful for Murray's knowledge of literary and social niceties when the publisher was able to steer her through the intricacies of the placing and wording of the dedication. After an anxious letter to Dr Clarke seeking to clarify whether it was 'incumbent' upon her to inscribe the work to the Prince, and his reply that it was not incumbent, but that she had 'permission' to do so, Austen wrote to Murray on 11 December to tell him that 'The Title page must be, Emma, Dedicated by Permission to H.R.H. The Prince Regent.'[54] Murray evidently replied by return of post to advise her that the dedication should be printed on a separate page, not on the title page, and to suggest a more elaborate and conventional wording, as eventually printed in the book:

To
His Royal Highness
The Prince Regent
this work is,
by His Royal Highness's permission,
most respectfully
dedicated,
by His Royal Highness's
dutiful
and obedient
humble servant
The Author.

Austen responded to Murray (again on the same day), saying:

> As to my direction about the title-page, it was arising from my ignorance only, and from my never having noticed the proper place for a dedication. I thank you for putting me right. Any deviation from what is usually done in such cases is the last thing I should wish for. I feel happy in having a friend to save me from the effect of my own blunder.[55]

Jane's visit to Carlton House led to a comical correspondence with the pompous and egotistical Dr Clarke, whose egregious self-importance must have reminded her more than a little of her own Mr Collins in *Pride and Prejudice*. His first suggestion was that she should 'delineate in some future Work the Habits of Life and Character and enthusiasm of a Clergyman – who should pass his time between the metropolis & the Country . . . Fond of, & entirely engaged in Literature – no man's Enemy but his own' (in other words, himself).[56] Austen declined in discreetly modest terms, claiming she did not know about 'Science & Philosophy', nor have the 'Classical Education, or at any rate a very extensive acquaintance with English Literature Ancient & Modern' which would be 'quite Indispensable for the person who wd. do any justice to your Clergyman'.[57] But with Collins-like self-assurance and pertinacity, Clarke continued to provide further suggestions for Austen's Clergyman, including a discussion of 'what good would be done if Tythes were taken away entirely . . . burying his own mother – as I did, . . . carry[ing] your Clergyman to Sea as the Friend of some distinguished Naval Character about a Court', and asking Murray to procure for Austen 'the Sermons which I wrote & preached on the Ocean'.[58] Finally, in March 1816 when he had become Private English Secretary to the Regent's future son-in-law Prince Leopold of Saxe-Cobourg, he suggested that her next work might be about the history of the 'august house' of Saxe-Cobourg and recommended Austen should dedicate her 'Volumes' to Prince Leopold.[59] Jane responded with a barely suppressed giggle that although she was 'fully sensible' that a historical work 'might be much more to the purpose of Profit or Popularity, than such pictures of domestic Life in Country Villages as I deal in', she could not compose such a thing without 'laughing at myself or other people'.[60]

Several of Dr Clarke's suggestions found their way into Austen's comic 'Plan of a Novel', reminiscent of her teenage satires, which she sketched out in early 1816.

Heroine to be the daughter of a clergyman, who after having lived much in the world had retired from it, and settled on a curacy with a very small fortune of his own. The most excellent man that can be imagined, perfect in character, temper, and manner. . . . Heroine a faultless Character herself –, perfectly good, with much tenderness and sentiment, and not the least Wit – very highly accomplished, understanding modern Languages and (generally speaking) everything that the most accomplished young Women learn, but

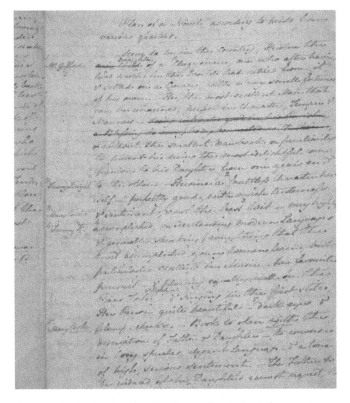

Figure 20 Jane Austen's *Plan of a Novel, according to hints from various quarters* (1815–16) sets out the details of an impossibly far-fetched and sentimental story, with names in the margin indicating the people who had offered suggestions for her work. 'Mr Gifford' appears first, on the top left. The Morgan Library & Museum, New York.

particularly excelling in Music – her favourite pursuit – and playing equally well on the Piano Forte and Harp – and singing in the first stile. Her Person, quite beautiful – dark eyes and plump cheeks. . . . The father induced, at his daughter's earnest request, to relate to her the past events of his life. Narrative to reach through the greater part of the first volume; as . . . it will comprehend his going to sea as chaplain to a distinguished naval character about the court; and his going afterwards to court himself, which involved him in many interesting situations, concluding with his opinion of the benefits of tithes being done away with. . . . At last, hunted out of civilized society, denied the poor shelter of the humblest cottage, they are compelled to retreat into Kamtschatka, where the poor father quite worn down, finding his end approaching, throws himself on the ground, and after four or five hours of tender advice and parental admonition to his miserable child, expires in a fine burst of literary enthusiasm, intermingled with invectives against the holders of tithes. Heroine inconsolable for some time, but afterwards crawls back towards her former country, having at least twenty narrow escapes of falling into the hands of anti-hero; and at last, in the very nick of time, turning a corner to avoid him, runs into the arms of the hero himself, who, having just shaken off the scruples which fettered him before, was at the very moment setting off in pursuit of her. The tenderest and completest *éclaircissement* takes place, and they are happily united.[61]

Names written in the margin of the manuscript indicate the sources or targets of Austen's satire, and as well as 'Mr Clarke' these include Jane's niece Fanny Knight, who had said she did not like the character of Mary Crawford and that 'she could not bear Emma'. Also in the margin 'Mr Gifford' appears next to the emendation of 'only child' to 'Daughter': perhaps reflecting Austen's impatience with some minute changes Gifford had made in editing *Emma*. Gifford had certainly, as we have seen, been critical of the punctuation and printing of Austen's previous novels, and it is possible that he may indeed have made substantial changes to the original text of *Emma*. It is difficult to tell precisely what condition Austen's manuscripts were in when they came into Murray's hands, since (unlike Byron's manuscripts which were carefully kept by the publisher) hers would have been routinely destroyed by the printers after setting the text. If, however, the manuscript of *Emma* was similar to the unpublished manuscripts of *The Watsons*, and the cancelled chapters of *Persuasion* and *Sanditon* (which survive), there was a good deal of capitalization of proper nouns, with no clear or regular paragraphing and no separation of speaking parts from one another.[62] Although Austen's satire may imply that she would have preferred to leave some aspects of her text *un* 'mended' by Gifford, it is certainly not true, as Henry Austen claimed in his 'Biographical Notice of the Author', that 'Every thing came finished from her pen', and likely that some of the 'correctness' of style and elaborate punctuation of the finished novels was added by Gifford's editorial pen.[63]

Like Byron, too, Austen must have had a healthy respect for Gifford's power and influence, both as Murray's advisor and as the editor of the *Quarterly*, with its print-run of 10,000 and readership of perhaps 50,000.[64] Thanks to Samuel Smiles' 1891 memoir of Murray and Andrew Nicholson's 2007 edition

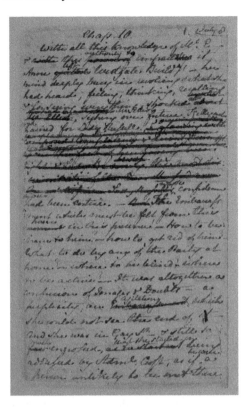

Figure 21 The first page of chapter 10 in the manuscript of the alternative (first) ending of *Persuasion* which was finished on 18 July 1816. Austen rewrote the chapter sometime before 6 August and the rewritten ending was published by Murray in the first edition of the novel in 1818. © British Library Board. All Rights Reserved/Bridgeman Images.

of the Murray-Byron correspondence, we now know a good deal more than Murray's authors ever did about the machinations he and Gifford undertook to procure good reviews for Murray's publications. Nicholson's notes show, for example, how hard Gifford worked to arrange a favourable review in the *Quarterly* for Byron's *The Giaour* in 1813.[65] Murray and Gifford also exerted themselves to obtain Walter Scott as a highly prestigious reviewer for *Emma* – although, as Claire Tomalin puts it, Murray introduced his request to Scott with 'a remark that consigns him to that circle of the Inferno reserved for disloyal publishers' (i.e. those who disparage their own authors' work) when he wrote: 'Have you any fancy to dash off an article on "Emma"? It wants incident and romance, does it not? None of the author's other novels have been noticed, and surely "Pride and Prejudice" merits high commendation.'[66]

Scott's review duly appeared in the *Quarterly* in 1816, and Austen had, as she put it rather coolly to Murray, 'no reason to complain of her treatment in it – except in the total omission of Mansfield Park.'[67]

Judicious compliments

Gifford and Murray also knew how and when to deploy judicious compliments to soothe and influence their authors, although both Byron and Austen saw through such ruses to some extent. Murray used praise from the beginning to mollify Austen, as is demonstrated by her full report to Cassandra about his first offer for *Emma*:

> Mr Murray's Letter is come; he is a Rogue of course, but a civil one. He offers £450 – but wants to have the Copyright of MP. & S&S included. It will end in my publishing for myself I dare say. – He sends more praise however than I expected. It is an amusing Letter. You shall see it.[68]

It would be intriguing to know exactly what 'praise' Murray sent in this case. A letter dictated by Henry Austen to Murray, probably on 20 or 21 October 1815, refers to 'The Politeness & Perspicuity of your letter' and continues:

> Your official opinion of the Merits of *Emma*, is very valuable & satisfactory. – Though I venture to differ occasionally from your Critique, yet I assure you the Quantum of your commendation rather exceeds than falls short of the Author's expectation & my own.[69]

Murray's methods (such as passing on compliments to his authors, lending and giving them publications and apologizing profusely when things went wrong) were all used with Byron as well as with Austen, who itemized them in a letter to Cassandra a few weeks later, on the day after she had written to Murray to say how she was 'disappointed & vexed by the delays of the Printers'.

> We sent the notes however, & I had a most civil one in reply from Mr M. He is so very polite indeed, that it is quite over-coming. – The printers have been waiting for Paper – the blame is thrown upon the Stationer – but he gives his word that I shall have no farther cause for dissatisfaction. – He has lent us *Miss Williams* [Helen Maria Williams' *A Narrative of the Events which have lately taken place in France. . .*] & *Scott* [Walter Scott's *Field of Waterloo*] & says that any book of his

will always be at *my* service. – In short, I am soothed & complimented into tolerable comfort.[70]

Austen's tone indicates some continuing scepticism, but such attentions must have come as a welcome change from the discourteousness of her previous publishers, and they worked well with most of Murray's authors. William St Clair describes how Murray 'became the first publisher in a modern sense', by dint of 'realising that he was essentially an entrepreneur who selected and put together packages of text, finance, and marketing' and 'withdrew from bookselling altogether'.[71] One of Murray's particularly successful marketing ploys was to provide a magnificent annual dinner, with 'oceans of wines', at the Albion Tavern in the City of London's Aldersgate Street for booksellers, printers, stationers, illustrators, editors and authors.[72] After the dinner, large discounts were offered for bulk orders, and Murray routinely sold books to the value of more than £20,000. 'Eh, man it was such a dinner and such drink, as nae words can describe', recalled the Scottish poet James Hogg after one of Murray's events, while Murray gleefully reported to Byron in 1816 that he had sold 'after the first Pint Five Thousand Pounds Worth of thy Poetry'.[73]

'So very inferior to what we had expected'

Murray's offer of the sum of £450 for the copyrights of *Emma*, *Mansfield Park* and *Sense and Sensibility* was firmly rejected by the Austens: the draft dictated by Henry on 20 or 21 October 1815 continues: 'The Terms you offer are so very inferior to what we had expected, that I am apprehensive of having made some great Error in my Arithmetical Calculation.'[74] With hindsight, however, it looks as if this was a fair offer from Murray. Jan Fergus estimates that Jane would almost certainly have done better to accept it rather than the option she chose instead, which was to risk the chance of profits by publishing on commission: an unusual form of publishing which, judging by their title pages, seems to have been chosen by the authors of as few as thirty-four of the 662 novels published in Britain in the 1810s.[75] In 1831 Murray was in correspondence with Cassandra about buying the copyrights of the novels he had published, but this seems to have come to nothing, and the following year the copyrights of all six major novels were acquired by Richard Bentley for his Standard Novels series for only £250, of which Cassandra received £210.[76]

Fergus describes the 'on commission' system as one in which 'the author was ultimately responsible for the cost of paper, printing and advertising;

the publisher kept accounts, distributed the books to the trade and charged a 10 per cent commission on each copy sold – a kind of royalty in reverse.[77] The understanding was that the author would bear any losses.[78] It was an unusual form of publishing for Murray and, in such a deal, he of course had an incentive to understate the income and overstate the costs of publication, and it is certainly true that Austen paid much more for *Emma*'s 'fine demy' paper (at thirty-seven shillings a ream) than for that used for *Persuasion* and *Northanger Abbey*, which was charged at only twenty-six shillings a ream.[79] Murray used his favourite printer, Thomas Davison of Blackfriars, to print some volumes of Austen's works as well as Byron's, but whereas her novels were published in runs of 1,750 copies or less, Byron's were produced in the tens of thousands: *The Bride of Abydos* (1813) for instance, sold some 6,000 copies in its first month and nearly 13,000 by the end of the year.[80]

Nevertheless, Murray's ledger entries show an initial profit to Austen of over £221 on *Emma* for 1,248 copies sold at a guinea each (twenty-one shillings: the weekly salary of a poor curate).[81] However, since there was a loss on the second edition of *Mansfield Park* of over £182, the amount that was owing to her overall was under £39, and on 21 October 1816 Murray issued a cheque to Austen for thirty-eight pounds, eighteen shillings and one penny.[82] As a further setback, Murray's cheque was a 'four-month bill' which was not payable until February 1817, and, since money was sorely needed by the Austens at this point, the endorsements on the cheque show that Austen had to discount 5 per cent of the sum in order to be able to bank it straight away.[83] *Emma* did eventually yield £385 for Austen and her heirs, before it was remaindered in 1821.[84]

Issues of social class and its part in the developing publishing market were embedded in both Austen's and Byron's relations with Murray, and self-consciousness about their own relative social status gave rise to tensions and embarrassment in both authors' dealings with him. By the early nineteenth century the old system of polite or courtly letters, where authors paid for the printing of their own works or were financially supported by a patron or by subscriptions, had largely given way to a new, publisher-based, market-centred literary system, in which authors were treated as professionals and paid for their work. But, as Fergus points out, 'the older aristocratic attitudes that saw print and payment as vulgar were surprisingly persistent among elite women and some men', and this social code was certainly one that exerted its pressure upon both Austen and Byron.[85]

In 1809 Byron had forcefully expressed his disdain for the new way of publishing in *English Bards and Scotch Reviewers*:

No! when the sons of song descend to trade,
Their bays are sear, their former laurels fade.
Let such forego the poet's sacred name,
Who rack their brains for lucre, not for fame:
Still for stern Mammon may they toil in vain!
And sadly gaze on Gold they cannot gain!
Such be their meed, such still the just reward
Of prostituted Muse and hireling bard![86]

Within the political and social system of the time, having enough wealth not
to have to work for one's living – and preferably that wealth held in one's own
land – was often called an 'independence' because it was considered to be
a sign of the necessary autonomy of thought and interest not only to write
real literature but also to take unbiased political decisions and to be a good
'statesman', including exercising one's vote in the House of Lords. As we have
seen, Byron's path to nobility was by no means straightforward, and it was
because of his insecurity about his status as a Lord, rather than his confidence
in it, that he was suspicious of anything that implied what would be (for him) a
step down in class to that of a professional writer, and led to his unwillingness
to accept any payment from Murray in the initial stages of their relationship.

'Spread over a dead flat'

Before he came to Murray, Byron had turned to privately commissioned
printing as a way of distributing his early poems without them being
officially 'published' through the means of trade. His first collection of
poems, *Fugitive Pieces* (1806) was issued in this way and revised again
for private printing as *Poems on Various Occasions* (1807). It was when it
entered the market with a publisher, as *Hours of Idleness* (1807), however,
that it attracted the scathing sarcasm of Henry Brougham's review in
the *Edinburgh*, which described the poems as 'spread over a dead flat'
and advised the author 'that he do forthwith abandon poetry'.[87] As Peter
W. Graham explains, this review 'taught [Byron] to distinguish private
poems, the occasional verses sent to friends or circulated to a coterie, from
candidates for publication'.[88] He was, however, caught out again in 1816,
when his bitter poems about his marriage separation, 'Fare Thee Well' and
'A Sketch from Private Life', were privately printed in a run of fifty copies by
Murray but immediately leaked (by Henry Brougham) to *The Champion*,
where they were published in April and, soon becoming anything *but*
'Private', were widely denigrated.[89]

But although to begin with Byron would not lower himself by accepting remuneration for his work, he nevertheless wanted the glory of the huge sums Murray was offering him, commenting in his journal of the 1,000 guineas suggested for *The Giaour* and *The Bride of Abydos*: 'I won't – it is too much, though I am strongly tempted, merely for the *say* of it. No bad price for a fortnight's work (a week each) what? – the gods know – it was intended to be called Poetry.'[90] Later, when Murray offered him £1,500 for *The Siege of Corinth* and *Parisina*, Byron instructed him to pay the money instead to the bankrupt radical philosopher William Godwin (father of Mary Shelley), with sums also for Samuel Taylor Coleridge and Charles Maturin.[91] Murray reacted by claiming he worked hard and it was 'heart-breaking to throw away [his] earnings' in this way, to which Byron responded that it was no business of his publisher's how he spent *his* money, and whether he paid it 'to a w[hore] or a hospital – or assisted a man of talent in distress'.[92]

When Byron asked Murray to give the copyright of *The Corsair* to Robert Dallas, it was Murray (who was concerned that it could be 'insinuated' that he had got the poem for nothing) who used a reference to the social inequality of the relationship as a means of upbraiding his aristocratic client.[93] 'Indeed my Lord this is not worthy treatment of one whom you have suffered to absorb – the humble servant in the faithful friend', he protested.[94] And in 1817, after Byron rebuked him for removing the last line of *Manfred*, Murray replied in distinctly passive-aggressive mode, adding his own nuances of class distinction:

> I sometimes feel a deep regret that in our pretty long intercourse I appear to have failed to shew, that a man in my situation may <be> possess the feelings & principles of a Gentleman – most certainly I do think that from personal attachment, I could venture as much in any shape for your service as any of those who have the good fortune to be ranked amongst your Lordships friends – & therefore do [*sic*] cut me up at a word as if I were your Taylor.[95]

Murray was still taking this rather uncomfortable stance after Byron's death, in 1824, during the heated discussions about the burning of the *Memoirs*, when, according to Hobhouse, he protested to Thomas Moore:

> here am I as a tradesman – I do not care a farthing about having your money, or whether I ever get it or not – but such regard have I for Lord Byron's honour and fame that I am willing and determined to destroy these MSS. . . . It is very hard that I as a tradesman should be willing to make a sacrifice that you as a gentleman will *not* consent to!![96]

Elsewhere, it is only too easy to notice the number of 'my Lords' and 'your Lordships' Murray sprinkles through his letters to Byron (twelve times in the thirty-six lines of his first letter, for example), and the servility with which the young aristocrat was treated by him.[97]

'The sweat of his brain'

Later, when Byron had moved to Italy and abandoned many of the social and financial scruples he had maintained while he was an active member of English aristocratic society and the House of Lords, he decided that there was 'no reason why a man should not profit by the sweat of his brain, as well as that of his brow', and began not only to accept money for his copyrights but also to bargain with Murray for them, securing 2,500 guineas for the copyright of canto 4 of *Childe Harold* after Murray had initially offered 1,500 guineas. He continued to write to Murray on friendly terms, however, using his letters as an opportunity to express many of his most intimate reflections and for retailing his amorous and other adventures. This caused considerable social discomfiture to several of Byron's friends, including Moore in particular. Perhaps, as the son of a Dublin grocer (albeit a graduate of Trinity College Dublin) Moore had his own class anxieties, since he objected strongly to the fact that some of Byron's most frank and engaging letters had been written, as he put it, to 'Murray, the bookseller – a person so out of his caste & to whom he writes formally, beginning "Dear Sir"'.[98] In fact Byron more often addressed his publisher as 'Dear Murray' – or 'Dear Moray' – although it is a mark of the later cooling of their relationship that he reverted to addressing Murray merely as 'Sir'.[99] After Byron's death, Moore and Hobhouse were reluctant to allow Murray's name to appear as a member of the committee formed to organize a monument for the poet. Murray 'is, after all, a tradesman, he has hardly a right to be there', Moore commented.[100]

Byron received nearly £20,000 from Murray over the ten years of their association, in contrast to the total of £668 that it has been calculated Austen received in all her literary earnings during her lifetime.[101] But Byron, too, was no match for Murray's canniness in matters financial and, in 1822, when Byron estimated the profits that Murray was making from his writings over the copyright period, he too felt exploited. St Clair notes, for example, that 'The five hundred guineas (£525) [Byron] was receiving for each of his poems was no more than Murray paid to the Reverend Henry Milman for religious verse dramas which sold far less well'.[102] 'I am worth any "forty on fair ground" of the wretched stilted pretenders and parsons of your advertisements', Byron wrote angrily on 23 September 1822.[103]

Another major issue which became a matter of contention between Byron and Murray was the difference in their politics: Byron's wish to use his poetry for some controversial political and polemical purposes, and Murray's pushback against this, which included making cuts and changes to the text before publication without Byron's consent. Even with *Childe Harold* cantos 1 and 2, where Byron was generally willing to make the changes suggested by his (then new) publisher, he specified that he would not allow Murray to alter anything 'to do with politics or religion'.[104] When in 1814 (as discussed in the Introduction) Byron found that Murray had withdrawn the controversial 'Lines to a Lady Weeping' from the second edition of *The Corsair* he threatened 'do not you – by any tremors or omissions – compromise me in any manner – for in that case – we should cease to be friends – which perhaps you don't much mind'.[105] Murray countered disingenuously that he had done it to maximize sales, and he did republish the 'Lines' in the fourth edition of *The Corsair* in mid-February 1814.[106] However in 1816 Murray evidently again felt that he was entitled to safeguard 'his' poet's popularity by removing two controversial lines (388–89) from *The Prisoner of Chillon* which contained a criticism of monarchy: 'Nor slew I of my subjects one / What Sovereign hath so little done?', and again Byron was furious: 'if he has made any alterations or omissions – I shall not pardon him', he wrote to Douglas Kinnaird.[107]

The difficulties with *Don Juan* were much greater, as discussed in Chapter 7, but the issue which finally drove Byron and Murray apart was not religious, social, political, moral, legal or even financial, but Byron's frustration at Murray's failure to keep him informed about the publication of his work, once he was dependent on Murray for news from England. Murray sometimes did not even acknowledge the receipt of a parcel of manuscripts which, as Byron said, had 'cost some pains in the composition, & great trouble in the copying', and if after publication Byron heard nothing from Murray about sales or reviews he would fear the worst: 'You say nothing of Manfred, from which its failure may be inferred', he wrote in 1817.[108] The tension increased dramatically in 1818 when Murray failed to communicate with Byron about canto 4 of *Childe Harold,* and on 30 June Byron threatened that if he did not receive a letter in the next ten days he would terminate their association.[109] Murray's response arrived just in time and they made up the quarrel, but the problems continued, and in 1822 Byron entered into a partnership with Shelley, Leigh Hunt and his brother John Hunt to publish a literary journal, *The Liberal.* It was through this radical publication, rather than through John Murray's, that cantos 6 to 16 of *Don Juan* were issued, along with other controversial late works of Byron's such as *The Vision of Judgment*, which mocked Poet Laureate Robert Southey's eulogy for George III and satirized the late king's attempts to get into heaven. In November 1822 Byron wrote to Murray to bid him a 'final farewell', citing 'your recent – & repeatedly rude neglect', and their parting received almost as much press coverage as the end of the Byron marriage had done in 1816.[110] 'Lord Byron and John Murray – the Prince of Poets and the Prince of Publishers – have long been on very indifferent terms', reported the *Literary Register*, 'and now, it appears, the divorce is utterly consummated.'[111]

'If I were alongside of him'

The volume of Murray's work had risen dramatically during the years that Byron was linked with him, and the number of publications issued by the firm had increased from twenty titles a year in 1810 to ninety-nine in 1816.[112] It is not surprising that both Austen and Byron felt frustrated by their publisher's delays and apparent neglect, although Austen wrote that '[a] short conversation may perhaps do more than much Writing', and Byron recognized that '[i]f I were alongside of him – I could deal with him'.[113] Murray too wished that Byron would 'return to London & come and talk all the day long – or send for me at night – as formerly'.[114] The existence of personal warmth and genuine friendship, alongside a constant background of busyness and haste, was part of Murray's character, and Byron paid tribute to it in 1817 in an affectionate ninety-line rhyming parody of a letter from Murray to Dr John Polidori. This satirized Byron himself:

> There's Byron – too – who once did better . . .
> I think he's lost his wits at Venice –
> Or drained away his brains as Stallion
> To some dark-eyed & warm Italian,

and ended with an imitation of Murray's special elaborate signature and the lines

> My hands so full– my head so busy –
> I'm almost dead – & always dizzy –
> And so with endless truth & hurry –
> Dear Doctor – I am yours
>   John Murray
> ('Epistle from John Murray to Dr Polidori', 33, 38–40, 89–93)[115]

Figure 22 Byron's imitation of John Murray's signature at the end of an affectionate ninety-line rhyming parody of a letter from Murray to Dr John Polidori, which also satirized Byron himself (1817). The John Murray Archive, National Library of Scotland.

The nuances of Austen's social relations with Murray may appear more slight and subtle than this, but they too reflect issues of class, and in particular the way in which the publication of a novel by a gentlewoman in this period could be seen as a violation of both sexual modesty and social caste. The threat to Austen's modesty had led her to begin correspondence with a previous publisher indirectly, through her brother's lawyer, and subsequently to present herself under a false name as a married woman ('Mrs Ashton Dennis'), while much of her correspondence with Murray was decorously conducted through her brother Henry.[116] It was for such reasons of social caste and modesty that Austen published all her novels anonymously, and Henry Austen claimed that 'so much did she shrink from notoriety, that no accumulation of fame would have induced her, had she lived, to affix her name to any productions of her pen'.[117] Kathryn Sutherland, however, describes this as 'a shrewd move for an ambitious author, reducing though not obliterating the focus on her female perspective as a writer'.[118] Eventually, Austen became inured to the idea that her identity was becoming publicly known, commenting to her brother Francis in September 1813 that 'the truth is that the Secret has spread so far as to be scarcely the Shadow of a secret now – & that I beleive [*sic*] whenever the 3d [novel] appears, I shall not even attempt to tell Lies about it'.[119] Nevertheless, she would have been anxious to preserve her position as 'a Lady' in the context of her dealings with Murray, since it was in just such a situation, where his position 'in trade' conflicted with her femininity and gentility, that her social status was most insecure. In *Pride and Prejudice* Elizabeth Bennet defends herself against the arrogance of Lady Catherine de Bourgh by pointing out that, although Darcy 'is a gentleman; I am a gentleman's daughter; so far we are equal.'[120] Actually, however, this comparison serves to draw attention to the way in which the description of gentility could cover an enormously wide range of situations, from Darcy's near-nobility to the precariously low financial and social expectations of the Bennet sisters. Austen, as the unmarried daughter of a deceased country clergyman was even further down the pecking order than Elizabeth Bennet, and that made her denomination as 'a Lady' all the more important to her.

At a crucial stage in the negotiations about the publication of *Emma* Henry Austen fell ill, and Jane was obliged to take over the correspondence with Murray herself. Humphrey Carpenter makes the point that Jane wrote 'inviting *him* to call, like the tradesman she considered him to be', and it is interesting to note the difference between the draft of her letter to the publisher on 3 November 1815, preserved in Austen's papers, where she wrote 'I must *beg* [my italics] the favour of you to call on me here', and the letter she actually sent, which was kept in the Murray archives, where she amended the word 'beg' to 'request', making a subtle but important difference to the tone.[121] Since, as we have seen, Murray certainly preferred to do business face-to-face with his clients, it seems likely that he may, as requested, have called on her at Henry's house in Hans Place, Chelsea.[122] The tone of Austen's subsequent letters to him is distinctly warmer, with references to 'the attention you have paid to my Convenience & amusement', and to her being 'much obliged' by his letter and 'very happy to feel everything arranged to our mutual satisfaction'. In her last letter to him from London she refers to him as 'a friend'.[123]

'Albeit a bookseller'

Perhaps by this stage Austen might have been prepared to modify her description of Murray as 'a Rogue' (albeit 'a civil one'). Like Byron's criticism of authors who 'rack their brains for lucre, not for fame', the portrayal of publishers as unscrupulous and greedy had by this time become a rather outdated cliché. Mary O'Connell shows how Charles Lamb, for example, characterized them as a 'rapacious, dishonest set' who despised authors, while Byron's friend the poet Thomas Campbell damned Murray with faint praise in a letter to Walter Scott as 'a very excellent and gentlemanlike man – albeit a bookseller'.[124] When Isaac D'Israeli, who was a close friend of Murray's, commented more moderately that publishers are 'but commercial men. A trader can never be deemed a patron, for it would be romantic to purchase what is not saleable', he put his finger on the key source of publishers' reputation for greed: namely, the way in which the production of books had moved into the hands and control of businessmen.[125]

Despite their comments, both Byron and Austen in fact viewed this situation realistically and with some irony. Both of them used the well-worn joke about an author's printed unread work ending up in undignified roles such as wrapping for bacon or in 'the pastry-cook's shop', or as the lining for hats and trunks, or even for use in the privy: 'I am apt to consider the trunk-maker as the sexton of authorship', Byron remarked.[126] Austen did not consider it as compromising her literary integrity when she struck what E. J. Clery calls 'mercenary poses' in letters to her family.[127] 'I have now therefore written myself into £250 – which only makes me long for more', she wrote to Cassandra, and 'I shall rather try to make all the money than all the mystery I can of it. – People shall pay for their knowledge if I can make them', she told her brother Francis in 1813.[128] Byron and Austen deployed different metals to metaphorically carry the same message: Byron initially excoriating poets in search of 'Gold', but later seeking the best price possible for his work, while Austen remarked that 'tho' I like praise as well as anybody, I like what Edward calls *Pewter* too'.[129]

In practice, therefore, despite Austen's slightly squeamish gentility and femininity, Byron's anxious nobility, and Murray's self-abasing tradesman pose, we might prefer to regard all three of them as competent and professional business-people: sometimes cautious and sometimes adventurous; often willing to take a gamble, and working (sometimes together and sometimes in competition) to make and market a commodity that they all, rightly, regarded as highly valuable, in material as well as in cultural terms.

Notes

1. The first edition of *Mansfield Park* was published by Thomas Egerton (1814) and the second edition by John Murray (1816).

2. O'Connell (2014) 81. *EBSR* 171–2, *LBCPW* 1.234.

3. Smiles 267–8.

4. O'Connell (2014) 200.

5. *JAL* 291, to Cassandra Austen, 17–18 October 1815.

6. *JAL* 305, to John Murray, 11 December 1815. Austen-Leigh ed. Sutherland 99.

7. *BLJ* 8.163, to John Murray, 30 July 1821.

8. Medwin 170.

9. *EBSR* 701, *LBCPW* 1.251.

10. *BLJ* 3.63, to William Gifford, 18 June 1813.

11. *BLJ* 11.117, to Douglas Kinnaird, 21 or 22 February 1824. For Byron's defence of Pope, see, e.g., 'Some Observations', *LBCMP* 111–17. *BLJ* 3.63–64, letter to William Gifford, 18 June 1813.

12. *Manfred* 3.4.151, *LBCPW* 4.102.

13. Graham (2004) 31.

14. Austen-Leigh ed. Sutherland 18. Austen certainly did 'venture upon' medicine in the unpublished *Sanditon*.

15. For biographical details of Whately see de Giustino 218–36.

16. Whately 359. Henry Austen quoted this passage in his 1833 'Memoir of Miss Austen', see Henry Austen in Austen-Leigh ed. Sutherland 153.

17. *DJ* 1.1, *LBCPW* 5.9.

18. Whately 361, 375.

19. Cochran, 'Byron's Correspondence with John Murray 3, 1820–1824' 105.

20. Kenyon Jones (with grateful thanks to David McClay). Sutherland (2013) 109–10.

21. Murray ed. Nicholson 13.

22. Sutherland (2013) 112–20.

23. *BLJ* 4.290, to Thomas Moore, 23 April 1815.

24. Wordsworth to Samuel Rogers, 15 August 1825, quoted in O'Connell (2014) 105.

25. Graham (2004) 30.

26. Graham (2004) 31. Clery (2017) 200.

27. Austen-Leigh ed. Sutherland 105–6.

28. Letter of 21 November 1814, quoted in Cochran (2009) 21.

29. Letter of 29 September 1815, National Library of Scotland, John Murray Archive, 42248, 'Various Letters to and from Gifford.'

30. Sutherland (2013) 108.

31. Corley (2012) 49.

32. Clery (2017) 245.

33. Barchas 206–10.

34. *BLJ* 6.26–9, to John Murray, 11 April 1818.

35. Sutherland (2013) 123.

36. *JAFR* 202.

37. Austen-Leigh ed. Sutherland 92.

38. *JAFR* 225.

39. Baillie's description and opinion as recorded in the Newton Hanson MS and published in Marchand (1957) 1.54.

40. Burton and Murdoch 6–7.

41. Moore (1830) 2.815. MacCarthy 262.

42. *LBCMP* 77, *Donna Josefa: A Fragment of a Skit on the Separation* (1817), lines 23–4.

43. Carhart chap. 4 np.

44. Jeffrey 265–6.

45. *BLJ* 5.203, to John Murray, 2 April 1817.

46. 'Lines to a Lady Weeping' 2, *LBCPW* 2.10. In 1821 Byron was less harsh about the Prince (by now King George IV): *LBCMP* 186, *Some recollections of my acquaintance with Madame de Staël,* lines 18–20, 4 August 1821, 'I shall not presume to be so treasonable – as to say that he is bad – but *if* he were – with the provocation he has had – I should only wonder that he is not worse.'

47. *BLJ* 2.182–83, to Walter Scott, 6 July 1812. See also Murray to Scott, 27 June 1812, MacCarthy 161.

48. Austen-Leigh ed. Sutherland 92. *JAFR* 225, quoting Caroline Austen 12. *JAL* 208, to Martha Lloyd, 16 February 1813.

49. Clery (2017) 90–2. Schuessler l.

50. *JAFR* 226.

51. *JAL* 297, to John Murray, 23 November 1815.

52. *BLJ* 6.123, to John Murray, 6 May 1819.

53. *JAL* 304, to Cassandra Austen, 2 December 1815.

54. *JAL* 296, to James Stanier Clarke, 15 November 1815. *JAL* 296, from James Stanier Clarke, 16 November 1815. *JAL* 304, to John Murray, 11 December 1815.

55. *JAL* 305, to John Murray, 11 December 1815.

56. *JAL* 296–7, from James Stanier Clarke, 16 November 1815.

57. *JAL* 306, to James Stanier Clarke, 11 December 1815.

58. *JAL* 307, from James Stanier Clarke, 21[?] December 1815.

59. *JAL* 311, from James Stanier Clarke, 27 March 1816.

60. *JAL* 312, to James Stanier Clarke, 1 April 1816.

61. Austen, 'Plan of a Novel' 1–12.

62. See Austen ed. Todd and Bree, 381–555 and Austen, *Jane Austen's Fiction Manuscripts*. There is at least one paragraph that appears both in the earlier draft and in the published version of *Persuasion*: the original has far less punctuation than the published text. Since it was published posthumously, Austen was not of course able to check the proofs of *Persuasion*. See Levy 191.

63. Scott expected Gifford to 'correct all obvious errors [in] and abridge' his review of *Emma*. Smiles 289.

64. Robert Southey, quoted by O'Connell (2014) 41.

65. Murray ed. Nicholson (2007) 43–4.

66. Tomalin 252, quoting Smiles 1.288.

67. *JAL* 313, to John Murray, 1 April 2016.

68. *JAL* 291, to Cassandra Austen, 17–18 October 1815.

69. *JAL* 293, Henry Austen to John Murray, 20[?]–21 October 1815.

70. *JAL* 298, to Cassandra Austen, 24 November 1815.

71. St Clair (2004) 170.

72. O'Connell (2014) 157.

73. O'Connell (2014) 157. Murray to Byron 13 December 1816 in Murray ed. Nicholson 181.

74. *JAL* 293, from Henry Austen to John Murray, 20[?]–21 October 1815.

75. Fergus (2011) 14. Clery (2017) 130.

76. Viveash (1995) 34.

77. Fergus (2011) 6.

78. Sutherland (2013) 108.

79. Gilson 68, 84 and 59.

80. O'Connell (2014) 121.

81. Le Faye (2002) 106.

82. Fergus (2011) 14.

83. Corley (2011) 134.

84. Fergus (2011) 14.

85. Fergus (2011) 3.

86. *EBSR* 175–82, *LBCPW* 1.234–5.

87. Brougham 2, 3.

88. Graham (2004) 29.

89. MacCarthy 274–5.

90. *BLJ* 3.212, *Journal*, 17 November 1813.

91. O'Connell (2014) 137.

92. *BLJ* 5.17, to John Murray, 22 January 1816.

93. Murray ed. Nicholson 82.

94. Murray ed. Nicholson 65.

95. Murray ed. Nicholson 241–2.

96. Hobhouse ed. Cochran, 33, 1824 Byron's Death and Funeral, 50.

97. Nicholson 3–4.

98. Moore 1.187 and 1.225, quoted in Murray ed. Nicholson 278.

99. Cochran, 'Byron-Murray 1816–1819' 2.

100. Moore *Journal* 3.939, quoted by O'Connell (2014) 200.

101. St Clair (2004) 162. Fergus (2011) 16.

102. St Clair (2004) 162.

103. *BLJ* 9.213, to John Murray, 23 September 1822.

104. *BLJ* 2.99, to John Murray, 14 September 1811.

105. Simmers and Lister 53–4. This letter from Byron to John Murray, dated 13 February 1814, was unknown before its publication in the *Byron Journal* in 2023.

106. O'Connell (2014) 127–8.

107. O'Connell (2014) 157. 12 January 1817, *BLJ* 5.159.

108. *BLJ* 7.77, to John Murray, 16 April 1820. *BLJ* 5.254, to John Murray, 7 August 1817.

109. *BLJ* 6.57, to John Murray, 30 June 1818.

110. *BLJ* 10.28, to John Murray, 6 November 1822.

111. O'Connell (2014) 194.

112. O'Connell (2014) 150.

113. *JAL* 295, to John Murray, 3 November 1815. *BLJ* 8.205, to Douglas Kinnaird, 11 September 1821.

114. Murray 373.

115. Byron to John Murray, 21 August 1817. *BLJ* 5.258–61.

116. *JAL* 174–5. Austen's letter to Crosby & Co, 5 April 1809, about *Susan*, and Le Faye's note *(JAL* 400).

117. Henry Austen (1833) in Austen-Leigh ed. Sutherland 140.

118. Sutherland (2013) 114.

119. *JAL* 231, to Francis Austen, 25 September 1813.

120. *P&P* vol. 3, chap. 14, 395.

121. Carpenter 88. *JAL* 295, draft of letter to John Murray, 3 November 1815 and letter to John Murray, 3 November 1815.

122. O'Connell (2014) 172.

123. *JAL* 305, to John Murray, 11 December 1815, and *JAL* 305, to John Murray, 11 December 1815.

124. O'Connell (2013) 160–1.

125. O'Connell (2013) 161.

126. James or Jane Austen, 52. *BLJ* 8.11–12.

127. Clery (2013) 132.

128. *JAL* 217, to Cassandra Austen, 3–6 July 1813, and *JAL* 231, to Francis Austen 25 September 1813.

129. *JAL* 287, to Fanny Knight, 30 November 1814.

CHAPTER 6
FICTION, FINANCES AND ENTAIL
'A LARGE INCOME IS THE BEST RECIPE
FOR HAPPINESS I EVER HEARD OF'[1]

I had a dream, which was not all a dream.
The bright sun was extinguish'd, and the stars
Did wander darkling in the eternal space,
Rayless, and pathless, and the icy earth
Swung blind and blackening in the moonless air;
Morn came and went – and came, and brought no day.

('Darkness' 1–6)[2]

Byron's poem 'Darkness' was a response to what came to be known as 'the year without a summer'. Because of the volcanic debris thrown up into the atmosphere in April 1815 by the massive eruption of Mount Tambora in the Dutch East Indies (modern Indonesia), temperatures in the northern hemisphere in the following year fell to the coldest on record. The glaciers failed to melt in summer, and there was frost in August and torrential rainfall leading to disastrous floods, ruined harvests and widespread famine. These meteorological events provided an apt metaphor for the turbulent political and economic climate in the period following Napoleon's final defeat at Waterloo in June 1815: particularly for those who, like Byron, Mary Godwin and Percy Bysshe Shelley, deplored the subsequent restoration of the French monarchy and the reversal of many of the revolutionary changes of the previous decades, and also for those who, like Henry Austen, were dependent on the war economy for their business and livelihood.

By 10 June 1816, Byron, fleeing England in the wake of the breakdown of his marriage and ensuing scandal, had arrived with his doctor John Polidori at the Villa Diodati (where John Milton had once stayed) in Cologny on Lake Geneva. A few minutes' walk away on the lakeside, the Villa Chapuis housed Mary Godwin (daughter of the writer and advocate of women's rights Mary Wollstonecraft and the radical philosopher William Godwin), who was living with Percy Bysshe Shelley, political campaigner, poet and already-married son of a baronet, and their four-month-old son William. With them (sometimes, but often running up the hill to visit Byron's bed at Diodati) was Clare Claremont, Mary's stepsister, who had provided the initial link between the two poets by briefly becoming Byron's lover in London in April, and then persuading Mary and Percy to travel to Geneva in pursuit of him.

'But it proved a wet, ungenial summer', Mary explained later, 'and incessant rain often confined us for days to the house.'[3] The group met in the evenings at Diodati and, after reading *Fantasmagoriana* – a collection of German ghost stories translated into French – Byron decreed that they should each write a ghost story.[4] Of the four that were begun, two went on to become famous Gothic novels: Mary's *Frankenstein* (1818) and Polidori's *The Vampyre* (1819) which was loosely based on a story begun by Byron about the eerie death of an English traveller in a Turkish cemetery. And, since then, the Diodati gathering has itself become a famous ghostly story in its own right, which has been widely retold and recreated in fiction, film and fantasy.

Three miles away in Geneva that summer, Henry Austen was living a quieter life. He was shepherding two of his brother Edward's teenage sons – Henry and William Knight – around Europe and socializing with the friends that Edward had made when he had visited Switzerland thirty years earlier.[5] Henry and Byron were, as Byron described it, 'among the 100000 visitors who broke loose from Great Britain in all directions' in the year after Waterloo.[6] News of the arrival of the notorious poet and tales of the goings-on at Diodati would soon have reached Henry through the hundreds of other English visitors in Geneva at this time.[7] Byron's old enemy Henry Brougham and the Poet Laureate Robert Southey were both there and alleged that Byron and Shelley were involved in a 'league of incest' with the supposed sisters Mary and Clare. Byron, acutely sensitive to the accusation of incest because of his relationship with Augusta, sent Brougham a challenge to a duel.[8]

Telescopes

Henry Austen may have felt some sympathy for Byron. Thanks to his own avid London theatre-going and the location of his office in Henrietta Street, close to the Covent Garden and Drury Lane theatres, and given the distinguishing mark of Byron's lameness, Henry may well have been able to recognize the famous poet by sight. But he would surely not have been among the English tourists who trained their telescopes onto the windows of the Villa Diodati from across the lake, waylaid his lordship on his evening drives and described him, Byron said, as 'a man-monster'.[9] And Henry, like Byron, was just then at an acutely painful turning point in his life. As with Byron's, the disasters that had led to his downfall were partly of his own making, and they had played out over almost exactly the same timescale. The collapse of Henry's Alton bank in late 1815, followed by his business failure and bankruptcy in early 1816, had caused not only distress and embarrassment to all the Austens, but also grievous financial problems for several members of the family, with serious repercussions for Jane herself. The year 1816 was to be a grim and dark one for the Austens and Byron alike.

Henry – the fourth of Jane's brothers, born in 1771 – was the one she was closest to ('her especial pride and delight' according to her niece Caroline), with whom she shared her literary interests and ambitions, her experiences of London and her sense of humour.[10] *Northanger Abbey*'s Henry Tilney is often thought of as having his basis in Henry Austen. '[H]e cannot help being amusing', Jane wrote in 1805, and 'Oh! what a Henry', she exclaimed delightedly when she heard in 1814 that he was attending a grand ball at White's Club and rubbing shoulders with the Prince Regent and other heads of state.[11]

After leaving St John's College, Oxford, Henry had joined the Oxfordshire Militia in 1793 and rapidly risen to lieutenant, lieutenant-captain and then captain, as well as becoming the Regiment's paymaster. When he left the militia in 1801 this experience enabled him to establish himself in London as an army agent and then to move into private banking enterprises in Hampshire, Kent, Somerset, Derbyshire and London.[12] He also expanded into tax collection, and in 1813 became Receiver General for Land and Assessed Taxes for Oxfordshire. His businesses did well for several years, but the end of the war brought widespread economic depression, while the reduction in the militia and army establishment meant that the regimental payroll handled by Austen & Co. fell from £85,513 in 1813 to £13,447 in 1817.[13] The Austen, Gray & Vincent bank in Alton, Hampshire, near Jane's home in Chawton, was one of the thirty-five English country banks that failed in 1815; this was followed by Henry's own bankruptcy and the collapse of his army agency and his London bank, Austen, Maunde and Tilson, in March 1816. He was summoned to prove his debts at a bankruptcy meeting on 19 March, and on 27 April (five days after Byron departed from London in disgrace, leaving the goods in his house at Piccadilly Terrace to be seized by bailiffs in lieu of rents) Henry was called to make a full disclosure of his estate, knowing that the death penalty was still in place for the concealment of assets.[14] He and his partners were lucky to avoid imprisonment in the Fleet debtors' prison.[15] Austen & Co's goods and chattels at the Henrietta Street office were valued at £100 and those in Henry's home at Hans Place at £200.[16] While Captain Wentworth's rise to riches from a relatively humble background might recall Henry's similar ascent, some of the details of financial mismanagement and the closing-in of debt around Sir Walter Elliot may also have been drawn by Jane from the later stages of Henry's banking career.

Henry received his certificate of discharge from bankruptcy on 8 June, and by September he had decided to pursue the other profession that was available to him as a graduate of the University of Oxford by becoming a clergyman like his father and his brother James. In December 1816 he was ordained deacon and installed as curate of Chawton, with an annual stipend of fifty-two guineas. He was ordained priest early in 1817. After Jane's death in July 1817 he – who had married a French Countess, handled sums in the hundreds of thousands of pounds and helped to fund and guarantee Jane's publishing ventures – must have been very grateful for the modest bequest of £50 in his sister's will.[17] Henry married again in 1820 and spent the rest of his life as a lowly paid clergyman of an 'Evangelical' cast; a schoolmaster and an author of sermons, who helped to manage his deceased sister's literary assets and carefully guarded the respectability of her reputation though his 'Biographical Notice of the Author' written in late 1817 and published in 1818, and the 'Memoir of Miss Austen' written in October 1832 and published in 1833.[18] He died in 1850.

'Worldly failure'

While acknowledging his 'worldly failure' in the letter he sent in November 1816 to the Bishop of Winchester seeking ordination, Henry described himself as 'conscious of no criminality'.[19] He blamed the bank failure on his partners in the Alton bank (who had deliberately syphoned off almost all the funds when they realized that danger was near) and accused in particular the Whig grandee, politician and erstwhile close friend of the Prince Regent, the Earl of Moira, to whom Henry had made large loans, and who had himself advanced vast sums of money to the Prince. Like Moira, nearly all Henry's important business clients and patrons were members of the elite Whig circle that Byron mixed with politically and socially, including Henry's close associate Lord Charles Spencer, a cousin of Lady Caroline Lamb.[20] Byron recorded an occasion in 1812 during the negotiations led by Moira (after the assassination of Prime Minister Spenser Perceval) with Lords Grey and Greville about forming a coalition ministry:

> In the debate or rather discussion afterwards in the House of Lords upon that very question – I sate immediately behind Lord Moira – who was extremely annoyed at G[rey]'s speech upon the subject – & while G. was speaking, turned round to me repeatedly – and asked me whether I agreed with him? It was an awkward question to me who had not heard both sides. – Moira kept repeating to me 'It was *not so* – it was so and so &c.' – I did not know very well what to think – but I sympathized with the acuteness of his feelings upon the subject.[21]

Moira and Byron may also have discussed their common experiences of seeing members of the Royal family in tears: comparing Byron's 'Lines to a Lady Weeping', addressed to Princess Charlotte in March 1812, with Moira's effect on the Regent himself, who is said to have been 'very nearly in convulsions' of tears when Moira described to him the desperate state of the country in May 1812.[22] One of the liberal causes Moira supported was, ironically, an improvement in the treatment of insolvent debtors, who were often sent to prison because they could not pay: a fate which clearly did not affect himself.[23] Following his failure to form and lead a coalition and the return of the Tories under Lord Liverpool, in November 1812 Moira was appointed Commander-in-Chief and Governor-General of India, and he sailed for India the following year,

Henry Austen was an exceptionally buoyant and resilient character and seems to have quickly regained his spirits after his financial disasters: but nevertheless, these had a profound impact on the fortunes of his family. Most seriously affected was his brother Edward, who was one of the 'sureties' for Henry's Receivership of Taxes post who had given a bond to the Crown to guarantee Henry's liability to pay over the taxes that were collected by him. In 1816 Henry was proved to owe tax to the amount of £44,800 and, although the sureties were given two years' respite while debts to Henry were collected, in February 1818 Edward had to pay out over £13,000, while the executors of the second surety, their uncle, James Leigh-Perrot (who had died in 1817) had to find more than £6,500.[24] The third guarantor, their second cousin Thomas Hampson, was for some reason not required to contribute. It was not until 1842 that Edward, and James Leigh-Perrot's executors, were able to complete the recovery of the debts owed to them via Henry, and it has been calculated that between them they lost some £12,000 in income over this period.[25]

Moira's machinations

Henry continued to blame Lord Moira for his bankruptcy, but (although they also lost some hundreds of pounds each) Captains Frank and Charles Austen may not have felt too sore about the Earl, since he had done his best to advance their Navy careers.[26] He had used his influence to try to obtain command of a frigate for Frank in 1805 (including an introduction and opportunity to meet Admiral Lord Nelson himself) and, through his approaches to two successive First Lords of the Admiralty, had succeeded in enabling Charles to receive his first naval command (of the sloop HMS *Indian* in the West Indies in 1804).[27] Moira's interventions were brokered by Major Charles James, Henry's covert business partner who was also Moira's agent, and there is no doubt that Moira's assistance to the Austen naval brothers was a direct quid pro quo for Henry's provision of large loans to the Earl.[28] Again, a hint of these shadowy dealings may have found their way into *Persuasion*, in the form of the off-stage scheming and speculating of William Walter Elliot: a part of the book which lacks detail, perhaps because Jane did not want what she wrote to reflect too closely on the circumstances of Henry's downfall.

Once the war had ended in June 1815, Frank was put on half pay from the Navy and neither he nor Henry could now afford to provide their mother and sisters with the £50 a year towards their living expenses that had been arranged when their father died in 1805. Again, Edward had to step in to help.[29] Charles also had woes of his own: in February 1816 his ship HMS *Phoenix*, which had been assigned to rid the Greek Archipelago of pirates of the type of Byron's Corsair, was damaged beyond repair in an accident near Smyrna (modern Izmir). Charles was court-martialled and, although he was acquitted in April 1816, he did not get another command for ten years. With a growing family of his own he struggled to make ends meet.[30] Jane herself (who fortunately had most of her earnings – £600 – safe in a Navy 5 per cent savings account) nevertheless lost what was for her a significant amount from the collapse of the Austen London bank: the £13.7s.0d profits from *Mansfield Park* and £12.5s.0d from *Sense and*

Sensibility.[31] Soon after the failure of Henry's bank, Mrs Austen, Cassandra and Jane each opened accounts at the oldest and safest bank in the country, Hoare's, at 37 Fleet Street, London. Founded by Sir Richard Hoare in 1672, and still run today by the same family, it had provided accounts for the Reverend George Austen as well as for Samuel Pepys, John Dryden, David Garrick, Eton College and Lord Byron.[32]

Also acutely threatening to the Austens at this time was a lawsuit brought by their neighbours in Chawton, John Knight Hinton and his half-sister Jane Baverstock, which challenged Edward's right to inherit the Manors of Chawton, Steventon and other estates that formed a large part of the fortune left to him by his adoptive parents Thomas and Catherine Knight. Together with Jane Baverstock's son James, described as 'a clever and rather scampish brewer of Alton', they were contending that they, rather than Edward, were the legal heirs to these properties.[33] A formal writ of ejectment was served on Edward in October 1814. The case caused acute embarrassment for Jane because the Hintons lived just across the road from Chawton Cottage and were on visiting terms with the Austens. Moreover, if he lost the case, Edward would have to forfeit nearly half of all his property overall, and Jane and her mother and sister would lose their home.[34]

The history of the case was that Mrs Elizabeth Knight (1674–1737) had entailed these Hampshire estates to her distant cousin Thomas Knight I (1701–80): in other words, she had conferred on him a life tenancy, with trustees who would pass on the estate at his death to his (male) 'heirs of the body'. Under the terms of her will, other relatives including the Hinton family were due to become her heirs should Thomas Knight's line die out. Thomas Knight I became connected with the Austen family when he married Jane Monk, second cousin of Jane's father, and in 1761 it was he who enabled the Reverend George Austen to become Rector of Steventon by presenting the Church living to him.[35] In 1757 Thomas Knight I joined with his son Thomas Knight II (1735–94) to perform a legal process called a 'common recovery', whereby the old entail was broken and a new settlement was made giving Thomas Knight II the life tenancy of the estates after his father's death. A further legal settlement took place in 1779 when Thomas married Catherine Knatchbull, and Thomas and Catherine Knight then adopted Edward Austen as their son in 1783. After Thomas Knight II's death in 1794, and Catherine Knight's transfer of the running of the estates to Edward in 1798, the Hintons evidently felt that Edward was receiving what they believed was rightly theirs, perhaps because he was an adopted son rather than an 'heir of the body' of the Knights. When Catherine Knight died in 1812 and Edward claimed his £8,000-a-year inheritance (changing his name from Austen to Knight, as legally required), the Hintons and Baverstocks began proceedings to claim the Chawton estates.[36] Instead of raising the issue of the adoption, however, they based their case on the argument that the legal procedure of the 'common recovery' in 1757 had been incorrectly carried out.[37]

In March 1814 Jane was writing confidently to Cassandra that 'Edward has a good chance of escaping his lawsuit', but in fact the matter dragged on until March 1818, eight months after Jane's death.[38] The claimants then dropped their case in exchange for a payment from Edward of £15,000 (approaching a million pounds in today's currency), so that all their claims on the estates 'should be for ever relinquished'.[39] Edward had to find the £15,000 and his legal costs on top of the financial burden of Henry's bankruptcy, as well as having to write off rents worth some £600 from tenant farmers who were struggling with the effects of the bad weather and the dip in the post-war economy.[40] To raise these sums he had to re-mortgage some of his properties elsewhere and also resorted to an action that was common among landowners who were short of cash, by felling a huge swathe of the Chawton Park Wood in order to sell the timber.[41] Ironically, when in 1811 Jane had taken Henry's banking partner James Tilson for a walk through Chawton Park, she had commented facetiously that 'Mr Tilson admired the Trees very much, but grieved that they should not be turned into money'.[42] In contrast, Fanny Price in *Mansfield Park* grieves for the avenue at Sotherton which is likely to be felled in landscaping 'improvements' by Mr Rushworth: '"Cut down an avenue! What a pity! Does it not make you think of Cowper? "Ye fallen avenues, once more I mourn your fate unmerited."''[43] According to one of the Austen nieces writing in the 1860s, Edward's timber felling 'occasioned the great gap in Chawton Wood Park, visible for 30 years afterwards, and probably not filled up again even now'.[44]

'Loquacious and laughing'

By the spring of 1817 (as Jane Austen entered the last few months of her life, in stressful family financial circumstances and with two unpublished novels – *Northanger Abbey* and *Persuasion* – 'on the Shelve') Byron's spirits, like Henry's, were beginning to revive after the disasters of 1816.[45] Writing to his friend Thomas Moore in March 1817, he asked him to convince Francis Jeffrey, editor of the *Edinburgh Review,* 'that I was not, and, indeed, am not even now, the misanthropical and gloomy gentleman he takes me for, but a facetious companion, well to do with those with whom I am intimate, and as loquacious and laughing as if I were a much cleverer fellow'.[46] 'I suppose now I shall never be able to shake off my sables in public imagination', he added regretfully. 'However, nor that, nor more than that, has yet extinguished my spirit, which always rises with the rebound.' Now settled in Venice, he was beginning what was to be a sustained affair with the 22-year-old Marianna Segati (wife of the 'Merchant of Venice' who was also his landlord), describing her as 'by far the prettiest woman I have seen here, and the most loveable I have met with any where'.[47] Relishing the Venetian carnival and his new life and location, Byron urged his friend and business manager Douglas Kinnaird to sell Newstead Abbey as quickly as possible, despite the current low prices for property. In July the Abbey was advertised for sale, and on 10 December 1817 Byron heard that it had been purchased by his former Harrow schoolfellow Major Thomas Wildman.[48] The total payment eventually received by the trustees (£97,972) put Byron on almost exactly the same footing as *Pride and Prejudice*'s Mr Bingley, who has 'inherited property to the amount of nearly an hundred thousand pounds' and has an income of 'four or five thousand a year'.[49]

After three previous failed attempts to dispose of Newstead, this sale at last brought Byron's years of financial insecurity to an end, although the proceeds would barely cover his commitments, in particular his over-generous marriage settlement of £60,000 to Lady Byron (whose own dowry of £20,000 had never been paid by her father, with the result that the Byron marriage was plagued by debt as well as all its other problems). Despite these and other liabilities, Byron was now largely in control of his finances.[50] Ironically, the effect was to make him much more careful with his money than he had ever been previously: bargaining fiercely with Murray for his copyrights, as seen in Chapter 5, keeping careful accounts and becoming positively parsimonious, as he joked to Kinnaird in January 1819:

> I have imbibed such a love for money that I keep some Sequins in a drawer to count, & cry over them once a week – and if it was not for a turn for women – (which I hope will be soon worn out) – I think in time that I should be able not only to clear off but [to] accumulate.[51]

Jane Austen and Lord Byron

The intricacies of entail

Byron was highly unusual and exceptionally lucky among British peers in being able to sell his ancestral estates like this. The sale of Newstead was made possible because of the specific way in which Byron had inherited it when his great-uncle the fifth lord had died in 1798. His story was in some ways a mirror-image of Edward Austen-Knight's: in Edward's case an apparent mistake in an entail settlement made more than fifty years previously threatened this entire part of his inheritance, whereas in Byron's case a mistake of a similar kind several decades earlier enabled him to inherit his estates without the restriction of an entail (in other words, without the legal obligation to pass on his estates intact to the next generation). He was therefore free to do what he liked with Newstead, including (initially) retaining and attempting to run the estate and (eventually) selling it and keeping the proceeds, before disbursing them to the Greeks and their struggle for independence and leaving the residue to Augusta.

Byron's ancestors had done all they could over several generations to ensure that Newstead and their other estates were passed down intact, and in doing this they were upholding not only family pride but also the basis of English aristocratic power in the late-seventeenth and eighteenth centuries. By concentrating their wealth on a single main heir (usually the eldest son) they accrued and securely held large estates, and this enabled the nobility, as a class, to rival and surpass the might of the monarchy. By the early nineteenth century this power was itself being challenged by the gentry and the middle classes (as explored in Austen's novels), and the working classes too were campaigning for political representation without the need for a property qualification. As John Beckett's summary of Byron's position puts it:

The Byron properties were exceptionally rare in 1798 in having no outstanding charges on them, and they were unusual in passing to an heir who inherited not as a life tenant (as the fifth Lord Byron had been) but as the owner of the fee simple. The sixth Lord Byron inherited Newstead debt free, and without any legal restraints. When he sold Newstead in 1817 he showed just why landed families did all they legally could to limit any single individual's freedom to manoeuvre. The careful planning of the fourth Lord Byron through his marriage settlements and his will, the 1747 legislation imposed by the Court of Chancery, and the resettlement of 1773 all counted for nothing.[52]

The entail system had broken down during the tenancy of Byron's great-uncle, the fifth lord (also known as the 'Wicked Lord', as discussed in Chapter 1). The fifth lord had gone through a resettlement of the estate with his son William Byron in 1773, but both his son and his grandson then predeceased him. The son died in 1776 and the grandson, William John Byron, was killed at the age of twenty-two by a cannonball at the Siege of Calvi in 1794, without having had time either to join with his grandfather to arrange a new settlement of the estate or to make his own will. On his grandson's death, the fifth lord believed that the 'fee simple' or absolute ownership of Newstead would revert to him, and he would be able to sell the estate and thus dig himself out of the mass of debt he had fallen into (perhaps Sir Walter Elliot harboured similar hopes of a surprise turn-around in his finances). The fifth lord set off to London to see John Hanson, a lawyer specializing in advice to aristocratic clients on this kind of issue, who may or may not have told his lordship that he had (as described in Chapter 4) already been consulted on the Byrons' affairs in the late 1780s by Mrs Catherine Byron, the poet's mother.

In 1794, however, Hanson had bad news for the fifth lord. When the settlement was completed in 1773, he told him, 'by some unaccountable inadvertence or negligence of the lawyers, the ultimate reversion of the fee-simple of the property, instead of being left, as it ought to have been, in the father as the owner of the estates, was limited to the heirs of the son'.[53] The 'heirs of the son' meant the nearest surviving male *after* the fifth lord, and, since the fifth lord's immediate next heirs were also dead, it was the ten-year-old George Gordon Byron, the future poet, who thus inherited Newstead with absolute ownership on the fifth lord's death in 1798.

When the fifth lord discovered in 1794 that after all he was still both poverty-stricken and powerless to do anything about it, he sank into despair and as a last resort tried to screw the last farthings that were available to him out of the Newstead estate. This included selling the furniture and almost all the contents of the Abbey and, like Edward Knight, felling and selling off the estate timber – but to a much more destructive extent. The 'numberless fine spreading oaks' were reduced to stumps, 'which remain an impediment to the traveller', one observer commented, while John Hanson described how 'Alas these fine trees were cut down, even the last one by his Lordship, and the Abbey, with its gardens, lakes, cascades and battlements . . . had all become dilapidated and neglected'.[54] A visitor in 1811 was distressed to find the estate still 'bare of wood, and presenting a scene rather of desolation than of improvement'.[55]

'Mouldering turrets'

The Newstead that Byron inherited was therefore a melancholy shadow of what it had once been, and the house was largely derelict. Byron strongly identified himself with the Abbey and, although he seems to have loved it all the more because of its forlorn state, this sense of melancholy clearly emerges in his youthful poems:

> Newstead! what saddening change of scene is thine!
>   Thy yawning arch betokens slow decay;
> The last and youngest of a noble line
>   Now holds thy mouldering turrets in his sway.
>
> Deserted now, he scans thy grey worn towers;
>   Thy vaults, where dead of feudal ages sleep;
> Thy cloisters pervious to the wintry showers,
>   These, these he views and views them but to weep.
>
>   ('Elegy on Newstead Abbey' 137–44)[56]

In *Childe Harold's Pilgrimage*, too, this melancholy identification with the half-ruined Abbey and his ancestors is still felt, but ironized by Spenserian language, self-mockery and perhaps a feeling of guilt about his own inadequate estate-management:

> Childe Harold was he hight: – but whence his name
> And lineage long, it suits me not to say;
> Suffice it, that perchance they were of fame,
> And had been glorious in another day:
> But one sad losel soils a name for aye,
> However mighty in the olden time;
> Nor all that heralds rake from coffin'd clay,
> Nor florid prose, nor honied lies of rhyme
> Can blazon evil deeds, or consecrate a crime.
>
>   (*Childe Harold's Pilgrimage* 1.19–27)[57]

The 'sad losel' of these lines is usually taken to be Harold/Byron's reference to himself, but in fact, in terms of damage to Newstead, the more likely candidate would have been the fifth lord, who had spoiled and mismanaged the estate and failed to pass it on in the good order in which he had inherited it. Later in the *Pilgrimage* Byron's sense of personal loss is much further complicated and extended into the classical topos of the fall of empires and the effects of time and neglect on human achievements.

Another disadvantage for Byron about the way in which his fortune had come to him was that the young lord had no older male relatives around him, and no one who could help train him in the business of managing his lands and his money. As a teenager he soon became the target of moneylenders who spotted that he was an extremely good bet – a young nobleman who, although cash-poor in his minority, when he turned twenty-one would gain control over substantial estates with no restrictions. He was an ideal person to lend money to at an extortionate rate of interest, knowing that in a few years he would have the wherewithal to pay it back. As Beckett puts it, Byron 'was always willing to help fund needy projects and to support ailing friends when he knew that behind his temporary cash-flow problems lay substantial capital assets that could one day be called upon to supply his needs'.[58] If the young Byron had been like other peers and aristocrats, he would have had an estate-holding father or uncle who knew and understood the dangers of mortgaging one's financial future, however rosy it might appear. Of course, Byron, like Tom Bertram in *Mansfield Park*, might have revolted against the over-strict parenting of an authoritarian father and racked up huge debts anyway. But as it was, apart from the dubious lawyer John Hanson, there was no father figure in his youthful life capable of fulfilling this role, and his mother warned, nagged and tried in vain to control him, up to her death in 1812. Had Byron had a son he would no doubt have tried harder to ensure that the ownership of his estate would pass – along with his title – to that son after his death. But once Byron's marriage separation made it unlikely that he would ever have a legitimate son, it became probable that his first cousin, George Anson Byron, would inherit the title. When in 1816 George Anson took Annabella's side in the marriage separation, the relationship between the cousins turned sour, and Byron felt little compunction about depriving him of Newstead. Because of the lack of entail, George Anson was powerless in 1817 or at any time to prevent George Gordon from selling the estate and disposing of it as he wished.[59]

Lairds and baronesses

If Byron was almost unique in inheriting his estates without any legal restraints, he was also unusual in being connected to several families in which the inheritance descended through women rather than through men. This almost always arose because it had been a feature of the original creation of the title, and it was generally restricted to baronies rather than to the higher orders of aristocracy such as dukes, marquesses and earls. It also seems to have been more often a feature of Scottish titles than of English ones. So Byron's mother, Catherine Gordon, inherited her father's title and estate in Aberdeenshire as the thirteenth laird of Gight, and when Byron's father John Byron married her he took her name by modifying his to 'John Byron Gordon', rather than the other way around. Gight castle became ruinous, and it seems unlikely that the young Byron ever visited it, proud though his mother was of her Gight and Gordon inheritance and her supposed descent from the Scottish royal family. Byron's father's first wife Amelia, former Marchioness of Carmarthen (Augusta's mother) also held a hereditary title, as well as a surname highly resonant to Austen readers. She was the only child of Robert Darcy, fourth Earl of Holderness, and through him she inherited the titles of twelfth Baroness Darcy de Knayth and ninth Baroness Conyers, although not her father's earldom. Byron followed in the same path by marrying Anne Isabella Milbanke who, through her uncle and then her mother, inherited a title with another strong Austen resonance, as eleventh Baroness Wentworth, although she continued to call herself Lady Byron. This title passed down through Byron's and Annabella's daughter Ada, Countess of Lovelace (of computer-programming fame) to Judith Blunt-Lytton (1873–1957) who, as the sixteenth baroness, did use the title 'Lady Wentworth', and the title continues in the Earl of Lytton's family today, although subsidiary to the earldom.

Byron and Austen evidently shared a personal interest in the law of entail and in the unexpected twists and turns of inheritance in general, although in their work they differ greatly in the way in which they discuss it. As noted in the Introduction, W. H. Auden was shocked by Austen's exceptionally forthright attitudes to 'brass', and the plots of all her novels hinge on matters of finance and expectations, clearly spelt out. *Northanger Abbey* features General Tilney's greed for what he believes is Catherine's great wealth, and then his revenge when he thinks she has fooled him, while *Sense and Sensibility* and *Pride and Prejudice* are based on the stark inequities of female inheritance. *Mansfield Park* explores an estate founded on the guilty principle of slavery and portrays Tom Bertram as a spendthrift and irresponsible heir. Emma's bossy character results in part from her consciousness of her own inherited wealth, while *Persuasion* compares the financial and other failings of the old, titled and entitled ranks with the energy and enterprise of the new professional and money-making classes. *Sanditon* is the most pointed of her writings in its specifics about the impending financial disaster of the resort and the greed of some of its characters. While Byron is less open and direct than Austen about the finances of individual protagonists, he nevertheless manages to slip in that Haidee is 'The greatest heiress of the Eastern Isles' (although 'so very beautiful was she, / Her dowry was as nothing to her smiles').[60] And in the 'English' cantos of *Don Juan,* where matters financial and legal do start to impinge on Juan's story, it is not long before Juan himself is characterized as not only 'a hero, young and handsome' but also 'Noble, rich, celebrated, and a stranger', and we learn within the first five lines about the spiritual Aurora Raby that she too is 'Rich, noble, but an orphan' (and therefore the perfect prey for a mercenary suitor).[61]

Plights and stratagems

And in matters of general comment such as the 'ubi sunt' stanzas at the end of canto 11 (before we are disingenuously warned to 'recollect the work is only fiction, / And that I sing of neither mine nor me') the financial plights and stratagems of the impoverished upper classes are mercilessly laid out in detail for our inspection.[62]

> They are young, but know not youth – it is anticipated;
> Handsome but wasted, rich without a sou;
> Their vigour in a thousand arms is dissipated;
> Their cash comes *from,* their wealth goes *to* a Jew; . . .

> Where are those martyred Saints the Five per Cents?
> And where – oh, where the devil are the Rents!

> Where's Brummel? Dished. Where's Long Pole Wellesley? Diddled. . . .

> Where are the Lady Carolines and Franceses?
> Divorced or doing thereanent. . . .
> Some die, some fly, some languish on the Continent,
> Because the times have hardly left them *one* tenant.

Some who once set their caps at cautious Dukes,
    Have taken up at length with younger brothers:
Some heiresses have bit at sharpers' hooks.

(*Don Juan* 11.593–643)[63]

Canto 12 opens with an apostrophe to 'Gold', the pleasures of misers, the joys of making money, and the power of the moneylenders who 'hold the balance of the world'; and wealth and privilege are a conspicuous element of the following cantos (12 to 17) which concern Juan's visit to Lord Henry Amundeville's estate at Norman Abbey.[64] This Abbey has been described by some critics as a fanciful version of Byron's own Newstead Abbey, but it is very different in one important respect. From Lord Henry's title (where the Christian name comes between the 'Lord' and the surname) we can tell that he is the younger son of a duke or marquess and that Lady Adeline Amundeville is similarly the daughter of a duke, marquess or earl. (Oddly, all the daughters of earls are styled 'lady', although the younger sons of earls are styled 'the Honourable', not 'lord', and this enables us also to work out that Darcy is the grandson of an earl on his mother's side, because his maternal aunt is 'Lady Catherine' while his cousin – a younger son of the title-holder – is just the Honourable Colonel Fitzwilliam.) So it appears that, although Lord Henry Amundeville is from a noble family, Byron needs, for plot reasons, to make him NOT an eldest son and a peer (who would automatically become a member of the House of Lords), because he wants to show him as 'a great electioneerer, / Burrowing for boroughs like a rat or rabbit' to become a member of the House of Commons.[65] But he also wants Lord Henry to be seen as the very secure and apparently long-term owner of a fine old house and a considerable estate – and this is a little puzzling since, as mentioned, Lord Henry is evidently a younger son.

Perhaps the situation is that the Amundevilles (whose name indicates their Norman ancestry) are so wealthy that the younger son or sons have inherited their own (perhaps entailed?) estates, separate from the family's main estate that would be held by Lord Henry's unidentified older brother the current duke or marquess (or their eldest son). Byron evidently wants to show Lord Henry on the one hand as an electioneer and on the other hand as a rich and rather self-satisfied noble estate-holder, and perhaps he did not fully work out (as Austen surely would have done) how this fictional circle could be squared. To quote Byron's narrator in canto 17 of *Don Juan* (among the last lines he ever wrote of the poem), 'I leave the thing a problem, like all things.'[66]

Entail as a plot device

For Austen, as for Byron, the consequences of entail and inheritance were part of her mental world from an early age. Although it was not until 1814 that the challenge to Edward's legacy caused painful anxiety to the family, the legal aspects of Edward's inheritance and the way in which it would change the family fortunes must have been avidly discussed by the Austens from as early as 1783 when he was adopted by the wealthy Knight family. Jane's interest in entail as a plot device is clearest, of course, in *Pride and Prejudice*, where Mr Bennet's Longbourn estate is entailed upon the next *male* heir, the dreadful Mr Collins, and so is not inheritable by Mr Bennet's five daughters who are therefore under an urgent imperative to find wealthy husbands. Some commentators have queried whether Austen got the legal details correct in this novel: why, for instance, could Mr Bennet not do a 'common recovery' with his heir Mr Collins, as the elder and younger Thomas Knights did to break the entail in 1757, and then reassign it to include financial portions for his daughters? And why, if the inheritance is exclusively through males, does Mr Collins have a different surname from the Bennets?[67] The answer to the first question is that Mr Collins is only the 'heir presumptive' to Longbourn, not the 'heir apparent', and so no 'common recovery' is available to him or Mr Bennet. According to the law, Mrs Bennet was judged to be still capable of producing a male heir until her dying day; or – if she were to die before her husband – Mr Bennet might remarry and have a son by his second wife. Mr Collins cannot be absolutely certain of his inheritance until Mr Bennet does actually die, and indeed this is also the situation in *Persuasion*, where William Walter Elliot is anxious to make sure that Sir Walter does not take a second wife – perhaps the widowed Mrs Clay – and beget a more direct male heir. This is why he (and Mr Collins too) plan to keep a close eye on the family they hope to inherit from by marrying one of the daughters, and thus persuading Sir Walter and Mr Bennet that their estates should be 'kept in the family' in every possible way.

A plausible answer to the second question about the different family surnames is that Austen may have imagined the original entail to have been set up by a man who had two daughters, with the inheritance going first through the elder daughter (who has married a Mr Bennet) to her son or grandson (the Mr Bennet of *Pride and Prejudice*) and then, if he has no male heirs, by descent through the younger daughter (who has married a Mr Collins, of whom the novel's Mr Collins is the grandson).[68] Such matters of inheritance are often illustrated by using the formula 'If A has two daughters, married to B and C . . .', and perhaps it is not too fanciful to imagine that someone explained this system to Austen in these terms: so that she imagined the original estate-holder as an (unnamed) Mr (A)usten, while his sons-in-law are Mr (B)ennet and Mr (C)ollins – with a magical Mr D(arcy) waiting in the wings to resolve the whole problem.

In *Sense and Sensibility* Elinor, Marianne and Margaret Dashwood are also excluded from inheritance by their father's uncle's settlement of his whole estate on their half-brother with an entail to his son, so that the Dashwood women are obliged to give up their previously affluent life in exchange for the relative poverty of their cousin's cottage in Devon. In *Persuasion*, as we have seen, Anne Elliot cannot inherit the estate from her father but comes under pressure to marry her cousin, who can, while in *Emma* the endogamous marriage of Emma (the heiress of £30,000) to her brother-in-law's brother Mr Knightley – although it deprives Isabella's son Little Henry of his position as heir to Donwell Abbey – produces a close family arrangement which wraps everything up even more neatly and tidily than any entail or other strict settlement might have done.

In *Pride and Prejudice* and *Sense and Sensibility* Austen clearly criticizes the way entail and the laws of inheritance privilege men and disadvantage women, and her attitude there seems firmly feminist. But when women in Austen's work do inherit or acquire wealth and power they are not generally portrayed positively. Emma Woodhouse is 'handsome, clever and rich', but also so complacently secure and entitled in her status as an heiress that she meddles potentially disastrously with other people's lives – although she does become wiser and kinder as the book goes on. Emma Watson, in *The Watsons*, by contrast, has been the victim of the imprudence of her aunt who, having brought her up among 'the elegancies of life' and to expect an inheritance of some eight or nine thousand pounds, has instead made a very imprudent marriage to a Captain O'Brien. Having gained control of the aunt's fortune, the captain is clearly determined to deprive the niece of her financial expectations as well. '"A pretty piece of work your Aunt Turner has made of it!"', opines Emma's brother Robert, the 'attorney at Croydon'. '"By heaven! a woman should never be trusted with money. I always said she ought to have settled something on you, as soon as her husband died." "But that would have been trusting *me* with money", replie[s] Emma; "and *I* am a woman, too –". "It might have been secured to your future use, without your having any power over it now"', is her brother's brusque response.[69] The exchange shows all too clearly Austen's familiarity with lawyers' attitudes and calculations with regard to women.

But worse than being insensitive or foolish, Austen's rich women can also be repulsively selfish. *Pride and Prejudice*'s Lady Catherine de Bourgh (who remarks that 'I see no occasion for entailing estates from the female line. It was not thought necessary in Sir Lewis de Bourgh's family') is a snob and a bully, intent on getting her own way with men and women alike.[70] *Sense and Sensibility*'s rich Mrs Ferrars wilfully disinherits her elder son Edward because of his choice of the relatively impoverished Elinor as his wife and the clergy as his profession. Lady Denham, in the unfinished *Sanditon*, is 'a very rich old Lady', 'very, very mean', who has acquired her money from one husband and her title from another, has a 'shrewd and self-satisfying air', 'knows the value of money' and boasts 'that though she had *got* nothing but her title from the family, still she had *given* nothing for it'.[71] With the possible exception of the affable but rather vulgar Mrs Jennings in *Sense and Sensibility*, it is hard to find a woman in Austen's work who is rich and uses her money with wisdom and kindness.

Lost legacies

This portrayal of mean and uncaring rich women takes us back in Austen's biography to Mrs Leigh-Perrot, who seems to have persuaded (or at least gone along with) her husband, James Leigh-Perrot, Mrs Austen's brother, in his will to deprive the Austen family of the legacies they expected and very clearly needed from their uncle. James Leigh-Perrot had inherited property and wealth from a distant relation (Mrs Austen's relation too). He and his wife Jane had no children of their own, and they were fond of the Austens and had often spoken of their intention to leave their estate to the eldest Austen son, James, with legacies to Mrs Austen and the other children. But when Mr Leigh-Perrot died in March 1817 it was discovered that he had left all his money in trust for his wife, with no immediate legacy at all for Mrs Austen (who sorely needed financial help) or anyone else in the family.[72] Jane was by now terminally ill, with what has been conjectured to be Addison's disease or perhaps Hodgkin's lymphoma or some other form of cancer, and any of these conditions would have been exacerbated by these stresses and anxieties. 'I am ashamed to say that the shock of my Uncle's Will brought on a relapse, & I was so ill on Friday night . . . that I could not but press for Cassandra's returning with Frank after the Funeral', she wrote to Charles in

March 1817. 'My Mother has borne the forgetfulness of *her* extremely well; . . . she thinks with you that my Uncle always looked forward to surviving her.'[73] In fact, however, it was Mrs Leigh-Perrot who survived Mrs Austen as well as both Jane and James Austen. When she died in 1836, the major part of her wealth was inherited by James's son, who added part of his great-uncle's surname to his own to become James Edward Austen-Leigh, author of the 1869 *Memoir* of his Aunt Jane.

If Jane had not predeceased Mrs Leigh-Perrot she would have received a share of the £6,000 left by her uncle to be bestowed (after his wife's death) on his nieces and nephews. This was a legacy which appears to have stemmed at least partly from the proceeds of enslaved labour, since Mrs Leigh-Perrot (neé Jane Cholmeley) was born in Barbados and reportedly inherited the plantation land (and the enslaved people attached to it) which had been owned by her father Robert Cholmeley (who died *c.* 1754).[74] The estate is presumed to have been sold by Mr and Mrs Leigh-Perrot and, with their combined wealth, they were able to live a very comfortable life at the house, Scarlets, they built in Berkshire, and at Great Pulteney Street in Bath.[75] Although by the 1800s the connections between the Leigh-Perrots and the Caribbean were probably no longer direct, one of their servants in England was of African descent and, when Jane visited them in Bath in 1801, she reported that 'Frank, whose black head was in waiting in the Hall window, received us very kindly; and his Master & Mistress did not shew less cordiality.'[76] Frank, whose surname is unknown, would have been one of a surprisingly large number of people of colour in Britain in this period: one contemporary claim put the number of 'Negro and East India servants' at 30,000 'at the lowest', and research by Kathleen Chater has identified several thousand individuals recorded in primary sources in Britain in the eighteenth century.[77]

This connection with the Cholmeleys is one of several which brought the Austens into an indirect relationship with slavery and the wealth generated by it. Another such connection was through the owners of an estate and enslaved people in Jamaica, the Hampsons, including Thomas Hampson who had stood as surety for Henry Austen's tax receivership. Henry's and Jane's great-grandfather on their father's side had been Sir George Hampson, fourth baronet of Taplow (who died in 1724), and his descendants the Austens and Hampsons remained close throughout Jane's life. Sir George Francis Hampson, the sixth baronet (1738–74), lived in Jamaica and was listed in the probate for his estate in 1781 as the owner of seventeen enslaved people.[78] Jane refers several times to meeting this son, Thomas Hampson, and his grandson George, later the eighth baronet, who was also a trustee of several Jamaican estates.[79] Thomas Hampson was actually the seventh baronet but did not use his title: apparently because of his republican views, which however did not stop him inheriting and enjoying the produce of his Jamaican estate and the labour of its enslaved people. It would be intriguing to know what was the (unidentified) 'scheme' which he suggested to the Austens in 1813 and which, Jane reported to Cassandra in November that year, 'We do not like'.[80]

James Langford Nibbs (1738–95), who met and became friends with Jane's father at St John's College, Oxford, owned a plantation in Antigua (like the Bertrams in *Mansfield Park*) and profited from the labour of enslaved people. In 1760 the Reverend George Austen officiated at the marriage of James Nibbs and Barbara Langford and became co-trustee of the Nibbs's marriage settlement. The trust documents specified how the ownership of the plantation and its profits should be dispersed among Nibbs's heirs, but George Austen had no direct management responsibilities for the plantation itself and received no direct financial or other benefits through his role as trustee. The other trustee, Morris Robinson, was an experienced lawyer (and also, incidentally, the brother of Elizabeth Robinson Montagu, the 'Queen of the Bluestockings'). In 1765 Nibbs became godfather to Jane's eldest brother James Austen, and from around 1781 to 1783 his second son, also James Langford Nibbs, was one of the early pupils at the Steventon vicarage, whose fees were presumably paid to the Austens from the proceeds of enslaved labour in Antigua.[81]

In the unfinished *Sanditon* Austen very briefly sketches her only character of colour: the seventeen-year-old Caribbean heiress Miss Lambe, described as 'a young West Indian of large fortune, in delicate health', whose arrival it is hoped will prop up the tottering economics of the resort.[82] It is only later she is described as 'half-mulatto' (meaning, probably, with one African-origin and three European-origin grandparents); and her skin colour or origins do not prevent Lady Denham, the most socially conservative character in the book (but also the most avaricious) from pursuing her as a potential wife for her nephew.[83] Austen's use of the name 'Lambe' may refer to an epigram by her favourite poet, the fervent abolitionist William Cowper, which was printed in the *Northampton Mercury* in 1792:

To purify their wine some people bleed
    A lamb into the barrel, and succeed;

No nostrum, planters say, is half so good,
To make fine sugar as a *negro's* blood.

Now *lambs* and *negroes* both are harmless things,
    And thence perhaps this wond'rous virtue springs,
    'Tis in the blood of innocence alone –
Good cause why planters never try their own.

('Epigram on the Slave Trade' 1–8)[84]

Cape Coast Castle

People of colour were also part of the domestic history of the Byron family. John, the first lord Byron, was painted in military dress around 1643 by William Dobson, and shares his portrait with a young boy of African descent represented as his groom, wearing a crimson velvet suit and holding the bridle of a horse. It is not known whether the boy was part of Lord Byron's household, but his status in England at this time is likely to have been difficult and ambiguous, because it was not until 1772 that Lord Justice Mansfield's ruling in the James Somerset case stated that slavery could not legally exist in England. There may also have been people of colour in the later Byrons' household, judging from a 1726 watercolour painting of the household at Newstead Abbey by Peter Tillemans (Figure 24).

Figure 23 *John Byron, 1st Lord Byron, with a boy of African descent*, by William Dobson (*c.* 1643). © Tabley House Collection/Bridgeman Images.

Figure 24 *Lord Byron's Household at His Seat Newsted* [sic] *Abbey* by Peter Tillemans (1726) appears to show that there were people of colour living at Newstead at this date. The fourth Lord Byron is seated left, Lady Byron is dancing centre left and their three infant sons are shown centre-right. Private collection. Photograph by Natalie Shaw, courtesy of Emily Brand.

And in 1752 John Byron, the poet's grandfather (who appears in this picture as a toddler) was sent by the Royal Navy with his ship the *St Albans* to patrol the West African coast and protect British merchants who were trading in ivory and enslaved people. Captain (later Admiral) Byron certainly saw the infamous Cape Coast Castle, where the British governors lived in luxury while African captives were held in terrible prison conditions before being shipped to the Americas. There is, however, no evidence that he personally was involved in trading enslaved people, and, like all other British naval officers, he would have been severely warned against the practice of making their own personal profit by transporting Africans to Barbados and selling them there as slaves.[85]

The wealth of Major Thomas Wildman, Byron's Harrow schoolfellow who purchased Newstead Abbey in 1817, was generated by the labour of more than three hundred enslaved people on the Quebec sugar plantation in Jamaica which Wildman inherited from his father in 1795. Wildman also used the 'compensation' funds, awarded to him and other owners of enslaved people at the time of the abolition of slavery in British lands in 1833, to restore and rebuild the Abbey.[86] Byron of course benefited personally from the proceeds of his sale of Newstead to Wildman in 1817 and, like the members of the Austen family who received Jane Leigh-Perrot's legacies, James Langford Nibbs's school-fees and Thomas Hampson's financial backing, he thus became an indirect beneficiary of slavery.

Byron's personal connections with African Americans included those with the bare-knuckle boxers Tom Molyneux and Bill Richmond, who coached him in boxing in London, and with Benjamin Lewis, a 26-year-old man of African descent who became his employee. Lewis had been previously engaged by the adventurer Edward Trelawny as a 'sailor-groom', and was taken on by Byron from the summer of 1823 at a wage of eight crowns a month to be 'head of the stables'.[87] Lewis travelled from Italy to Greece with Byron and used his 'smattering of French and Italian', as well as his knowledge of horses and cooking, to support Byron there. Byron is said to have been 'very partial' to Lewis, and there is a record of him teasing his servant by pretending to rebuke him for asking Byron to arrange for two Black women, enslaved by the Turks and starving, to be given comparatively safe quarters in the seraglio at Missolonghi.[88] While Byron spoke of his Italian servants to Trelawny as 'men to look at, but of no use under any emergency', he described 'your negro' as 'worth them all'.[89] Lewis was present at Byron's death in Missolonghi in April 1824 and also at his funeral in Nottinghamshire in July, but he died of smallpox two months after arriving in England.[90]

Culture and imperialism

As part of the argument of his famous study of *Culture and Imperialism* (1993) Edward W. Said controversially claimed that *Mansfield Park* promotes 'a domestic imperialist culture without which Britain's subsequent acquisition of territory would not have been possible', and proposes that Sir Thomas Bertram's plantation wealth, based on slavery, 'mak[es] possible his values to which Fanny Price (and Austen herself) finally subscribes [*sic*]'.[91] There have, however, been many studies challenging Said's arguments and showing how, on the contrary, Austen depicts the values and morality of the Bertram family to be seriously undermined by the poisonous source of the wealth they take for granted.[92] The name Austen chose for the appalling Mrs Norris appears deliberately to recall Robert Norris, a trader who defended slavery in his 1789 account of the slave trade, while the novel's title may refer to Lord Mansfield and his judgement, mentioned above.[93] In an 1813 letter to her sister Cassandra, Jane playfully described herself as having been 'in love' with the anti-slavery writer and campaigner Thomas Clarkson.[94] The exchange between Jane Fairfax and Mrs Elton in *Emma* uses a comparison of the 'governess trade' to the transatlantic trade in enslaved Africans which makes it clear that Austen could take for granted her readers' agreement that this trade was a guilty one, and even the vulgar Mrs Elton is anxious to distance herself and her family from the stigma of supporting the slave trade, although Jane Fairfax's contention that there may be as much misery among the 'victims' of the governess trade as there is among those traded as slaves surely turns a blind eye to the horrors of real slavery.[95] In *Persuasion*, too, there is the vexed question of whether the 'property of her husband in the West Indies', which Captain Wentworth helps the cheerful Mrs Smith to reclaim, involves (as seems highly likely) the ownership of enslaved people.[96]

Jane Fairfax's phraseology – the 'sale . . . of human flesh' – is also used in one of Byron's critical references to the topic.[97] In canto 5 of *Don Juan* young Juan and his companion are sold as slaves (a 'yoke of human cattle') by a merchant who then goes off to dine, leading the narrator to 'wonder if his appetite was good' and 'also his digestion?'.

> Methinks at meals some odd thoughts might intrude,
>   And conscience ask a curious sort of question,
> About the right divine how far we should
>   Sell flesh and blood.
>
> (*Don Juan* 5.233–8)[98]

Matt Sandler has made the case for what he calls Byron's works' 'transformational influence on the emergence of African American literature', arguing that 'nineteenth-century African American writers drew on Byron to mount critiques of slavery, . . . to displace the moral coordinates of conventional representations of Blackness, . . . and to mark their poetic deviance from within the tradition of revolutionary liberalism'.[99] Black abolitionists deployed the Byronic ideal of the male liberator and freedom fighter, who was not marked by social status and hereditary entitlement, to achieve their ends. Sandler points out the 'extraordinary array' of African American writers who cited Byron's lines from *Childe Harold* canto 2, stanza 76, so that it became the 'cultural *lingua franca*' of Black abolitionists:

> Hereditary bondsmen! Know ye not
> Who would be free themselves must strike the blow?
>
> (*Childe Harold's Pilgrimage* 2.720–21)[100]

Frederick Douglass

In particular, the famous African American orator, writer and statesman Frederick Douglass made wide use of this quotation and this concept, citing it both in his memoir of escape from slavery and treatise of abolition, the *Narrative of the Life of Frederick* Douglass (1845), and in his novella *The Heroic Slave* (1853). And as Margie Burns has shown, Douglass and other reformers and abolitionists also used the traditional phrase 'pride and prejudice' as a specific 'sign and signal' of opposition to enslavement and the slave trade.[101]

More than half a century after Captain Byron's naval duties on the Slave Coast, a very different note on slavery was struck by another future admiral, Jane's brother Frank, who wrote in his diary: 'Slavery, however it may be modified is still slavery and it is much to be regretted that any trace of it should be found to exist in countries dependent on England, or colonized by her subjects.'[102] This comment, made in around 1807, was not reported for another 100 years, but it appears to be the product of a world that had changed greatly from that of Captain Byron in the 1750s, and seems to have been written at the time that the Act for the Abolition of the Slave Trade was being piloted through the British Parliament by William Wilberforce. When the Act came into force, Francis and Charles Austen and their Royal Naval colleagues were tasked with patrolling the seas to try to prevent (instead of to protect, as Captain Byron had done) the trading of enslaved people across the Atlantic. Thanks to research by Devoney Looser, we know that in 1826 Charles Austen's ship HMS *Aurora* captured a ship that was carrying more than 250 enslaved people, most of whom were 'rescued' but had the uncertain fate of becoming 'freed blacks' or *emancipados*, in Cuba.[103]

And in 1840, seven years after the official abolition of slavery in British lands, both Austen and Byron family members were participating actively in the anti-slavery movement, when Henry Austen and the widowed Lady Byron were among some 500 people (nearly all white) who attended the first meeting of the World Anti-Slavery Convention in London that year.

'The Reverend H.T. Austen', who by then was aged 69 and had recently retired as Perpetual Curate of Bentley, Hampshire, was listed among the 200 British delegates, as one of the two representatives for Colchester, Essex.[104] The terms of the meeting limited delegates to 'gentlemen' and specified that women would not be admitted; and eight (white) female delegates from Philadelphia and Massachusetts were forbidden to take part as delegates. There were, however, many women abolitionists present as 'guests', and these included Lady Byron, the poet's widow. Along with the novelist Amelia Opie, she is one of the women featured prominently in Benjamin Robert Haydon's painting of the Convention being addressed by Austen's hero the

Figure 25 Lady Byron (third from the right in the second row) is one of the women featured prominently in Benjamin Robert Haydon's painting of the *World Anti-Slavery Society Convention of 1840*. Henry Austen was also present, and it is possible that a so-far unidentified portrait of Jane's brother may appear in the background. © National Portrait Gallery, London.

elderly Thomas Clarkson. And, although Henry Austen is not listed in the key to the painting, many of the people who appear in it are unnamed, and it does not seem impossible that a so-far unidentified portrait of Jane's brother may appear somewhere in the background.

Notes

1. *MP* vol. 2, chap. 4, 248.

2. *LBCPW* 4.40–1.

3. 'Introduction to *Frankenstein*' 1831, Mary Shelley 454. See *JAL* 315, to James Edward Austen, 9 July 1816: the weather is 'really too bad, & has been so for a long time, much worse than anybody *can* bear, & I begin to think it will never be fine again'.

4. Anonymous (trans. Benoît Eyriès), *Fantasmagoriana*.

5. Clery (2017) 289.

6. 'Italy, or not Corinna', *LBCMP* 86.

7. Sophy Mackie, a young Englishwoman who travelled in Europe with her family in 1815 and 1816, mentioned in her journal that both Byron

and Polidori were in the area around Geneva. See Dow and Seth, 'Fickle Fortunes', np.

8. MacCarthy 295–6.

9. Medwin 11.

10. Caroline Austen in Austen-Leigh ed. Sutherland 175.

11. *JAL* 103, to Cassandra Austen, 8–11 1805. *JAL* 264, to Cassandra Austen, 23 June 1814.

12. Caplan (1998) 70.

13. Avery-Jones 9.

14. Caplan (1998) 87.

15. Avery-Jones 12.

16. Caplan (1998) 87. Avery-Jones 21 describes Henry's 'contents' as being valued at £1,843.

17. *JAFR* 248.

18. Henry Austen in Austen-Leigh ed. Sutherland 135–43 and 145–54.

19. Caplan (2010) 109.

20. Clery (2017) 151.

21. *BLJ* 9.27, 'Detached Thoughts' (15 October 1821–18 May 1822), no. 44.

22. Creevey 1.158.

23. Bennett 132: 'In some of his politics Moira was simply ahead of his time, advocating the abolition of slavery before Wilberforce made it a popular cause and espousing fairer treatment for Irish Catholics and insolvent debtors.' Thorne np: 'On 22 May 1787 Rawdon advocated relief of imprisoned debtors; the ensuing bill was lost in 1788'.

24. Avery-Jones 22.

25. Avery-Jones 23.

26. Corley (1998) 144.

27. Southam (2000) 94.

28. Bennett 135.

29. Slothouber 23.

30. Corley (1998) 144.

31. *JAFR* 234.

32. Clery (2017) 108, 283.

33. *JAFR* 216.

34. *JAFR* 217.

35. See Grover (2014).

36. Slothouber 19–20. See Grover (2013). Hildebrand (1982) claims that 'the annual income of Godmersham was £5,000; and of Chawton, approximately £10,000', but these amounts are considerably higher than estimated elsewhere.

37. See Grover (2014).

38. *JAL* 260, to Cassandra Austen, 5–8 March 1814.

39. Edmund Yaldon White, quoted in *JAFR* 217.

40. Slothouber 29.

41. *JAFR* 217. Slothouber 23.

42. *JAL* 193, to Cassandra Austen, 6 June 1811.

43. *MP* vol. 1, chap. 6, 66.

44. Austen-Leigh and Knight 171.

45. *JAL* 333, to Fanny Knight, 13 March 1817.

46. *BLJ* 5.185–6, to Thomas Moore, 10 March 1817.

47. *BLJ* 5.148, to Thomas Moore, 24 December 1816.

48. Hobhouse ed. Cochran 26, Venice 1817 183.

49. Beckett 223. *P&P* vol. 1, chap. 1, 4. *P&P* vol. 1, chap. 4, 16. 'nearly an hundred thousand'.

50. Beckett 192–8.

51. *BLJ* 6.98, to Douglas Kinnaird, 27 January 1819.

52. Beckett 83.

53. Beckett 81 and 308, quoting *Notes and Queries* 8, no. 192 (2 July 1853).

54. Beckett 72–3.

55. Beckett 72.

56. *LBCPW* 1.111.

57. *LBCPW* 2.9.

58. Beckett 223–4.

59. Beckett 280.

60. *DJ* 2.1018–20. *LBCPW* 5.128–9.

61. *DJ* 11.585–6, *LBCPW* 5.487. *DJ* 15.345, *LBCPW* 5.601.

62. *DJ* 11.700–1, *LBCPW* 5.492.

63. *LBCPW* 5.488–90.

64. *DJ* 12.17–40, *LBCPW* 5.495–6.

65. *DJ* 16.601–2, *LBCPW* 5.641.

66. *DJ* 17.97, *LBCPW* 5.661.

67. Treitel 563–6.

68. Treitel 566.

69. *The Watsons,* Austen ed. Todd and Bree 122.

70. *P&P* vol. 2, chap. 6, 185.

71. *Sanditon,* Austen ed. Todd and Bree 150.

72. Clery (2017) 283.

73. *JAL* 338, to Charles Austen, 6 April 1817.

74. UCL/Cholmeley.

75. Huxtable 97.

76. *JAL* 81–2, to Cassandra Austen, 6 May 1801.

77. Gerzina 42, Chater (2009).

78. UCL/Sir George Hampson.

79. *JAL* 105, 23 April 1805; *JAL* 183, 25 April 1811; *JAL* 212, 24 May 1813; *JAL* 254, 7 November 1813; *JAL* 260, 8 March 1814; *JAL* 271, 23–4 August 1814 (all to Cassandra Austen); *JAL* 273, to Martha Lloyd, 2 September 1814; *JAL* 531, biographical index.

80. *JAL* 254, to Cassandra Austen, 7 November 1813.

81. Looser (2021).

82. *Sanditon,* Austen ed. Todd and Bree 200.

83. *Sanditon,* Austen ed. Todd and Bree 202.

84. Cowper ed. Milford 376. The use of animal blood as a purification agent in winemaking continued until 1997, when it was banned because of bovine spongiform encephalopathy (BSE). See 'French wine scare over cattle blood' by Susannah Herbert, *Daily Telegraph*, 25 June 1999, 7.

85. John Byron Order Book (Private Collection) quoted in Brand 99.

86. Brown 61. Seymour 1–3.

87. Langley Moore 374.

88. Parry 157–8.

89. Trelawny 2.86.

90. Langley Moore 427.

91. Said 114, 73.

92. *MP* vol. 2, chap. 3, 231. For challenges to Said see in particular White 4 and throughout.

93. See Kenyon Jones (2010).

94. *JAL* 198, to Cassandra Austen, 24 January 1813.

95. *Emma* vol. 2, chap. 17, 325.

96. *Persuasion* vol. 2, chap. 12, 274. While Collins Hemingway argues that 'a Slave Island Does Not Mean Slavery' and presents other possibilities for the source of Mrs Smith's 'incumbrances', Erin M. Goss points out how unlikely it would be that such a property 'in the West Indies' did not include enslaved people. Susan Allen Ford makes the case that, in creating Mrs Smith, Austen may have been thinking of the novelist Charlotte Smith, who wrote about slavery in her novels and was known to have suffered financially from her husband's profligacy and her inability to access the profits from a West Indian property.

97. *Emma* vol. 2, chap. 17, 325.

98. *LBCPW* 5.250.

99. Sandler 39.

100. *LBCPW* 2.69.

101. Burns np.

102. Hubback 192.

103. Looser (2022).

104. Looser (2021). Clery (2017) 314, 316.

CHAPTER 7
PROSE, POETRY, PRIVATE AND PUBLIC
'WHO WOULD WRITE, WHO HAD ANY THING BETTER TO DO?'[1]

In 1832 Henry Austen revised his 'Biographical Notice' about his sister (published with the first edition of *Northanger Abbey* and *Persuasion* in 1818), to provide a short biography of Jane for the new edition of *Sense and Sensibility* in Richard Bentley's Standard Novels series, published in 1833. The new 'Memoir of Miss Austen' was even more reticent than the 1818 'Notice' had been: it continued to craft a demure, pre-Victorian, 'Angel in the house' Jane Austen, with 'perfect placidity of temper', but left out, for instance, the information from 1818 about Jane's fondness for dancing; her gift for reading aloud and 'the comic muse', and an amusing remark in one of her last letters about the fashion for short petticoats (see Introduction).[2] There was now no mention of what the earlier Henry had called the 'stanzas replete with fancy and vigour' on Winchester races, composed only three days before her death.

Henry also included a new anecdote designed to show Jane's social propriety and seemly public reticence, which recounted how when 'Miss Austen' was visiting London soon after the publication of *Mansfield Park*,

> a nobleman, personally unknown to her, but who had good reasons for considering her to be the authoress of that work, was desirous of her joining a literary circle at his house. He communicated his wish in the politest manner, through a mutual friend, adding, what his Lordship doubtless thought would be an irresistible inducement, that the celebrated Madame de Staël would be of the party. Miss Austen immediately declined the invitation. To her truly delicate mind such a display would have given pain instead of pleasure.[3]

This has been often interpreted specifically as Jane's refusal to meet Madame de Staël, baronne de Staël-Holstein: a central figure of European literary and intellectual networks and superstar author of *Corinne, ou de l'Italie* (1807).[4]

De Staël's story of a doomed love affair between a Scottish nobleman and the Italian artist and poet-performer Corinne combined her highly influential views on the role of the woman artist and her hopes that Italy might unite to become a great nation once again.[5] Her own private life, which included several lovers and children by different fathers, was somewhat notorious, and might well have given Austen pause about meeting her; although Jane certainly read the English translation of *Corinne*, enjoyed it and recommended it to an acquaintance.[6]

Henry's new anecdote illustrates what seems to have been Jane's genuine reticence about appearing in public as an author, and this chapter uses this incident as a stepping-off point to consider the place of social niceties in Austen's and Byron's views of themselves as authors; their relationships with de Staël and the coincidence between their and her presentation of particular ideas about the feelings of women left behind by men. It also discusses the way in which Austen's and Byron's friends and families sought to protect their literary and social reputations in the light of the appearance of works of a very different character to those they had become known for; it explores their writings in what might be thought of as the other's medium (i.e. Austen in verse and Byron in narrative prose), and it traces their negotiation through 'private' and 'public' publishing methods and the effects of these on their output.

Austen perhaps need not have worried unduly about a meeting with de Staël in 1814, because it seems most unlikely that de Staël would have wished to meet her. According to the *Memoirs* of Sir James Mackintosh (1833), on reading *Pride and Prejudice*, de Staël said she 'found no interest in it' and dismissed it as 'vulgaire'.[7] Claire Tomalin helpfully glosses de Staël's comment as meaning 'too close to the English provincial life she detested for its narrowness and dullness, its emphasis on duty and its stifling of wit and brilliance', and one can see those qualities at work in Henry's 'Memoir', if not in Jane's novels themselves.[8]

Byron, too, was sought after by literary hosts and hostesses to meet de Staël when she visited England between 1813 and 1814. He encountered her first at Lady Jersey's on the very day she arrived (20 June 1813) and again at Sir Humphry Davy's the next evening, and on many occasions thereafter; and, perhaps, if Austen had accepted the 'polite' nobleman's invitation to join his 'literary circle', she and Byron too might have met there.[9] No concerns about the personal propriety of associating with de Staël stood in Byron's way, of course, but although he had a genuine and warm regard for her, her intellect and her works, he did not share her views of Napoleon and he was exasperated by her prolix and self-centred literary talk: 'this same lady writes octavos and *talks* folios' he complained in his journal in November 1813.[10] '[R]eally her society is overwhelming – an avalanche of glittering nonsense – all snow and sophistry'.[11] But two years later, in 1816 when Byron was in Switzerland, ostracized by English society after his marriage breakdown, it was perhaps de Staël's dislike of what she saw as the narrowness of English manners and morals that prompted her to welcome him so warmly to her own house at Coppet. 'In her own house she was amiable; in any other person's, you wished her gone, and in her own again', Byron commented.[12]

Lovers' letters

Austen, Byron and de Staël shared John Murray as their publisher and, perhaps because of this, the three of them have been brought together in critical discussions about whether any of them borrowed from each other or from other common sources for the similar ways in which they imagined and expressed the thoughts and feelings of women left behind by their lovers.[13] 'We certainly do not forget you so soon as you forget us', Anne Elliot tells Captain Harville in a key conversation towards the end of *Persuasion*, where she is able to give words to her deepest feelings:

> It is, perhaps, our fate rather than our merit. We cannot help ourselves. We live at home, quiet, confined, and our feelings prey upon us. You are forced on exertion. You have always a profession, pursuits, business of some sort or other, to take you back into the world immediately, and continual occupation and change soon weaken impressions. . . . Your feelings may be the strongest . . . but the same spirit of analogy will authorise me to assert that ours are the most tender. . . . You have difficulties, and privations, and dangers enough to struggle with. You are always labouring and toiling, exposed to every risk and hardship. Your home, country, friends, all quitted. Neither time, nor health, nor life, to be called your own. It would be too hard, indeed . . . if woman's feelings were to be added to all this.[14]

Byron's Julia in canto I of *Don Juan* (1819) makes the same point while writing to her lover Juan after he has been forced to leave her, and she is disgraced and confined to a convent:

'Man's love is of his life a thing apart,
 'Tis woman's whole existence; man may range
The court, camp, church, the vessel, and the mart,
 Sword, gown, gain, glory, offer in exchange
Pride, fame, ambition, to fill up his heart,
 And few there are whom these can not estrange;
Man has all these resources, we but one,
To love again, and be again undone.'

(*Don Juan* 1.1545–52)[15]

Byron's editor Jerome McGann speculates that *Persuasion* may actually have been Byron's source for this stanza ('a book which Murray published, and which he may very well have sent to Byron, not long before this paragraph was written').[16] But, as he mentions, critics have also noticed that both Austen's and Byron's passages show a likeness to de Staël's statements in *De l'influence des passions* (1796): 'Love is the sole passion of women. Ambition, even the love of glory, are so little suited to their nature, that very few of them turn their attention to these objects. . . . The history of the life of women is an episode in that of men'; and in *Corinne* (1807): 'How fortunate men are to go to war, to risk their lives, to give themselves up to the passion for honour and danger! But there is nothing outside themselves that relieves women. Their lives, unchanging in the presence of misfortune, are a very long torture.'[17] Hobhouse believed Byron's lines owed something to de Staël and noted 'Coppet to wit' beside this stanza on his proof copy of *Don Juan*.[18] Byron described how he read *Corinne* 'again and again' and he certainly knew it very well: his annotations appear in a copy of an Italian translation of *Corinne* belonging to Teresa Guiccioli, where he also wrote a love letter to Teresa.[19]

Ovid's *Heroïdes*

As Karen Caines has suggested, another very probable source for Byron (and for de Staël) is Ovid's *Heroïdes*, written in Latin in the last decade BCE. These 'Letters of Heroines' (where, as Gillian Beer notes, 'the rhetoric accorded to the women is assertive and assured', and 'presented without irony or demurral') would certainly have appealed to de Staël, and the name of her heroine, *Corinne*, may be drawn from that given by Ovid to his lover in his *Amores*.[20] The rather clumsy Loeb Classical Library translation of the letter which Ovid's priestess Hero writes to her lover Leander reads as follows:

> You men, now in the chase, now in the genial acres of the country, consume long hours in the varied tasks that keep you. Either the market-place holds you, or the sports of the supple wrestling-ground, or you turn with bit the neck of the responsive steed; and now you take the bird with the snare, now the fish with the hook; and the later hours you while away with the wine before you. For me who am denied these things, even were I less fiercely aflame, there is nothing left to do but love.[21]

Although he does not mention Ovid, McGann categorizes Julia's letter as 'an eloquent statement of a deeply traditional set of ideas', and some of the same thoughts and feelings can be found elsewhere in the *Heroïdes* (where, however, heroines such as Dido, Ariadne, Medea, Phyllis and Penelope are generally less forbearing and more critical of their absent partners). Alexander Pope's *Eloisa to Abelard* (1717) draws on this tradition and provides another possible source for Austen, Byron and possibly for de Staël, although Pope's heroine, unlike Ovid's, is entrammelled in sexual guilt.[22] Jocelyn Harris suggests a similarity with Anna Letitia Barbauld's 'The Origin and Progress of Novel-Writing' (1810) where Barbauld asks why women novelists 'are apt to give a melancholy tinge to their compositions'. Men, she suggests, 'mixing at large in society, have a brisker flow of ideas'; and whereas men experience feelings 'more transiently' and with 'fewer modifications of delicacy', women 'nurse those feelings in secrecy and silence'.[23]

But if Austen and Byron did use the same sources, or if Byron drew some of his ideas for Julia's letter from *Persuasion*, there are certainly differences in the ways in which the two authors interpret and express them. Anne's statement to Harville is moving not only because of its poignant evocation of her own feelings and her fidelity to her lost lover but also because of the sympathy she voices for the feelings of men – the 'difficulties', 'privations' and 'dangers' that they must endure: 'always labouring and toiling, exposed to every risk and hardship', she says. 'It would be too hard, indeed . . . if woman's feelings were to be added to all this.' Austen, like Anne, had experienced acute anxiety about loved ones away fighting for their country; and while Anne honours Harville and Wentworth, Austen revered her two sailor brothers Frank and Charles in similar circumstances. Byron's Julia, on the other hand, views masculine activities solely in terms of the way in which they 'estrange' men from women: the 'court, camp, church, the vessel, and the mart, / Sword, gown, gain, glory' offer a man 'Pride, fame, ambition' as 'resources' to 'fill up his heart'. Her (accurate) prophecy for Juan is that he 'will proceed in beauty, and in pride, /Beloved and loving many'. In fact, however, Byron seems vehemently to have disagreed with de Staël's statement in *Corinne* that men are 'fortunate . . . to go to war, to risk their lives, to give themselves up to the passion for honour and danger', since this is where he scribbled 'No – No' in the margin as he read it, and his own feelings were perhaps more like Anne's than Julia's.[24] It may be that his intention at this point in *Don Juan* (where Juan is about to embark on his next adventure) is to subtly reduce our sympathy for Julia by having her ignore the actual suffering and emotions of men, using her lack of empathy for them to increase our criticism of her. And he seems further to diminish Julia's tragedy by his deliberate focus on the physical (and evidently carefully chosen by Julia and by Byron) characteristics of her note itself:

> This note was written upon gilt-edged paper
>> With a neat crow-quill, rather hard, but new; . . .
>> The seal a sunflower; *'Elle vous suit partout,'*
> The motto, cut upon a white cornelian;
> The wax was superfine, its hue vermilion.

> (*Don Juan* 1.1576–7 and 1582–84)[25]

By reifying Julia's concern with the material elements of her farewell to Juan, Byron implies that she is dramatizing her sorrow, and that she may even have an eye to increasing her lover's pain by expressing her own, unlike Anne's self-denying wish to minimize this suffering: 'It would be too hard, indeed . . . if woman's feelings were to be added to all this.' If Byron is indeed picking up on Austen's text, he turns round that word 'hard' to face completely in the opposite direction, so that Julia's 'rather hard' neat crow-quill seems selected deliberately to further wound her departing lover. In the poem, her letter itself lives on in its physical form to participate ironically in two further mock-heroic moments in Juan's life: the next when Juan takes it out and apostrophizes his love for Julia just before he becomes sea-sick and 'gr[ows] inarticulate with reaching', and finally when it provides the paper for the grim lottery to decide which of the shipwrecked men is to be killed and eaten when they turn to cannibalism after their food runs out.[26]

Ovid in Latin

Byron certainly knew Ovid's *Epistolae Heroïdum* in Latin. His famous swim across the Hellespont on 3 May 1810 was undertaken to emulate Leander's legendary crossings to visit his lover, and Hobhouse noted in his diary: 'write this in the Dardanelles at anchor. Byron & Ekenhead . . . now swimming across the Hellespont – Ovid's Hero to Leander open before me'. Byron later added a more prosaic note in the same place, 'the current very strong and cold, some large fish near us when half-way across, we were not fatigued but a little chilled'.[27] Elsewhere he and Hobhouse used a Latin phrase from Ovid's 'Penelope to Ulysses' as shorthand in their letters: 'ipse veni!' from *nil mihi rescribas attinet: ipse veni* – 'writing back is pointless: come yourself'.[28]

The question of whether Austen could have read Ovid – or any other text – in the original Latin has been much debated. Classicists such as Mary De Forest maintain that 'it seems probable that her father, who knew classical literature thoroughly, and who taught Latin to students both inside and outside his family, would have taught her a language that we know he passionately valued'.[29] Such an argument is not supported by Austen's (admittedly comically self-denigrating) claim that she knew 'only her own mother tongue' and did not have the 'Classical Education, or . . . a very extensive acquaintance with English Literature, Ancient & Modern' that she would need to enable her to write like a clergyman.[30] The few Latin or Greek phrases used in her novels – such as *minutiae* (by Elinor and Anne); *panegyric* (Elizabeth and Darcy); *in propria persona* (Fanny); *dramatis personae* (Tom Bertram); *eulogium* (Henry Crawford) and *amor patriae* (Frank Churchill) – are not of the sort that could only be used by those who knew the classical languages.[31] Elsewhere, the inscription *Ex dono mei Patris* ('a gift from my father') on the notebook containing 'Volume the Second' of Austen's juvenilia, and the (inaccurate) quotation of the phrase *Propria qu[a]e Maribus* (from the 'Eton Latin Grammar') in a letter to Cassandra about some verses sent to her nephew Edward, seem to be the only Latin phrases we have from Austen's pen.[32]

The case is not completely closed on Austen's ability to tackle Ovid in Latin, however, because in 1966 Zachary Cope suggested that an anonymous letter signed by 'Sophia Sentiment', published in James's and Henry Austen's Oxford literary magazine *The Loiterer* in 1789, was actually by Jane, and this piece carries a Latin epigraph that is a quotation from Ovid's *Heroïdes* itself: *Non venit ante suum nostra querela diem* ('My complaint comes not before its time', from letter 2, 'Phyllis to Demophon').[33] Cope's suggestion has, however, been disputed, partly on the grounds that Jane was only thirteen at this time, but mainly that Sophia Sentiment's mockery of women's poor 'sentimental' taste in literature is much more likely to have originated with James or Henry than with Jane.[34] The Phyllis and Demophon episode in the *Heroïdes* may, however, have provided Byron with inspiration for the second, third and fourth, 'Haidee', cantos of *Don Juan*, since these, like Ovid's story, feature an idyll on a lonely island where a young princess welcomes a shipwrecked stranger to her bed. Unlike Demophon, however, Juan does not abandon Haidee willingly but is forcibly torn away from her and sold into slavery.

Another possible basis for the theory that Austen as well as Byron was influenced by the *Heroïdes* is that, of course, Austen may have read it in an English translation. Austen's most likely source for this is the collection supervised and prefaced by John Dryden: *Ovid's Epistles Translated by Several Hands* (1680); and other volumes by Dryden and Ovid (though not the *Epistles*) are listed in the 1818 *Alphabetical Catalogue for Godmersham Park Library*.[35] In this collection the letter from Hero to Leander was translated by Nahum Tate, who was to become Poet Laureate in 1692:

With such delight I read your Letter o're,
Your Presence only could have giv'n me more.
Excuse my Passion if it soar above
Your thought; no Man can judge of Woman's love.
With Bus'ness you, or Pleasures may sustain
The Pangs of Absence, and divert the Pain.
The Hills, the Vales, the Woods, and streams are stor'd
With Game, and Profit with Delight afford.
Whilst Gins for Beasts, & Snares for Fowl you set,
You smile, and your own amorous Chains forget.
Ten thousand helps besides effect your Cure,
Whilst Women's sole Relief is to endure.

(*Ovid's Epistles Translated by Several Hands*, no. 8,
'Hero's answer to Leander', 1–12)[36]

Although the premise is the same, Anne's statement is (again) infinitely more expressive: while Hero imagines in some detail the rustic sports that might distract Leander, Anne conjures up the lover's state of mind and soul: 'Neither time, nor health, nor life, to be called your own.' Harville, and Wentworth listening nearby, are both deeply moved, and her intensely eloquent expression of her feelings and her sympathy leads directly to Wentworth's marriage proposal and decisively turns the story towards its happy ending.

Austen's world turned upside down

This passage dates from the last year of Austen's life: it is part of the brilliant new ending for *Persuasion* which she completed in August 1816 and might be termed the 'perfection' of Austenian writing. But although she was already ill, Jane did not intend to rest on her laurels even at this point, and the substantial fragment of *Sanditon*, which she started in January 1817 and continued drafting until only a few weeks before her death, is very different in characterization, plot and style from the novels that preceded it, and instead returns to a more openly burlesque and satiric tone and approach which connects back to her very earliest work. The 'Juvenilia', most of which were written while she was still a teenager, certainly come as a shock to the reader who turns from Anne's admirable, selfless, thoughts and feelings (often expressed in Austen's most skilful free indirect speech, imperceptibly merging and separating the narrator and the character) to the ruthless and exuberant comedy of her youthful writings. Here, as E. J. Clery says, 'you will find the world associated with her turned upside down, as the young apprentice undertakes a rip-roaring demolition of the sentimental tradition of fiction she inherited: mantraps in the shrubbery, elopements and adultery in abundance, assault and battery, murder and suicide, civil war and even cannibalism.'[37]

Peter Sabor concludes that this 'anarchic energy, violence, and irreverence' makes Austen's early writings 'quite unlike the work of any of her contemporaries', and so it is initially even more surprising to find that, with very few allowances, Clery's sketch could also be used to describe Byron's work in *Don Juan* – which includes some of the latest and most mature of *his* writing.[38] Here too 'the world associated with [him is] turned upside down', so that the soulful Romantic persona and plaintive travelogue of the *Childe Harold* tradition, and the gloomy post-Gothic Byronic heroes of *Manfred* and the 'Oriental Tales', are discarded in favour of the witty, knowing narrator and realistic story of *Don Juan*. Here Byron too undertakes a 'demolition' of a literary genre (in his case, the 'Romantic' one he himself had had a major hand in creating) and turns to presenting a modern narrative full of sudden, violent and destructive events such as cannibalism, sometimes recounted in a positively gleeful tone:

> The surgeon, as there was no other fee,
> Had his first choice of morsels for his pains;
> But being thirstiest at the moment, he
> Preferr'd a draught from the fast-flowing veins:
> Part was divided, part thrown in the sea,
> And such things as the entrails and the brains
> Regaled two sharks, who follow'd o'er the billow –
> The sailors ate the rest of poor Pedrillo.
>
> (*Don Juan* 2.609–16)[39]

Like Austen's juvenilia, *Don Juan* contains 'elopements and adultery in abundance, assault and battery, murder and suicide, civil war and even cannibalism' – and also in fact, in canto 16, a mention of 'two poachers caught in a steel trap / Ready for jail, their place of convalescence'.[40] The resemblance between Austen's juvenile work and Byron's most mature does, I suggest, run deep and, although Byron can never have read Austen's teenage and unpublished writings, and she did not live long enough to sample *Beppo* or *Don Juan*, there is a similarity of spirit and purpose in this work: an insouciance of manner (sometimes contrasted with very weighty themes); a common love of burlesque, satire and irony; a reverence for Augustan writers and modes, and that shared sense of humour which, as Peter W. Graham points out, singles out the two of them from among their contemporaries. The teenage girl and the worldly wise male poet, writing at the beginning and the end of the three decades denominated 'Romantic' in English literature, turn out to have much in common.

Friends and family

In the first place, Austen's juvenilia and Byron's *Don Juan* share certain aspects of their reception history. The initial publication of both was fraught with problems: and for similar reasons, as members of Austen's family and

Byron's close friends and colleagues opposed making public works that were radically different from those on which the writers had built their existing reputations. In both cases the family and friends feared that the publication would offend current public sensibilities and fundamentally damage and coarsen the image of 'their' author, detrimentally changing her or his literary standing for posterity. The increasing personal reticence of Henry Austen's two biographical notes about Jane, and Tomalin's gloss of de Staël's 'vulgaire' accusation, demonstrate some of the forces that were already in play in 1817 and which had become stronger by 1832: the way in which British society (progressively dominated by the middle classes) was becoming more strait-laced and prudish about what was aired in public, and in which women were imagined (and expected to appear) as increasingly modest, home-loving, gentle and demure. Austen's published novels could in fact sit relatively easily in this milieu: the delicacy with which she approached issues such as licentiousness, violence, crime, extra-marital sex, illegitimacy, and sensuality and sexuality in general were able to meet the new, increasingly 'higher', standards of public morality that pertained in the two decades following her death and then in the Victorian era. But hidden away in the homes of her descendants (together with the drafts of *The Watsons* and *Sanditon,* and a collection of her poems and charades) was another Jane Austen: the teenage author of the startling epistolary novel with its rakish and Machiavellian heroine Lady Susan, and twenty-seven short fictional pieces in which, as Peter Sabor puts it, 'murder, suicide, violence, theft, verbal abuse, gluttony and drunkenness all play a prominent part'.[41] This young Jane Austen, as A. Walton Litz points out, is a product neither of the Rousseauian claim (in *Emile,* 1762) that 'there is no original sin in the human heart', nor of the later Victorian cult of the child as innocent and of 'blessed immaturity'.[42] These were, moreover, pieces which Austen evidently valued, and which she carefully kept even when she was producing her mature work: turning back over the decades to the collection – which had been copied out in her beautiful copperplate handwriting in three manuscript notebooks, grandly entitled 'Volume the First', 'Volume the Second' and 'Volume the Third' – to correct the spelling and make small amendments: some as late as 1809 and 1811.[43]

In her teenage writings Austen is not only entirely open about the issues which the mature novels handle with reticence, but she also positively revels in bringing them and other reprehensible characteristics to the fore in the anarchic world they inhabit. Violence (leavened by humour) is common: Anna Parker of 'A Letter from a Young Lady' has 'murdered my father at a very early period of my life', has since murdered her mother and is now about to murder her sister; Lucy in 'Jack and Alice' has her leg caught in a man-trap; Sir George and Lady Harcourt in 'Henry and Eliza' punish the idleness of their haymakers by cudgelling them, while Eliza herself has her fingers bitten off by her hungry children after she has thrown them out of the prison window.[44] 'The beautifull [*sic*] Cassandra' knocks down a pastry-cook in order to get at his ices; Edward and Augustus of 'Love and Freindship [*sic*]' die 'weltering in their blood' after a carriage accident, and 'Frederic and Elfrida's intimate neighbours do not scruple 'to kick one another out of the window on the slightest provocation'.

What Sabor calls 'sexual knowingness' is also very evident. Even in 'Frederic and Elfrida', written when Austen was probably only eleven, there is a running joke about Elfrida's fear of the marriage bed which makes her postpone her wedding for many years, while 'Love and Freindship' (written a few years later) nonchalantly introduces at least six illegitimate children.[45] As explored in Chapter 4, the teenage author of 'The History of England' (1791) was also very knowing about male same-sex desire, and when, in 'Love and Freindship', she reports how Edward and Augustus 'flew into each other's arms', exclaiming 'my Life! My Soul' and 'my Adorable Angel', they do, as Sabor puts it, 'go far beyond conventional eighteenth-century expressions of male friendship', while the pathos of the scene famously causes Laura and Sophia to 'faint . . . Alternately on a Sofa.'[46]

'Generally intended to be nonsensical'

These writings continued to be held privately by succeeding generations of the Austen family, and the first mention of them in public was in *A Memoir of Jane Austen* written by Jane's nephew James Edward Austen-Leigh and published at the end of 1869 (dated 1870). Austen-Leigh referred to 'copy books . . . containing tales, some of which must have been composed while she was a young girl', described the stories as 'of a slight and flimsy texture . . . generally intended to be nonsensical' and added that 'it would be as unfair to expose this preliminary process to the world, as it would be to display all that goes on behind the curtain of the theatre before it is drawn up'.[47] '[T]he family have, rightly, I think, declined to let these early works be published', he added.[48]

The public mention of these writings, however, soon led to pressure on the family to release them, and in the second edition of the *Memoir* (1871)

Austen-Leigh published *Lady Susan* and *The Watsons*; a portion of *Sanditon;* an edited version of 'Plan of a Novel' (see Chapter 5), and five of Jane's poems, but he provided only a tiny sample from the juvenilia 'Volumes' themselves, in the form of the miniature drama entitled (appropriately in the circumstances) 'The Mystery'. The point of this playlet is that the audience never learns anything about the plot because it is all conducted in whispers. Like the girls 'fainting alternately on a Sofa', it was inspired by Sheridan's *The Critic*.[49]

> Mrs Hum:[bug]) And what is to become of? . . .
> Daphne) Oh! that's all settled. (whispers [to] Mrs Humbug)
> Fanny) And how is it determined?
> Daphne) I'll tell you (whispers [to] Fanny)
> Mrs Hum:) And is he to? . . .
> Daphne I'll tell you all I know of the matter.
>   (whispers [to] Mrs Humbug and Fanny)
> Fanny) Well! Now I know everything about it, I'll go away.
> Mrs Hum: And so will I. . . .
>   (Exeunt).[50]

The nineteenth-century Austens were aware not only of the need to preserve the image of Jane as a decorous Victorian author, but also of their duty to protect her reputation in the way she herself might have wished to. The *Quarterly Review* intoned in 1870 about the 'wholesome truth' that 'the work that [an author] has judged discreet to withhold from public view . . . ought to be sacred from being pored over and printed by posthumous busybodies'.[51] James Edward Austen-Leigh was anxious about releasing *Lady Susan* in particular because 'If it should be judged unworthy of the publicity now given it, the censure must fall on him who has put it forth and not on her who kept it locked in her desk'.[52]

Since the family could, at this stage, still control the release of the juvenilia, the scene from 'The Mystery' was all that the public were able to see or hear of the contents of Austen's teenage 'Volumes' for the next fifty years. It was not until 1922 that 'Volume the Second' was published, under the title of *Love and Freindship* and edited by G. K. Chesterton, who in his introduction referred to the works as 'nursery jests' and remarked that he would willingly have left *Lady Susan* in the wastebasket.[53] 'Volume the First' was issued in 1933 and 'Volume the Third' finally saw the light of day in 1951, with the manuscript remaining in the Austen-Leigh family until 1976.[54] As late as 1989 Joan Austen-Leigh, great-granddaughter of James Edward, felt that the juvenilia 'could well have been left, not in the wastebasket but in a drawer, for study by scholars, who I venture to suspect are pretty much the only people who ever really peruse them'.[55]

Times and tastes were changing, however, and, as early as 1922, Zona Gale, reviewing *Love and Freindship* for the *New York Times Book Review*, had remarked delightedly: 'here she is – this Jane Austen of library shelves and bookcases – here she is, human, laughing, alive, taken unaware, as she must so often have longed to be taken. Never before has she quite escaped from the Rectory.'[56] And since 1989 the history of the reception of Austen's juvenile work has in fact shown a completely different trajectory to that predicted by Joan Austen-Leigh: with the juvenilia taken up in particular by feminist scholars including Sandra Gilbert and Susan Gubar, who celebrated their heroines' 'exuberant assertiveness, their exploration and exploitation of the world, their curiously honest expression of their needs, their rebellious rejection of their fathers' advice'.[57] Lady Susan's philandering, independent and mercenary ways, as well as her attractive though reprehensible personality, are now enjoyably read as a female version of the Restoration rake, and as an example of Austen's perspectives on gender roles and acceptable behaviour.[58] A successful film version of *Lady Susan* appeared in 2016 (confusingly, under the title 'Love and Friendship'), written and directed by Whit Stillman and starring Kate Beckinsale; and a multi-series television drama by Andrew Davies, based on *Sanditon*, was aired in 2019 and 2022. The Jane Austen we now know incorporates this laughing and outspoken teenage writer, as well as the mature author of the novels, who had learned (partly through her own early writing) how to retain her own distinctive voice while submitting to the need for decorum, feminine modesty and reticence; how to conform herself while creating and presenting characters who do *not* conform, and how to be pointed, narratively brilliant, satirical, humorous, challenging and sometimes startling, as well as continuing to be reassuring, comforting and acceptable.

The struggle for *Don Juan*

Other writers were also, of course, the victims of a 'Victorianising' cover-up: notably Percy Shelley, whose family over two generations struggled to create a saintly image of the poet by selecting, excising, rewriting and destroying part of the surviving archive, leading to Matthew Arnold's memorable characterization of Shelley as 'a beautiful and ineffectual angel, beating in the void his luminous wings in vain'.[59] The story of the reception and publishing history of *Don Juan* was, however, played out over quite a different timescale from that of Shelley's work and Austen's juvenilia: largely during Byron's lifetime between 1819 and 1824, and with Byron (unlike Austen) active on his own behalf against those who declared his work 'unpublishable'. When sending the manuscript of the first two cantos of *Don Juan* from Italy to England he was concerned that the 'damned Cant and Toryism of the day may make Murray pause', but actually the response from the publisher and the Tory critics was highly favourable, and in fact it was Byron's Whig friends who 'paused'. In March 1819 Murray described these two cantos as 'exceedingly good' and praised 'the power with which you alternately make ones [*sic*] blood thrill & our Sides Shake'. 'It probably surpasses in talent any thing that you ever wrote', he added.[60] The Tory writer and critic John Gibson Lockhart, too, regarded *Don Juan* as 'out of all sight the best of your works; . . . by far the most spirited, the most straightforward, the most interesting, and the most poetical'. '[E]very body thinks as I do of it', he added, 'although they have not the heart to say so. Old Gifford's brow relaxed as he gloated over it; Mr Croker chuckled. . . . The whole band of *The Quarterly* were delighted.'[61]

As Lockhart hinted, however, many people who relished the poem in private were wary about praising it in public, and this was particularly true of Whigs such as Hobhouse, who was standing for a seat in Parliament and may have been fearful of its effect on his own reputation (as a known close friend of Byron) in the eyes of his voters. In January 1819 he wrote to Byron outlining why *Don Juan* was 'impossible to publish', citing 'the sarcasms against the lady of Seaham' (Lady Byron, whom Byron satirized as the hypocritical Donna Inez), 'the licentiousness and in some cases downright indecency of many stanzas', 'the flings at religion', 'the slashing right and left at other worthy writers of the day', and 'the immoral turn of the whole poem'. He advised 'a total suppression' of it and persuaded Byron's Whig friends Scrope Berdmore Davies and Douglas Kinnaird to concur with him.[62] Murray's response was to try to get Byron to agree to cut or change some sections, but Byron flatly refused to have the poem censored: 'You shan't make *Canticles* of my Cantos. The poem will please if it is lively – if it is stupid, it will fail – but I will have none of your damned cutting & slashing.'[63]

The fundamental difficulty was, again, the rising influence of more prudish tastes, reflecting what Murray called 'the character of the Middling

Classes in the country [which] is certainly highly moral – and we should not offend them'.[64] A crucial factor for the publisher was the advice of the barrister John Bell that 'considering the general nature of the subject the warmth of description in some parts & the scriptural allusion in others *in the present temper of the times* a court will not afford its protection to this book' (my italics).[65] So although Murray nevertheless took the risk of publishing the work, the way in which he did so seriously undermined its reputation. The first two cantos were issued in July 1819 in grand quarto format (like that of *Childe Harold)* costing over a guinea a copy, but without including the name of the author (which Byron did not mind) but also without the publisher's imprint (which incensed Byron). There were also large gaps in the text in places, and rows of asterisks replacing some passages. Murray advertised it enthusiastically – for example, at the top of the front page of *The Times*: 'TOMORROW DON JUAN' – but also without saying whose work it was or acknowledging that he was the publisher.[66] This stance implied that he did not believe the courts would uphold his copyright because of the 'corrupting' or 'immoral' nature of the publication and was in effect an open invitation to pirate publishers. Mary O'Connell points out the prophetic nature of Byron's lines in canto 3 of *Don Juan*:

> Words are things, and a small drop of ink,
> Falling like dew, upon a thought, produces
> That which makes thousands, perhaps millions, think.

> (*Don Juan* 3.793–95)[67]

Ironically, thanks to the way in which Byron's text was stolen, printed and cheaply reprinted by pirate publishers, *Don Juan* reached and presumably 'corrupted' a far greater audience than if it had been published by Murray alone. More than 100,000 copies of it were sold – at very low prices and often in a paper-saving format which made them look like tiny prayer-books – during Byron's lifetime, and he lived to see its readership reach well over a million by 1824.

Murray's fearful mode of publishing *Don Juan* hammered another nail into the coffin of his and Byron's relationship and publishing association and marked in particular the gulf between their stances because of the difference between the environments in which they now operated. In continental Europe, especially in Italy, from the late 1810s revolutionary ideas and movements had developed in opposition to aspects of the conservative settlement of the Treaty of Vienna, and these were widely explored in culture and especially in literature. But in Britain, despite a widespread disdain for George IV as Regent and King, there was in this decade relative political stability and increasing conservatism in literary and cultural life. The short-lived 1822 literary journal *The Liberal*, which was conceived by Shelley and realized after his death by Byron and Leigh Hunt in Pisa, wore its politics not only on its sleeve but also in its subtitle: 'Verse and Prose *from the South*' (my italics) emphasizing the difference in the political and literary atmospheres of the two locations. Designed to promote the internationalist tendencies of its writers, multilingualism, cultural pluralism and a dialogue with continental literature, the 'Italianized Cockney magazine' reflected Byron's espousal of the cause of the Ravenna Carbonari 'freedom-fighters' and later, of course, that of Greek liberation.[68] Having lived abroad since 1816, mainly in Italy, Byron came to be increasingly impatient of what he (like de Staël) thought of as the 'cant' of British society, and increasingly *un*willing to do as Austen had done by accommodating himself to the conservative British market, and indeed becoming more and more vehement in his satire of it. Perhaps, however, if Austen had lived, she too might have dared to do something more similar to what Byron did, and the 1817 draft of *Sanditon* seems to show her turning away from the romantic, happy-ending, marriage plot formula she had developed so successfully and becoming more ruthless, exuberant, abrupt and directly satirical of contemporary society and individuals.[69]

'Begin at the beginning'

In stanzas 6–7 of the first canto of *Don Juan* Byron explains his method of narration in this poem:

Most epic poets plunge in 'medias res,'
    (Horace makes this the heroic turnpike road)
And then your hero tells, whene'er you please,
    What went before – by way of episode . . .

That is the usual method, but not mine –
    My way is to begin at the beginning;
The regularity of my design
    Forbids all wandering as the worst of sinning.

And therefore I shall open with a line
    (Although it cost me half an hour in spinning)
Narrating somewhat of Don Juan's father,
And also of his mother, if you'd rather.

In Seville was he born . . .

(Don Juan 1.41–57)[70]

Although Byron's ironic tone might lead us to expect otherwise, in fact *Don Juan's* narrative *is* 'regular' in this aspect of its design: moving through the chronology of Juan's life step by step, without 'episodes' to tell us 'What went before', or sudden revelations of past events that might explain or throw light on the present. This directness and lack of narrative 'wandering' is crucially necessary, because of the lavish amount of digression of other kinds that Byron allows himself in his epic poem, and his claim to 'regularity of design' actually *only* applies to the 'begin-at-the-beginning' mode of narration, not to the poem's general way of proceeding. Byron develops a highly nuanced interchange between the narrator, the poet, the protagonist and the reader, aspects of which may remind us of Austen's free indirect discourse, and in which the interruption of Juan's story by authorial digressions helps to keep the reader eager to find out 'what happened next'. This sequential story provides the firm framework upon which Byron builds his sprawling poetic edifice and, along with the brilliant resolution of the complexities of the regular *ottava rima* scheme, links the bulky, unpredictable whole together in a way which for the reader is pleasingly reliable.

If Byron was looking for a model of reliable and aesthetically developed chronological narrative, he could certainly have found it in Austen's mature novels. Unlike the multi-layered verse narrative of Byron's *The Giaour* (where, after plunging in *in medias res*, the story is told through the individual perspectives of several narrators, Muslim and Christian, and where, as Bernard Beatty points out, the bias of the narrators 'force[s] the reader to attend to narrative as a problem'), or the nested narrative of a Gothic novel such as Mary Shelley's *Frankenstein* (where the Arctic explorer Robert Walton recounts to his sister his meeting with Victor Frankenstein, who in turn tells his life story and then introduces the words of the Creature), the story-telling of Austen's novels appears at first sight wonderfully clear and straightforward.[71] Using a third-person omniscient narrator, and the past tense, it too generally develops in natural, chronological, time, with the reader and the heroine usually learning new information or experiencing new events at the same pace. The narration does become more complicated in *Emma*, where the viewpoint of the not-always-reliable heroine is part of the theme of Emma's growth from rather complacent self-confidence and bossiness to real self-knowledge. The reader, who has probably *not* been fooled by Emma's conviction that Mr Elton's amorous campaign is directed at Harriet, may find that their confidence about being able to guess the rest of the plot is undermined when they eventually learn of the Frank Churchill/Jane Fairfax connection (although Mr Knightley is allowed to see this long before Emma suspects it) and then the revelation to Emma herself of her love for Mr Knightley. In a 1998 lecture considering *Emma* as a detective story, the celebrated writer in this genre P. D. James admitted that when she first read the novel as a girl she did not see the clues which lead to the denouement.[72] Like an ingenious murder-mystery narrator, Austen directs our attention to misleading clues and an over-elaborate explanation for the 'crime', while the actual 'culprits' hide in plain sight. Byron too can hide a guilty couple where, we later realize, they are very visible: in his case Juan's mother Donna Inez and Julia's husband Don José, and he uses his *not* omniscient narrator, the nosey neighbour, to present clues of which he does not apparently see the significance, while the reader, knowingly, does.

And Austen's broadly linear, chronological narration does not prevent her as author from rather disconcertingly stepping in with comments made directly to 'the reader', interrupting the story to chat about novels, the characteristics of heroines and the handling of the plot in a way that may recall Byron's much more active authorial intervention. In her teenage 'History of England' ('By a partial, prejudiced and ignorant Historian', 1791) Austen had experimented from the title page onwards with the persona of the intrusive narrator, and continued throughout to comment knowingly on her own unscholarliness and prejudices: 'During his reign, Lord Cobham was burnt alive, but I forget what for'; 'The Character of this Prince has been in general very severely treated by Historians, but as he was a *York,* I am rather inclined to suppose him a very respectable Man.'[73] The preponderance of direct authorial interventions in *Northanger Abbey* attests to the relative earliness of its composition and its likeness to the juvenilia. Two of these interventions are particularly well-known: Austen's spirited defence of the novel as a genre (at some length) in volume 1, chapter 5, and, at the end of the book, a reminder of the fictionality of the author's whole enterprise:

The anxiety, which in this state of their attachment must be the portion of Henry and Catherine, and of all who loved either, as to its final event, can hardly extend, I fear, to the bosom of my readers, who will see in the tell-tale compression of the pages before them, that we are all hastening together to perfect felicity.[74]

Austen, when she chooses, can be quite as tricky as Byron is in the way she plays with the reader and the narratorial role while continuing to maintain the regular progression of the story.

Prose versus verse

The most obvious gulf between Austen's work and Byron's lies, of course, in their primary choice of medium: Austen's for prose and Byron's for verse; although, as noted in the Introduction, W. H. Auden praised Byron's ability to write verse that emulated a 'higher art than poetry altogether', namely that of the novel. Comparing what each of them chose to try in the medium characteristic of the other does, however, point up some interesting parallels. The Austen family habit of composing verse seems to have originated with Mrs Austen, who with her 'sprack wit' was a highly skilful light versifier.[75] In skill and polish Jane's rhymes (most of which were written between 1805 and 1812) do not match her mother's, and most of them are small, personal, occasional pieces, designed for simplicity of form and content:

Chawton, July 26. – 1809. –
My dearest Frank, I wish you joy
Of Mary's safety with a Boy,
Whose birth has given little pain
Compared with that of Mary Jane. –[76]

One specimen of Austen's verse, however – 'On Sir Home Popham's sentence – April 1807' – strikes a political note which sounds somewhat like Byron, although more personal and less epigrammatic in style:

Of a Ministry pitiful, angry, mean,
A Gallant Commander the victim is seen . . .
    To his Foes I would wish a resemblance in fate;

That they too may suffer themselves soon or late
The Injustice they warrant – but vain is my spite,
They cannot so suffer, who never do right. –

('On Sir Home Popham's sentence – April 1807', 1–8)[77]

The most moving of Austen's poems are the elegiac verses 'To the memory of M[rs.] Lefroy, who died Dec:[r] 16. – my birthday. – written 1808. –', which may remind us of Austen's fondness for William Cowper's work in this vein, such as *On the Receipt of My Mother's Picture out of Norfolk* (1790). Austen's poem seeks in vain to find meaning in the coincidence between the dates of her own birth and her friend's death:

The day returns again, my natal day;
What mix'd emotions with the Thought arise!
Beloved friend, four years have passed away
Since thou wert snatch'd forever from our eyes. – . . .

Fain would I feel an union in thy fate,
Fain would I seek to draw an omen fair
From this connection in our Earthly date.
Indulge the harmless weakness – Reason, spare. –

('To the memory of Mrs· Lefroy . . .', 1–4 and 49–52)[78]

Similarly, one of Byron's last poems, whose subject was his unrequited love for the Greek youth Lukas Chalandritsanos, uses a very personal note of loss and regret, addressing the loved one, like Austen, as 'thee' and 'thou', and introducing a moment of self-reproach and harsh realism at the end:

I watched thee on the breakers, when the rock
Received our prow, and all was storm and fear,
And bade thee cling to me through every shock;
This arm would be thy bark, or breast thy bier. . . .

Thus much and more; and yet thou lov'st me not,
And never wilt! Love dwells not in our will.
Nor can I blame thee, though it be my lot
To strongly, wrongly, vainly love thee still.

('[Love and Death]', 1–8 and 21–24)[79]

The poem on Winchester races, which Austen composed only three days before her death is (like much of her prose work in her last year) satirical, humorous and challenging. While *Sanditon* mocks her own ill-health with a sceptical take on invalidism and the supposed health benefits of fashionable seaside resorts, 'Winchester races' goes daringly much further, to mock death itself and resurrection too, as St Swithin upbraids the citizens of 'Venta' (Winchester) for their failure to ask his leave for holding the races, and threatens that he will punish them by making it rain on their race meetings:

'Oh subjects rebellious, Oh Venta depraved
When once we are buried you think we are dead
But behold me Immortal. – By vice you're enslaved
You have sinn'd and must suffer.'

('When Winchester races first took their beginning', 13–16)[80]

The dead saint

Although Austen's brother Henry had had what was later regarded as the bad taste to mention these 'stanzas replete with fancy and vigour' in his 1818 biographical notice, Jane's niece and nephew Caroline and James Edward Austen-Leigh were horrified by the idea of the poem becoming public. Caroline protested that for 'reasons of taste . . . the joke about the dead saint, & the Winchester races, all jumbled up together, would read badly as amongst the few details given of the closing scene', while James Edward made no mention of it in his *Memoir* of his aunt and never allowed it to be published. It did not become public, in fact, until some other Austen descendants, the Hubbacks, included it in their study of *Jane Austen's Sailor Brothers* in 1906.[81]

Part of the appealing 'vigour' of Austen's poem lies in its versification: its jaunty anapestic rhythm which seems designed to mimic the racehorses cantering by. A similar effect was achieved by Byron in one of his 1815 *Hebrew Melodies* collection, 'The Destruction of Sennacherib':

The Assyrian came down like the wolf on the fold,
And his cohorts were gleaming in purple and gold;
And the sheen of their spears was like stars on the sea,
When the blue wave rolls nightly on deep Galilee.

('The Destruction of Sennacherib', 1–4)[82]

Byron's poem is still among the most often-quoted examples of this unusual metre, and it is possible that Austen was recalling it when she conjured up her Winchester races. Any doubts she may really have had about death and resurrection were, however, aired only in a humorous and private poem which she expected would never be published. Byron used no such circumspection, and his late work, particularly his 1821 drama *Cain*, became notorious for voicing challenges to religious orthodoxy such as Lucifer's cynical prophecy about the doctrine of atonement:

> 'perhaps he'll make
> One day a Son unto himself – as he
> Gave you a father – and if he so doth
> Mark me! – that Son will be a Sacrifice.'
>
> *(Cain 1.1.163–6)*[83]

This was, or had been, Byron's own argument as well as Lucifer's, first broached in an 1811 letter to his friend the Reverend Francis Hodgson:

> [T]he basis of your religion is *injustice*; the *Son of God*, the *pure*, the *immaculate*, the *innocent*, is sacrificed for the *guilty*. . . . You degrade the Creator, in the first place, by making Him a begetter of children; and in the next you convert Him into a tyrant over an immaculate and injured Being, who is sent into existence to suffer death for the benefit of some millions of scoundrels, who, after all, seem as likely to be damned as ever.[84]

These and similar arguments aired in *Cain* led even Byron's close friend Thomas Moore to 'regret, for many reasons, you ever wrote it' and to speak out against the 'desolating' conclusions to which it might lead 'the young, the simple, – all those whose hearts one would like to keep unwithered'.[85]

Byron experimented with writing prose fiction throughout his life, but although Moore claimed that he had seen 'a portion, to the amount of nearly a hundred pages, of a prose story, relating the adventures of a young Andalusian nobleman', and Hobhouse recorded how he had 'read the beginning of a novel of B's – he adumbrates himself – Don Julian', it appears that Byron never completed a work in this genre.[86] The only prose fiction that was published in his lifetime was 'Augustus Darvell: A Fragment of a

Ghost Story' – the beginning of the eerie tale of an English traveller who dies suddenly in a Turkish cemetery and seems to have a doppelganger – which was sent to Murray for publication after Polidori's *The Vampyre* was issued by another publisher in 1819 with the claim that it was by Byron. Several of the pieces that survive recall Austen's juvenilia in tone (brisk, burlesque, apparently inconsequential); in length (usually brief and unfinished) and in purpose (using a mocking veneer of novelistic features and of romanticism to satirize human folly and sentimental fictional genres). Although Byron's 'Tale of Calil' (1816) does have a deeper purpose as a critique of the savagery of war and specifically of Talleyrand's betrayal of Napoleon, its language and presentation is strongly reminiscent of some of the young Austen's nimble social vignettes which use an apparently sentimental narrator to give brusque facts and to end statements on a sardonic note. So Calil's wife is 'deeply lamented, . . . till Calil married again, which he did at last, though inconsolable for many weeks'; 'the day was delightful – the night was sublime – and the next morning all Samarcand woke with the headache'; and 'he considered all this with the deepest attention for three minutes – and in the end – like a true patriot changed his politics and his road at the same moment.'[87]

'Italy, or not Corinna' (1820), subtitled 'a travelling Romance by an "Ecrivain en poste"', satirizes the vogue for continental travel after Napoleon's defeat in 1815, contrasting de Staël's glamorization of Italy with the hackneyed travelogues of British travellers such as William Sotheby and his family ('Mr Solemnboy the poet Mrs Solemnboy and the six Miss Solemnboys') whose 'letters . . . were full of past and present description with very little assistance from Coxe's Guide-book'.[88] The allusive names invented for Byron's characters here – such as Solemnboy, Amundeville and Clutterbuck – compare well with the evocative placenames dreamed up by the teenage Austen, including Crankhumdunberry, Pammydiddle and Kilhoobery.[89]

'Expectorating a romance'

The most innovative in form among Byron's prose fictions and the earliest that is now extant is 'Bramblebear and Lady Penelope: A Chapter of a Novel', written around 14 November 1813, when Byron recorded in his journal that he had 'some idea of expectorating a romance, or rather a tale in prose'.[90] Byron's fictional letter (which purports to be one of a sequence from 'Darrell' to his friend 'G.Y.') describes a country-house party where the beautiful, pious and apparently chaste Lady Penelope, wife of the dull and absurd Bramblebear, is pursued by 'as many suiters as her namesake'. Like Byron's other fictional heroes, Darrell clearly embodies something of the author, and Byron's role as fictional letter-writer allows him to represent himself under the double aspect of observer and observed, narrator and protagonist, in the context of the flirtation he was currently conducting under similar circumstances with Lady Frances Wedderburn-Webster.[91] By 17 November, however, he was less confident: 'I began a comedy and burnt it because the scene ran into *reality;* – a novel, for the same reason. In rhyme, I can keep more away from facts'; and on 23 November he recorded 'I ran into *realities* more than ever; and some would have been recognized and others guessed at'.[92] Perhaps trying to prevent the work being recognized as his, Byron gave the draft of what is presumably the first letter (which ends 'More in my next') to his relative Robert Charles Dallas, saying, 'Now, do you go on', proposing that he and Dallas should write alternate fictional letters to make up a full novel. Dallas, however, felt it would be impossible for him to adopt 'either the style or the objects he [Byron] had in view', and instead he used Byron's draft as the opening letter for a novel of his own, published in 1820.[93] Andrew Nicholson describes Byron's idea for an epistolary novel to be written by two people as an '[e]xtraordinarily original conception: to realize a fictional correspondence, or perhaps rather to fictionalize a "real" correspondence', and it certainly shows that, for Byron in 1813 the epistolary novel was a form still well worth exploring.[94]

For Austen, however, whose engagement with epistolary form had been much more extensive, her experimentation with letters as the basis for a novel was well and truly over by 1813. Sometime after 1805 she revived her mid-1790s novella-of-letters, *Lady Susan*, and it may have been then that she decided (apparently because of frustration with the epistolary medium) to finish it off in a third-person direct narrative: 'This Correspondence, by a meeting between some of the Parties & a separation between the others, could not, to the great detriment of the Post Office Revenue, be continued longer'.[95] In 1797 she began converting her draft of 'Elinor and Marianne' into the non-epistolary *Sense and Sensibility;* between 1798 and 1803 she was working on 'Susan' (later to become *Northanger Abbey*) – her first novel to be written from the beginning in non-epistolary form – and by 1811 she had started to convert 'First Impressions', apparently originally written in letter form, to *Pride and Prejudice* in third-person narrative, with its publication following in January 1813. Neither Byron nor Austen abandoned the epistolary form entirely, however: Byron used it to great effect in Julia's letter in *Don Juan*, and Austen included letters in her novels both as a way of conveying information needed to speed up the denouement (as in Frank Churchill's long letter of explanation towards the end of *Emma*) and as a way of fleshing out characters such as Mr Collins, with his wonderfully pompous and obtuse epistles in *Pride and Prejudice*.[96]

Austen's narrative techniques were admired from early on: as we have seen in Chapter 5, as early as 1821 Richard Whately was approving her use of third-person rather than first-person narrative. In fact Austen uses the best effects of both third- and first-person narrative in her free indirect discourse, creating an illusion by which the third-person narrative transmits the intimate subjectivity of fictional characters. Byron's technical skills, including his methods and skills of narration, were noted by his contemporaries (Francis Jeffrey commented on the 'unparalleled rapidity of narrative' in *The Giaour*), and even in the 1930s, when his reputation was at its lowest, T. S. Eliot in his largely denigratory 1937 essay nevertheless praised Byron's 'extraordinary ingenuity in story-telling', particularly in the 'Tales' and *Don Juan*, where he 'combined exoticism with actuality and developed most effectively the use of *suspense*'.[97] Byron should be admired for his ability to 'avoid . . . monotony by a dextrous turn from one subject to another', Eliot admitted grudgingly, and 'has the cardinal virtue of being never dull'.[98] Bernard Beatty notes 'the careful management of information, supplied and withheld, through which Byron controls our reactions to characters and events', and Peter Knox-Shaw points out how Byron excels in using 'a series of sharp, subjective impressions caught by a third person (either the poet or a fictional narrator) to register an intense emotional state in the protagonist'.[99]

Published or not?

The place of 'public' and 'private' writing genres in both Austen's and Byron's oeuvre has been much discussed, and studies such as Michelle Levy's of literary manuscript culture in Romantic Britain remind us of the great variety of modes that existed on this continuum in this period. Both Austen and Byron wrote for coterie audiences as well as for the public, and between them over their lifetimes they experimented with almost every method conceivable for sharing their work with others.[100] Byron's journals, for example, were private at the time of writing but from as early as

1814 were being sent to Moore for preservation and eventual publication, while Austen's juvenilia were presented in home-made 'Volumes' with the kind of front-matter (such as dedications) and chapter headings ('Chapter the First') that imitated printed books. Austen experimented with different publishers and publishing methods for her novels and was unlucky with both the sale of the valuable copyright of *Pride and Prejudice* to Egerton and the unusual, not-very-profitable 'on commission' system used for *Emma* with Murray. Byron learnt the hard way about the difference between printing for private distribution and publishing for potential profit when *Hours of Idleness* (1807) was damned by Henry Brougham's review in the *Edinburgh* (see Chapter 5), while his supposedly privately printed poem about Lord Elgin and the Parthenon Marbles, 'The Curse of Minerva' (1812), and the verses about the dissolution of his marriage – 'Fare Thee Well' and 'A Sketch from Private Life' (1816) – were leaked by the printers and made public. Austen can never have envisaged that her deathbed comic poem about St Swithin would be published by her descendants, while Byron's autobiography, which he confidently expected would shape his posthumous reputation, was burnt unseen by his friends. Two of Austen's six novels remained unpublished at her death, and more than half (208) of the total of Byron's now-known 410 poems were not published during his lifetime.[101]

'Public' and 'private' considerations also drive the content and style of the individual works of both authors and adumbrate the issue of their future fame. Levy draws attention to the 1808 *Edinburgh Review*'s (very long) article about Scott's *Marmion*, and its criticism of Scott's 'allusions to objects of temporary interest' which it describes as 'instances of bad taste, and additional proofs that the author does not always recollect, that a poet should address himself to more than one generation': in other words, to the public and not just the private reader.[102] Levy suggests that Austen knew this review (she was certainly reading *Marmion* at the time) and that she 'seems to have taken these comments to heart [by] removing, almost, it seems, under compunction many of the topical elements of her fiction before it crossed over into print'.[103] It is a mark of the rising status of the novel, and of Austen's faith in it, that she should subject her own prose to an even more severe discipline about excluding 'objects of temporary interest' than Scott did in his verse, and that she should be so scrupulous about appealing to 'more than one generation'.

But she was not wrong to do so. Although critics now scour Austen's novels for topical references to her own time, it is a considerable part of her appeal to most modern readers that they do not need to know the topical or political details of the historical background to her writing to appreciate her fiction. Her process of removing contemporary references from her narrative, and her narrowing down of creative options from a much wider range of possibilities to achieve the relative timelessness of her novels seems, as Levy suggests, to be a consequence of her bending to the demands of print, as opposed to private publication.[104]

Byron took the opposite course, and used verse to comment on many topical issues, not only in shorter poems such as 'The Curse of Minerva', 'Lines to a Lady Weeping', 'Napoleon's Farewell' and 'The Age of Bronze', but also in *Childe Harold* and, of course, in *Don Juan*. Poets such as Scott and Byron, whose 'allusions to objects of temporary interest' now need to be researched to be understood and appreciated by modern readers, are far less appealing in our century than Austen is. Because of this – and also because of the length at which the male writers (and a few female ones, such as de Staël) confidently allowed themselves to address their readers – their work is less taught both to school-students and to undergraduates than that of novelists such as Austen or generally shorter-writing poets such as Keats, who had radically different views of the role of poetry. History has, however, had its revenge on the 'Big Guys' of both sexes, and many of those who were widely read, reviewed, discussed, courted, quoted, flouted and given attention of all kinds during their lifetimes are now obliged to step back and give precedence to what the journal of the Jane Austen Society of North America has called the 'moderately successful provincial woman writer, who was destined to become one of the world's best-known and most beloved novelists'.[105]

Notes

1. Byron, *Journal*, 24 November 1813, *BLJ* 3.220.

2. Henry Austen in Austen-Leigh ed. Sutherland 145–54.

3. Henry Austen in Austen-Leigh ed. Sutherland 149–50.

4. Dow and Seth, 'Fickle fortunes' np.

5. Dow and Seth, 'Fickle fortunes' np.

6. *JAL* 160–1, to Cassandra Austen, 27–28 December 1808.

7. Mackintosh (1835) 472, quoted in Austen-Leigh ed. Sutherland 111.

8. Tomalin 243.

9. *LBCMP* 184, 493.

10. *BLJ* 3.207, *Journal*, 16 November 1813.

11. *BLJ* 3.244, *Journal*, 18 February 1814.

12. *LBCMP* 222.

13. *LBCPW* 5.680. The prices paid by Murray to de Staël were far higher than those offered to Austen. In 1813 de Staël received £1,500 for *De l'Allemagne* (*Germany*), while in 1815 Austen was offered £450 altogether for the copyrights of *Emma, Mansfield Park* and *Sense and Sensibility*.

14. *Persuasion* vol. 2, chap. 11, 253–4.

15. *LBCPW* 5.71. In their edition, Stauffer and Sachs (2022) reverse the next two stanzas (lines 1553–60 and 1561–9) so that they are in the order Byron intended them to be.

16. McGann's commentary, *LBCPW* 5.680.

17. De Staël (1807) 358 and de Staël (1796) 146.

18. *LBCPW* 5.680.

19. *BLJ* 3.232, *Journal*, 5 December 1813. *LBCMP* 223.

20. Karen Caines, private correspondence March–April 2015. Beer 130.

21. Ovid *Heroïde*s 19.

22. See Pope (1720).

23. Harris 219.

24. *LBCMP* 223.

25. *LBCPW* 5.72.

26. *DJ* 2.144–5 and *DJ* 2.591–2, *LBCPW* 5.94–9 and 5.112.

27. *LBCMP* 205 and 524, with grateful thanks for this reference to Karen Caines.

28. Ovid, *Heroïdes* 1, quoted in Hobhouse ed. Graham.

29. De Forest (1988) np.

30. *JAL* 306, letter 132(D) to James Stanier Clarke, 11 December 1815.

31. De Forest (2018) 109.

32. *JAL* 170, to Cassandra Austen, 24 January 1809. The official title of the 'Eton Latin Grammar' was *The Introduction to the Latin Tongue* by M. Pote and E. Williams (1758). The full quotation is: 'Propria quae maribus tribuuntur, mascula dicas' ('Proper names which are given to Males, or Hees, are masculine'). Austen writes 'que' for 'quae'. See Austen ed. Todd and Bree 720.

33. Cope 143–51. James or Jane Austen 50.

34. See Tomalin 63. Le Faye supports Cope's arguments in Le Faye (1998) 31 and *JAFR* 68.

35. Richard Tate np. There is no reference to Hero and Leander in the 1801 edition of *Elegant Extracts in Prose* that Jane gave to her niece Anna.

36. Nahum Tate, 'Hero's answer to Leander', in Dryden (ed.) 68–9.

37. Clery (2022) 9.

38. Austen ed. Sabor lxvii.

39. *LBCPW* 5.113.

40. *DJ* 16.61 and 529–30, *LBCPW* 5.638.

41. Austen ed. Sabor lxii.

42. Litz 1–3.

43. Austen ed. Sabor xxxii.

44. Austen ed. Sabor lxiii, 223, 24, 43, 54, 129, 42 and 6.

45. Austen ed. Sabor 11–12. The dates given here for items in the juvenilia are those proposed in Austen ed. Sabor xxviii–xxix.

46. Austen ed. Sabor lxii, 114.

47. Austen-Leigh ed. Sutherland 39–40, 43.

48. Austen-Leigh ed. Sutherland, 43.

49. McAleer 15.

50. Austen ed. Sabor 72.

51. *Quarterly Review* 128 (January and April 1870) 200, quoted Austen ed. Todd and Bree xxxvii.

52. Austen-Leigh (2009) 'Preface' to *Lady Susan*, 202: 'I have lately received permission to print the following tale from the author's niece, Lady Knatchbull, of Provender, in Kent, to whom the autograph copy was given. . . . The tale itself is scarcely one on which a literary reputation could have been founded: but though, like some plants, it may be too slight to stand alone, it may, perhaps, be supported by the strength of her more firmly rooted works.'

53. Joan Austen-Leigh 178.

54. Austen ed. Sabor xxxvii.

55. Joan Austen-Leigh 178.

56. Gale 24, quoted in Austen ed. Sabor xlviii.

57. See Gilbert and Gubar 148–85. Gilbert and Gubar 115–16, quoted in Austen ed. Sabor liv.

58. Teerlink i.

59. Arnold 168.

60. Murray ed. Nicholson 273.

61. Lockhart 32.

62. O'Connell 177–8. Murray ed. Nicholson 297.

63. *BLJ* 6.105, to John Murray, 6 April 1819.

64. Murray ed. Nicholson 297.

65. O'Connell 182.

66. O'Connell 180–1.

67. O'Connell 197. *LBCPW* 5.192–3 Jane's eldest brother James used the same metaphor when he wrote in *The Loiterer* 1,1: 'of all chymical mixtures, ink is the most dangerous'.

68. Schoina 216.

69. Doody 101.

70. *LBCPW* 5.10–11.

71. Beatty 101.

72. James 200.

73. Austen ed. Sabor 176–9.

74. *NA* vol. 2, chap. 16, 259.

75. *JAFR* 99.

76. Austen ed. Todd and Bree 249.

77. 'On Sir Home Popham's sentence – April 1807' 1–8, Austen ed. Todd and Bree 246.

78. 'To the Memory of Mrs Lefroy . . .' 1–4 and 49–52, Austen ed. Todd and Bree 247–9.

79. *LBCPW* 7.81–2.

80. Austen ed. Todd and Bree 255.

81. Austen ed. Todd and Bree xxxiv.

82. *LBCPW* 3.309.

83. *LBCPW* 6.237.

84. *BLJ* 2.97, to Francis Hodgson, 13 September 1811.

85. Moore to Byron, 19 February and 16 March 1822: Dowden (1964) 2.503–5.

86. *LBCMP* 347.

87. *LBCMP* 51–8 and 324–9.

88. *LBCMP* 85–7 and 355–8.

89. Austen ed. Sabor 4, 13, 47.

90. *LBCMP* 46–8 and 315–17. *BLJ* 3.205, *Journal*, 14 November 1813.

91. *LBCMP* 46–8.

92. *BLJ* 3.209, *Journal*, 17 November 1813, and *BLJ* 3.217, *Journal*, 23 November 1813.

93. *Sir Francis Darrell; or, The Vortex: A Novel.* Austen would not have approved of the title. On 28 September 1814 (*JAL* 277) she wrote to her niece Anna

about her draft of a novel: 'Devereux Forester's being ruined by his Vanity is extremely good; but I wish you would not let him plunge into a "vortex of Dissipation". I do not object to the Thing, but I cannot bear the expression; – it is such thorough novel slang – and so old, that I dare say Adam met with it in the first novel he opened.'

94. *LBCMP* 316.

95. Austen ed. Sabor 75. Levy 188.

96. *Emma* vol. 3, chap. 14, 476–83. *P&P* vol. 1, chap. 13, 48 and vol. 3, chap. 15, 401.

97. Beatty (2022) 38.

98. Eliot 198–200.

99. Beatty (2022) 38. Knox-Shaw 67–8.

100. Levy 172.

101. Levy 141.

102. Anonymous 35.

103. Levy 207. *JAL* 131, to Cassandra Austen, 20–22 June 1808.

104. Levy 207–8.

105. Dow and Seth 'Fickle fortunes' np.

CONCLUSION
'A GREAT STRUGGLE ABOUT WHAT THEY CALL "*CLASSICAL AND ROMANTIC*"'

Austen's apparent decision to follow the *Edinburgh Review*'s advice to eschew 'allusions to objects of temporary interest' and to 'address [her]self to more than one generation' is an example of her respect for Augustan principles. Samuel Johnson's view was that 'Whatever withdraws us from the power of our senses; whatever makes the past, the distant, or the future predominate over the present, advances us in the dignity of thinking beings'.[1] During Austen's and Byron's lifetime, however, the source and purpose of poetry came to be identified in a very different way from that advocated by the *Edinburgh*. Where eighteenth-century poetics had praised the general and envisaged the writer as addressing a cultivated and homogeneous audience, the generations following looked for the source of poetry in the intensity of the poet's own feelings, individual perceptions and unique experience, taking as his (or occasionally her) subject matter the workings of their own mind. Similar principles came to be pursued in architecture, music and visual art as well as literature, and William Blake's marginal comment on Sir Joshua Reynolds's *Discourses* (1778) expresses the change with characteristic bluntness: 'To Generalize is to be an Idiot. To Particularize is the alone Distinction of Merit'.[2]

Although the term 'romance' was sometimes used as a subtitle by Austen's and Byron's contemporary poets and novelists, it was generally not given to works that would later be designated literarily 'Romantic', or ones that concerned a 'love interest' in the modern sense of the term, but to creations or collections with medieval, chivalric and historical backgrounds. Scott was a pioneer in using this 'romance' label in English: his *Minstrelsy of the Scottish Borders* consisted of 'Historical and romantic ballads' collected by him from local traditions, while the first (anonymous) collected edition of his Waverley novels was entitled 'Romances by the author of *Waverley*'.[3] In the preface to *Marmion* (subtitled 'A Tale of Flodden Field, A Romance in Six Cantos') Scott explained that he called his poems 'romantic' in order to pre-empt any suggestion that he was claiming to write an epic. Byron adopted the Spenserian form of the word when he subtitled the two first cantos of *Childe Harold* a 'Romaunt'. Austen, on the other hand, firmly rejected the idea of writing a (prose) romance. When advised by the Prince Regent's librarian that 'any Historical Romance illustrative of the History of the august house of Cobourg, would just now be very interesting', she protested (as we have seen in Chapter 5) that she 'could no more write a Romance than an Epic Poem'.[4]

> I could not sit seriously down to write a serious Romance under any other motive than to save my Life, & if it were indispensable for me to keep it up & never relax into laughing at myself or other people, I am sure I should be hung before I had finished the first Chapter.

'Romanticism' is not a term Austen would have been familiar with, and Byron too was puzzled by it. At Coppet in 1816 he had met Madame de Staël's constant companion August Wilhelm von Schlegel, whose Vienna lectures on fine art and literature (1808–9) played a key role in defining Romanticism by distinguishing its 'organic' qualities from the supposedly 'mechanical' character of classicism and neo-classicism. These lectures were not widely known in translation until later, however, and in 1820 Byron wrote in his draft dedication of *Marino Faliero* to Goethe:

> I perceive that in Germany, as well as in Italy, there is a great struggle about what they call *'Classical and Romantic'* terms which were not subjects of Classification in England – at least when I left it four or five years ago. Some of the English scribblers (it is true), abused Pope and Swift, but the reason was that they themselves did not know how to write in either prose or verse – but nobody thought them worth making a sect of. Perhaps there may be something of the sort sprung up lately – but I have not heard much about it, and it would be such bad taste that I should be very sorry to believe it.[5]

In equating the lately sprung-up 'Romantic' with 'bad taste', Byron was striking the same note as that of a well-known essay of 1804 by John Foster, 'On the Application of the Epithet Romantic'. Foster, a Baptist minister, was a major contributor to the *Eclectic Review*, and may well (judging on stylistic grounds) have been the 1807 reviewer of Byron's *Hours of Idleness* there.[6] *Essays, in a Series of Letters to a Friend* ran through at least thirty-five English and American editions in the next two decades, and in it Foster described 'romantic' as 'a convenient exploding word, of more special deriding significance than the other words of its order, such as wild, extravagant, visionary . . . always understood to deny sound reason to whatever it is fixed upon', and, like Cervantes' Don Quixote, occupying 'a dubious frontier space between the rational and the insane'.[7]

Not surprisingly, neither Byron nor Austen identified themselves as 'Romantics' or saw themselves as belonging to a British or European 'Romantic movement'. Byron grouped Wordsworth, Coleridge and Southey together under the epithet 'Lakers' because of their common residence in the Lake District, and accepted the *Quarterly*'s identification of Keats and Leigh Hunt as 'Cockney poets', supposedly born within the sound of the church bells of St-Mary-le-Bow in the City of London's Cheapside.[8] Austen made no mention of Blake, Coleridge, Shelley or Keats in her work or letters, and allowed Wordsworth only a brief appearance as the 'true soul of poetry' in the list reeled off by the 'downright silly' character Sir Edward Denham in *Sanditon* (1817).[9] Byron himself was omitted from one of the twentieth century's defining critical texts on Romanticism, M. H. Abrams's *Natural Supernaturalism* (1971), because of his satirical take on the Romantic characteristics of his contemporaries.[10] Elsewhere, however, he has continued to be classed as a leading Romantic, not only for his literary work (particularly *Childe Harold's Pilgrimage*, with its visionary qualities, its preoccupation with the past, its focus on isolation and melancholy and its intense representation of the self), but also because of his dramatic life story, with its passions, its challenges to the establishment, its sexual transgressions and its commitment to freedom through his active involvement in the struggles for Italian nationalism and the liberation of Greece. The increasing number of critical studies that have considered Austen alongside her Romantic contemporaries have cited Romantic features such as her focus on the interiority of individual characters including Fanny Price and Anne Elliot; the development of her heroines from youth to maturity in the tradition of the *bildungsroman*; her great celebration of the natural world and her evocation of autumnal nature as pathetic fallacy for Anne's melancholy in *Persuasion*.[11]

Romantic siblings

In terms of another commonly perceived characteristic of Romanticism – its preoccupation with incest – it is well known that both Austen and Byron gave exceptional value to sibling relationships. Byron participated in dangerous reality as well as in fiction in this preoccupation, while Austen, writing of the bond between Fanny and William Price in *Mansfield Park*, celebrates the way in which their shared childhood is 'a strengthener of love, in which even the conjugal tie is beneath the fraternal'.[12] In her marriage plots she often favoured endogamous attraction over exogamous allure, and her novels include many romances that seem to escape being incestuous only by a whisker. Elinor and Edward in *Sense and Sensibility*, and Emma and Mr Knightley in *Emma*, are brothers- and sisters-in-law, while Fanny and Edmund in *Mansfield Park* are first cousins brought up more or less as siblings. In real life, too, Jane's brother Henry married their first cousin the glamorous widow Eliza de Feuillide, while Byron's paternal grandparents were first cousins, and his half-sister Augusta was the wife of their first cousin George Leigh.

In Byron's work his love for his half-sister is often the subject of tortured and despairing – if fictional – expression, as in his 1816 play *Manfred*:

> *Manfred:* She was like me in lineaments – her eyes,
>   Her hair, her features, all, to the very tone
>   Even of her voice, they said were like to mine;
>   But soften'd all, and temper'd into beauty . . .
>   I loved her, and destroy'd her!
> *Witch:* With thy hand?
> *Manfred:* Not with my hand, but heart – which broke her heart –
> It gazed on mine, and wither'd.
>
> (*Manfred* 2.2.105–19)[13]

But what often comes across, in Byron's as well as in Austen's writing, is the domestic comfortableness of the relationship with a sibling or near relation and the enjoyment of that sense of familiarity, and it is this tone that characterizes Byron's letters to Augusta in 1816, not long after the wreck of his marriage and his self-exile from England:

> What a fool was I to marry – and *you* not very wise – my dear – we might have lived so single and so happy – as old maids and bachelors; I shall never find any one like you – nor you (vain as it may seem) like me. We are just formed to pass our lives together, and therefore – we – at least – I – am by a crowd of circumstances removed from the only being who could ever have loved me, or whom I can unmixedly feel attached to. Had you been a Nun – and I a Monk – we might

have talked through a grate instead of across the sea – no matter – my voice and my heart are ever thine.[14]

Another Romantic preoccupation for both Austen and Byron, deftly analysed by Peter W. Graham, is their common penchant for the Gothic and its ambiguities, so that in *Northanger Abbey* Gothic conventions reveal truth in spirit if not in fact, while the 'Norman Abbey' cantos of *Don Juan* use Gothic slipperiness to teach us that in a mixed world we should neglect the reality of neither mind, soul nor body (as represented by the three women linked romantically with Juan: the intellectual Lady Adeline, the spiritual Aurora Raby and the fleshly Duchess of Fitz-Fulke).[15] Austen's Northanger Abbey is made ghostly by Catherine's own Radcliffe-inspired perceptions, while in Byron's Norman Abbey Juan is presented as a young, foreign visitor who is subjected to the social and political complexities of a grand English house party. After he has heard the spooky 'Ballad of the Black Friar' sung to him by his hostess, Juan retires to his room in the far reaches of the supposedly haunted abbey and is visited in his bedroom two nights running at midnight by a figure in a monk's habit. The second night's figure turns out to be the seductive Duchess of Fitz-Fulke, dressed in a monk's habit; but we never learn whether the figure on the *first* night was also the Duchess in disguise – or in fact a 'real' ghost. Given Byron's and Austen's different sense of propriety, however, there is a very different outcome to their two haunted abbey stories: whereas Austen's novel concludes with an exemplary marriage between her heroine and a handsome young clergyman, Byron's ends with the two protagonists decidedly the worse for wear when they meet at breakfast the morning after.

But Byron certainly did not set out to be a 'Romantic' and, as we have seen, he maintained a profound respect for many aspects of eighteenth-century culture and literature, seeking to emulate its realism, irony, wit, humour and sociability in his social life, letters, criticism and verse, especially in his later work. Neither Byron nor Austen aimed to idealize or idolize human nature, as many of the Romantics did: Byron's Manfred characterizes humanity as 'half dust half deity / alike unfit to sink or soar', while Austen declared that 'pictures of perfection as you know make me sick & wicked'.[16] For both of them reality took precedence over imagination, and for Byron even in the midst of fantasy 'truth is always strange; / Stranger than fiction', and, he surmised, 'if it could be told, / How much would novels gain by the exchange!'[17] They shared what Graham calls a 'sharp-eyed empirical way of showing human beings and their institutions in all their social and psychological subtlety'; and if they *are* to be classified as Romantics, it is, as Graham demonstrates, as 'the two great Romantic writers with a sense of humor'.[18]

If Romanticism is not especially useful here as a concept to define these authors – to differentiate them from their contemporaries, or to show how they related to each other in their lives or writing – perhaps it may be more helpful to categorize them both simply as 'Regency' people and writers. This approach makes use of a historical label they would both have understood themselves, and, although strictly applied only to Prince George's tenure as Regent between 1811 and 1820, it is now often used more widely to relate to culture, art, politics, fashion, institutions and even television drama series set anywhere between 1790 and Queen Victoria's accession in 1837. Both Austen and Byron, as we have seen, were at the heart of this era and could claim personal links with the Prince Regent, and both took as a primary element of their work the critique of this period's characteristics and developments, with Byron often deploying exotic material to contemplate the history and politics of his own time and place, and Austen ostensibly avoiding politics but dwelling with minute precision on the modifications in the class structure and other social changes that defined these decades. This is the context in which I have tried to show Austen and Byron, both together and apart, as characteristic of this intriguing period, and to argue that the continuing appeal of their work and the ongoing interest in their lives and the Regency era brings them into relationship and touching distance not only with each other but with us as well.

Notes

1. Johnson (1791) 346.

2. Blake's annotation to 'Rubens' in Sir Joshua Reynolds's *Discourses*, in Blake ed. Keynes 3.13.

3. St Clair (2004) 211–16.

4. *JAL* 312, to James Stanier Clarke, 1 April 1816.

5. Rejected 'Dedication' to *Marino Faliero*, 14 October 1820, *LBCPW* 4.546–7.

6. Anonymous (*Eclectic Review* 1807) 700–2.

7. Foster, Essay 3, 'On the Application of the Epithet Romantic', letter 1, 241–2.

8. 'Dedication' to *Don Juan*, 6, *LBCPW* 5.3. *BLJ* 8.102, to John Murray, 26 April 1821.

9. *Sanditon* chap. 7, 176.
10. Abrams 13.
11. See Brownstein, Deresiewicz, Fischer, Lau and Wootton.
12. *MP* vol. 2, chap. 6, 273–4.
13. *LBCPW* 4.74.
14. *BLJ* 5.96, to Augusta Leigh, 17 September 1816.
15. *DJ* 16.393–448, *LBCPW* 5.633–5.
16. *Manfred* 1.2.40–1, *LBCPW* 4.63. *JAL* 335, to Fanny Knight, 23–25 March 1817.
17. *DJ* 14.801–3, *LBCPW* 5.388.
18. Graham (2008) 1.

BIBLIOGRAPHY

Abrams, M. H., *Natural Supernaturalism*. New York: Norton, 1971.

Anonymous, (trans. Jean-Baptiste Benoît Eyriès), *Fantasmagoriana, ou Recueil d'histoires d'apparitions de spectres, revenans, fantômes, etc.*; Tome premier (Paris: F. Schoel, 1812).

Anonymous, 'Art. VII. *Hours of Idleness*, a Series of Poems, Original and Translated. By George Gordon, Lord Byron, a Minor', *Eclectic Review* 3 (November 1807): 700–2. https://ir.vanderbilt.edu/handle/1803/1826 (accessed 17 January 2023).

Anonymous, 'Art XI. *Childe Harold's Pilgrimage*. A Romaunt. By Lord Byron . . . 1812', *Eclectic Review* 8, no. 2 (June–December 1812): 630–41.

Armstrong, James, *Romantic Actors, Romantic Dramas: British Tragedy on the Regency Stage*. Cham: Palgrave Macmillan, 2022.

Arnold, Matthew, *Essays in Criticism: Second Series*. London: Macmillan, 1888.

Auden, W. H., 'Byron: The Making of a Comic Poet', *The New York Review*, 18 August 1966, np.

Auden, W. H., 'Letter to Lord Byron'. Originally published in *Letters from Iceland* by W. H. Auden and Louis MacNeice. London: Faber and Faber, 1937; revised text in *Longer Contemporary Poems*, ed. David Wright. Harmondsworth: Penguin, 1966. https://www.arlindo-correia.com/lord_byron.html (accessed 25 November 2022).

Austen, Caroline Mary Craven, 'My Aunt Jane Austen: A Memoir' (1867), in J. E. Austen-Leigh, *A Memoir of Jane Austen: And Other Family Recollections*, ed. with an Introduction and Notes by Kathryn Sutherland, 163–82. Oxford: Oxford World's Classics, 2002, reissued 2008.

Austen, Henry, 'A Memoir of Miss Austen' (1817), in J. E. Austen-Leigh, *A Memoir of Jane Austen: And Other Family Recollections*, ed. with an Introduction and Notes by Kathryn Sutherland, 145–54. Oxford: Oxford World's Classics, 2002, reissued 2008.

Austen, Henry, 'Biographical Notice of the Author' (1833), in J. E. Austen-Leigh, *A Memoir of Jane Austen: And Other Family Recollections*, ed. with an Introduction and Notes by Kathryn Sutherland, 135–43. Oxford: Oxford World's Classics, 2002, reissued 2008.

Austen, James, *The Complete Poems of James Austen, Jane Austen's Eldest Brother*, ed. David Selwyn. Chawton: The Jane Austen Society, 2003.

Austen, James, *The Loiterer, number 1, Saturday January 31st 1789*, 1. Oxford: Printed for the Author, 1789. http: www.theloterer.org/loiterer/no1.html (accessed 26 November 2022).

Bibliography

Austen, James or Jane Austen, 'To the AUTHOR of the LOITERER', in *The Loiterer, number 9, Saturday March 28th, 1789*, 50–2. Oxford: Printed for the Author, 1789. http://www.theloiterer.org/loiterer/no9.html (accessed 26 November 2022).

Austen, Jane, *Emma*, ed. Richard Cronin and Dorothy McMillan. *The Cambridge Edition of the Works of Jane Austen*. Cambridge: Cambridge University Press, 2005.

Austen, Jane, *Jane Austen's Fiction Manuscripts. Two Chapters of Persuasion: Diplomatic Display*. London: British Library, MS Egerton 3038. https://janeausten.ac.uk/manuscripts/blpers/1.html (accessed 13 January 2023).

Austen, Jane, *Juvenilia*, ed. Peter Sabor. *The Cambridge Edition of the Works of Jane Austen*. Cambridge: Cambridge University Press, 2006.

Austen, Jane, *Later Manuscripts*, ed. Janet Todd and Linda Bree. *The Cambridge Edition of the Works of Jane Austen*. Cambridge: Cambridge University Press, 2008.

Austen, Jane, *Mansfield Park*, ed. John Wiltshire. *The Cambridge Edition of the Works of Jane Austen*. Cambridge: Cambridge University Press, 2005.

Austen, Jane, 'Manuscript Copy of Byron's Poem "Napoleon's farewell" in the Hand of Jane Austen, *c.* 1815'. University of Southampton, Special Collections, MS 8. https://archives.soton.ac.uk/records/MS8 (accessed 9 December 2022).

Austen, Jane, *Northanger Abbey*, ed. Barbara Benedict and Deirdre Le Faye. *The Cambridge Edition of the Works of Jane Austen*. Cambridge: Cambridge University Press, 2006.

Austen, Jane, *Persuasion*, ed. Janet Todd and Antje Blank. *The Cambridge Edition of the Works of Jane Austen*. Cambridge: Cambridge University Press, 2006.

Austen, Jane, *Plan of a Novel, According to Hints from Various Quarters*. New York: Morgan Library & Museum, MS. MA 1034.1. https://www.themorgan.org/literary-historical/81844 (accessed 20 November 2022).

Austen, Jane, *Pride and Prejudice*, ed. Pat Rogers. *The Cambridge Edition of the Works of Jane Austen*. Cambridge: Cambridge University Press, 2006.

Austen, Jane, *Sense and Sensibility*, ed. Edward Copeland. *The Cambridge Edition of the Works of Jane Austen*. Cambridge: Cambridge University Press, 2006.

Austen-Leigh, J. E., *A Memoir of Jane Austen: Together with 'Lady Susan': A Novel*. Cambridge: Cambridge World Classics, 2009.

Austen-Leigh, J. E., 'A Memoir of Jane Austen (1871)', in *A Memoir of Jane Austen: And Other Family Recollections*, ed. with an Introduction and Notes by Kathryn Sutherland, 1–134. Oxford: Oxford World's Classics, 2002, reissued 2008.

Austen-Leigh, Joan, 'The Juvenilia: A Family "Veiw"', in *Jane Austen's Beginnings: The Juvenilia and Lady Susan*, ed. J. David Grey, 173–80. Ann Arbor: UMI Research Press, 1989.

Austen-Leigh, Richard Arthur, ed., *Austen Papers, 1704–1856*. Colchester: Spottiswoode, Ballantyne & Co., 1942.

Austen-Leigh, William and Richard Arthur Austen-Leigh, *Jane Austen: Her Life and Letters, A Family Record*. London: Smith, Elder & Co., 1913.

Austen-Leigh, William and George Montagu Knight, *Chawton Manor and its Owners*. London: Smith, Elder & Co., 1911.

Avery-Jones, John F., 'Henry Austen's Tax Debt as Receiver-General of Taxes for Oxfordshire', *Persuasions On-Line* 43, no. 1 (winter 2022). https://jasna.org/

publications-2/persuasions-online/volume-43-no-1/avery-jones/ (accessed 13 January 2023).

Bader, Ted, 'Mr. Woodhouse is not a Hypochondriac!', *Persuasions On-Line* 21, no. 2 (summer 2000). https://jasna.org/persuasions/on-line/vol21no2/bader.html (accessed 18 March 2023).

Barchas, Janine, *Matters of Fact in Jane Austen: History, Location and Celebrity*. Baltimore: Johns Hopkins University Press, 2012.

Barron, Stephanie, *Jane and the Madness of Lord Byron*. London: Bantam, 2010.

Barry, Elizabeth, 'Jane Austen and Lord Byron: Connections', *Persuasions* 8 (1986): 39–41.

Beatty, Bernard, *Reading Byron*. Liverpool: Liverpool University Press, 2022.

Beckett, John, *Byron and Newstead: The Aristocrat and the Abbey*. Cranbury: Associated University Presses, 2001.

Beer, Gillian, '"Our unnatural No-voice": The Heroic Epistle, Pope, and Women's Gothic', Modern Humanities Research Association, *The Yearbook of English Studies* 12, 'Heroes and the Heroic', Special Number (1982): 125–51.

Bennett, Ellie, 'Who was Eliza Hall Part 2 – Jane Austen and Jamaica', Blog posted 15 October 2017. Portraits of Jane Austen: Who was Eliza Hall Part 2 – Jane Austen and Jamaica (janeaustenportraits.blogspot.com) (accessed 21 November 2022).

Bennett, Stuart, 'Lord Moira and the Austens', *Persuasions* 35 (2013): 129–52.

Blake, William, *The Writings of William Blake*, ed. Geoffrey Keynes. London: Nonesuch Press, 1925.

Bond, Geoffrey and Christine Kenyon Jones, *Dangerous to Show: Byron and His Portraits*. London: Unicorn, 2020.

Bone, Drummond, ed., *The Cambridge Companion to Byron*. Cambridge: Cambridge University Press, 2004.

Bordman, Gerald, ed., *The Oxford Companion to American Theatre*. Oxford: Oxford University Press, 1984.

Boswell, James, *Life of Johnson, Unabridged*, ed. Robert William Chapman, introduced by Pat Rogers. Oxford: Oxford University Press, 1998.

Boyes, Megan, *Love without Wings: A Biography of Elizabeth Pigot*. Derby: J.M. Tatler & Son Ltd, 1988.

Boyes, Megan, *My Amiable Mama: A Biography of Mrs Catherine Gordon Byron*. Derby: J.M. Tatler & Son Ltd, 1991.

Brand, Emily, *The Fall of the House of Byron: Scandal and Seduction in Georgian England*. London: John Murray, 2020.

Brougham, Henry, 'Critique, from the *Edinburgh Review* on Lord Byron's Poems, which occasioned "English Bards and Scotch Reviewers"', 2–8. London: W.T. Sherwin, 1820. https://catalog.hathitrust.org/Record/008915813 (accessed 25 November 2022).

Brown, Simon, 'Engaging New Audiences at Newstead Abbey', *Social History in Museums* 43 (Social History Curators Group, 2019): 61–5.

Brownstein, Rachel M., 'Jane Austen and Lord Byron 1813–1815', *Persuasions* 16 (1994): 175–84.

Bibliography

Bull, John [*pseud.* John Gibson Lockhart], *Letter to the Right Hon. Lord Byron.* Edinburgh: William Wright, 1821. https://lordbyron.org/doc.php?choose =JoLockh.1821.JohnBull.xml (accessed 22 November 2022).

Burns, Margie, "'Pride and Prejudice": Jane Austen, Frederick Douglass, and Louisa May Alcott', *Persuasions On-Line* 41, no. 2 (summer 2021). https://jasna .org/publications-2/persuasions-online/volume-41-no-2/burns/ (accessed 15 January 2023).

Burton, Anthony and John Murdoch, *Byron: An Exhibition to Commemorate the 150th Anniversary of His Death in the Greek War of Liberation, 19 April 1824,* catalogue. London: Victoria and Albert Museum, 1974.

Butler, Marilyn, *Jane Austen and the War of Ideas.* Oxford: Clarendon Press, 1975, new introduction 1987, reprinted 1999.

Byrne, Paula, *Jane Austen and the Theatre.* London: Hambledon and London, 2002.

Byron, George Gordon Noel, Lord, ed. Peter Cochran, 'Byron's Correspondence and Journals 09: From Venice, November 1816–December 1817'. https:// petercochran.files.wordpress.com/2009/02/09-venice-1816-18174.pdf (accessed 23 November 2022).

Byron, George Gordon Noel, Lord, ed. Peter Cochran, 'Byron's Correspondence with John Murray, 2: 1816–1819'. http://petercochran.files.wordpress.com/2011 /01/byron-and-murray-1816-1819.pdf (accessed 23 November 2022).

Byron, George Gordon Noel, Lord, ed. Peter Cochran, 'Byron's Correspondence with John Murray, 3: 1820–1824'. https://petercochran.files.wordpress.com /2010/09/byron-and-murray-1820-18241.pdf (accessed 23 November 2022).

Byron, George Gordon Noel, Lord, *Letters and Journals,* ed. Rowland E. Prothero, 6 vols. London: John Murray, 1898–1904.

Byron, George Gordon Noel, Lord, ed. Peter Cochran, *Marino Faliero, Doge of Venice, An Historical Tragedy, in Five Acts, by Lord Byron.* http://newsteadabbeybyrons ociety.org/works/downloads/marino_faliero.pdf (accessed 11 December 2022).

Caplan, Clive, 'Jane Austen's Banker Brother: Henry Thomas Austen of Austen & Co., 1801–1816', *Persuasions* 20 (1998): 69–90.

Caplan, Clive, 'The Missteps and Misdeeds of Henry Austen's Bank', *The Jane Austen Society Annual Report* 2010: 103–9.

Carhart, Margaret Sprague, *Life and Work of Joanna Baillie.* New Haven: Yale University Press, 1923. https://electricscotland.com/history/baillie/index.htm (accessed 21 November 2022).

Carpenter, Humphrey, *The Seven Lives of John Murray: The Story of a Publishing Dynasty.* London: John Murray, 2009.

Chater, Kathleen, *Untold Histories: Black people in England and Wales during the period of the British slave-trade, c.1660-1807.* Manchester: Manchester University Press, 2009.

Clery, E. J., *Jane Austen, The Banker's Sister.* London: Biteback, 2017.

Clery, E. J., 'Jane's Juvenilia: The Burlesque Works that Baffled Jane's Own Family', *Times Literary Supplement,* 8 April 2022: 9.

Clery, E. J., 'Old Ways for Publishing to be Difficult: Jane Austen in the Literary Marketplace', *The Author* 124, no. 4 (2013): 131–2.

Cobbett, William, *Rural Rides,* 2 vols. London: Dent, 1853.

Cobbett, William, 'The Collision', *Weekly Political Register* 81 (August 1833): page not given. https://archive.org/stream/dli.bengal.10689.14202/10689.14202_djvu .txt (accessed 13 January 2023).

Cochran, Peter, ed., *Byron in London*. Newcastle: Cambridge Scholars Publishing, 2008.

Cochran, Peter, 'Byron's Library: The Three Book Sale Catalogues', 2009. https:// petercochran.files.wordpress.com/2009/03/byrons_library.pdf (accessed 23 November 2022).

Cochran, Peter, 'Review of "*The Letters of John Murray to Lord Byron*, edited by Andrew Nicholson"'. http://petercochran.files.wordpress.com/2010/03/letters-of -john-murray3.pdf (accessed 23 November 2022).

Cochran, Peter and Shona M. Allan, eds, *Byron at the Theatre*. Newcastle: Cambridge Scholars Publishing, 2008.

Coleridge, Henry Nelson, *Specimens of the Table Talk of Samuel Taylor Coleridge*, 2nd edn. London: John Murray, 1836.

Cope, Zachary, 'Who was Sophia Sentiment? Was she Jane Austen?', *Book Collector* 15 (Spring 1966): 143–51.

Copeland, Edward and Juliet McMaster, *The Cambridge Companion to Jane Austen*, 2nd edn. Cambridge: Cambridge University Press, 2011.

Corley, T. A. B., 'Jane Austen and Her Brother Henry's Bank Failure 1815–16', *The Jane Austen Society Report 1998 (Collected Reports 1996–2000)*: 139–50.

Corley, T. A. B., 'Jane Austen and John Murray: Response to a Lecture by Kathryn Sutherland', *The Jane Austen Society Annual Report* 2012: 47–50.

Corley, T. A. B., 'Jane Austen's Dealings with Her Publishers', *The Jane Austen Society Annual Report* 2011: 127–38.

Cowper, William, *The Complete Poetical Works*, ed. H. S. Milford. London: Oxford University Press, 1911.

Creevey, Thomas, *The Creevey Papers: A Selection from the Correspondence and Diaries of the Late Thomas Creevey M.P.*, 2 vols, ed. Sir Herbert Maxwell. London: John Murray, 1903.

Crompton, Louis, *Byron and Greek Love: Homophobia in 19th-Century England*. London: Faber and Faber, 1985.

Cruikshank, George, *Forty Illustrations of Lord Byron*. London, J. Robins, 1824–5.

Daiches, David, 'Jane Austen, Karl Marx, and the Aristocratic Dance', *The American Scholar* 17, no. 3 (1948): 289–96.

Davidson, Hilary, 'Reconstructing Jane Austen's Silk Pelisse, 1812–1814', *Costume* 49, no. 2 (2105): 198–223.

De Forest, Mary, *Jane Austen: Closet Classicist*. CreateSpace Independent Publishing Platform, 2018.

De Forest, Mary, 'Jane Austen and the Anti-Heroic Tradition', *Persuasions* 10 (1988): 11–21.

De Giustino, David, 'Finding an Archbishop: The Whigs and Richard Whately in 1831', *Church History* 64, no. 2 (June 1995): 218–36.

Deresiewicz, William, *Jane Austen and the Romantic Poets*. New York: Columbia University Press, 2004.

Doody, Margaret Anne, 'Jane Austen, that Disconcerting "child"', in *The Child Writer from Austen to Woolf*, ed. Christine Alexander and Juliet McMaster, 101–20. Cambridge: Cambridge University Press, 2005.

Dow, Gillian, 'Theatre and Theatricality; Or, Jane Austen and Learning the Art of Dialogue', *Persuasions* 43 (2021): 111–27.

Dow, Gillian with Catriona Seth (curators), 'Fickle Fortunes: Jane Austen and Madame de Staël', report of *Reimagining Reputations* exhibition at Chawton House Library, *Persuasions On-Line* 38, no. 1 (2017). https://jasna.org/publications-2/persuasions-online/vol38no1/dow-simpson-seth-intro/exhibit-2-article/ (accessed 13 January 2023).

Drabble, Margaret, 'Foreword', in *Jane Austen's Beginnings: The Juvenilia and* Lady Susan, ed. J. David Grey, xiii–xiv. Ann Arbor: UMI Research Press, 1989.

Dryden, John, ed., *Ovid's Epistles Translated by Several Hands*. London: Jacob Tonson, 1680.

Eliot, Sir Charles, *Turkey in Europe*, 2nd edn. London: Frank Cass & Co., 1908.

Eliot, T. S., 'Byron (1937)', in *On Poetry and Poets*, 193–206. London: Faber and Faber, 1957.

Erdman, David V., 'Byron's Stage Fright: The History of His Ambition and Fear of Writing for the Stage', *ELH* 6, no. 3 (1939): 219–43. https://www.jstor.org/stable/2871556 (accessed 21 March 2022).

Farrell, Stephen, 'Knatchbull, Sir Edward', in *The History of Parliament: The House of Commons 1820–1832*, ed. D. R. Fisher, 2009 (Crown copyright and The History of Parliament Trust 1964–2020). http://www.historyofparliamentonline.org/volume/1820-1832/member/knatchbull-sir-edward-1781-1849 (accessed 25 November 2022).

Fergus, Jan, 'The Professional Woman Writer', in *The Cambridge Companion to Jane Austen*, ed. Edward Copeland and Juliet McMaster, 2nd edn, 1–20. Cambridge: Cambridge University Press, 2011.

Fischer, Doucet Devin, 'Byron and Austen: Romance and Reality', *The Byron Journal* 21 (1993): 71–9.

Ford, Susan Allen, 'Learning Romance from Scott and Byron: Jane Austen's Natural Sequel', *Persuasions* 25 (2003): 72–88.

Ford, Susan Allen, 'Mrs. Smith, Charlotte Smith, and West Indian Property in *Persuasion*: A Note', *Persuasions On-Line* 41, no. 2 (summer 2021). https://jasna.org/publications-2/persuasions-online/volume-41-no-2/ford/ (accessed 13 January 2023).

Foster, John, *Essays in a Series of Letters to a Friend*, 2 vols, 3rd edn. London: Longman, Hurst, Rees, and Orme, 1806.

Foyster, Elizabeth, *The Trials of the King of Hampshire: Madness, Secrecy and Betrayal in Georgian England*. London: One World, 2016.

Franklin, Caroline, *The Female Romantics: Nineteenth-century Women Novelists and Byronism*. New York: Routledge, 2012.

Gale, Zona, 'Jane Austen Outdoes Daisy Ashford; A Review by Zona Gale', *New York Times, Section B*, 17 September 1922: page not given. https://www.nytimes.com/1922/09/17/archives/jane-austen-outdoes-daisy-ashford-a-review-by-zona-gale.html?searchResultPosition=1 (accessed 16 January 2023).

Gay, Penny, *Jane Austen and the Theatre*. Cambridge: Cambridge University Press, 2002.

Gerzina, Gretchen, *Black London: Life before Emancipation*. New Brunswick: Rutgers University Press, 1995.

Gilbert, Sandra M. and Susan Gubar, 'Jane Austen's Cover Story', in *The Madwoman in the Attic: The Woman Writer and the Nineteenth-Century Literary Imagination*, 148–85. New Haven: Yale University Press, 1979.

Gilson, David, *A Bibliography of Jane Austen. New Introduction and Corrections by the Author*. Winchester: St Paul's Bibliographies, 1997.

Gleckner, Robert and Bernard Beatty, *The Plays of Lord Byron: Critical Essays*. Liverpool: Liverpool University Press, 1997.

Goss, Erin M., 'Characterized by Violence: On Goodness and the Profits of Slavery', *Persuasions On-Line* 41, no. 2 (summer 2021). https://jasna.org/publications-2/persuasions-online/volume-41-no-2/goss/ (accessed 13 January 2023).

Graham, Peter W., 'A Tale of Two Abbeys: Byron, Austen, and Ambiguities of the Gothic.' Unpublished paper given at *Austen & Byron: Together at Last*, a joint meeting of the Byron Society of America and the Jane Austen Society of North America, Union Theological Seminary, New York City, 3 May 2008.

Graham, Peter W., 'Byron and the Business of Publishing', in *The Cambridge Companion to Byron*, ed. Drummond Bone, 27–43. Cambridge: Cambridge University Press, 2004.

Graham, Peter W., 'Childe Harold and Fitzwilliam Darcy, or A Tale of Two Two-Hundred-Year-Old Heroes', *Persuasions* 35 (2013): 169–81.

Grimaldi, Joseph, *Memoirs of Joseph Grimaldi*, ed. 'Boz' [Charles Dickens], 2 vols. London: Richard Bentley, 1838.

Grover, Christine, 'Edward Knight's Inheritance: The Chawton, Godmersham, and Winchester Estates', *Persuasions On-Line* 34, no. 1 (2013). https://jasna.org/persuasions/on-line/vol34no1/grover.html (accessed 9 December 2022).

Grover, Christine, 'Pride, Prejudice, and the Threat to Edward Knight's Inheritance', *Persuasions On-Line* 35, no. 1 (2014). https://jasna.org/persuasions/on-line/vol35no1/grover.html (accessed 9 December 2022).

Gullette, Margaret Morganroth, 'Annals of Caregiving: Does Emma Woodhouse's Father Suffer from "Dementia"?' *Michigan Quarterly Review* 48, no. 1 (winter 2009): 1–2. http://hdl.handle.net/2027/spo.act2080.0048.115 (accessed 18 March 2023).

Harding, D. W., *Regulated Hatred and Other Essays on Jane Austen*, ed. Monica Lawlor and L. C. Knights. London: Bloomsbury, 2000.

Harris, Jocelyn, 'Anna Letitia Barbauld, Jane Austen's Unseen Interlocutor', in *Anna Letitia Barbauld: New Perspectives*, ed. William McCarthy and Olivia Murphy, 204–20. Peterborough: Bucknell University Press, 2013.

Hawkins, Frederick William, *The Life of Edmund Kean*, 2 vols. London: Tinsley Brothers, 1869.

Hemingway, Collins, 'When a Slave Island Does Not Mean Slavery: An Audit of Mrs. Smith's Encumbered Funds', *Persuasions* 40 (2018): 213–20.

Heydt-Stevenson, Jill, *Austen's Unbecoming Conjunctions: Subversive Laughter, Embodied History*. Basingstoke: Palgrave Macmillan, 2005.

Heydt-Stevenson, Jill, "'Slipping into the Ha-Ha": Bawdy Humor and Body Politics in Jane Austen's Novels', *Nineteenth-Century Literature* 55, no. 3 (2000): 309–39.

Hildebrand, Enid G., 'Jane Austen and the Law', *Persuasions* 4 (1982): 34–41.

Hobhouse, John Cam (Lord Broughton de Gyfford), *Byron's Bulldog: The Letters of John Cam Hobhouse to Lord Byron*, ed. Peter W. Graham. Columbus: Ohio State University Press, 1984.

Hobhouse, John Cam (Lord Broughton de Gyfford), *Hobhouse's Diary*, ed. Peter Cochran. https://petercochran.wordpress.com/hobhouses-diary/ (accessed 25 November 2022).

Hobhouse, John Cam (Lord Broughton de Gyfford), *Recollections of a Long Life, With Additional Extracts from His Private Diaries*, ed. Charlotte Carleton and Lady Dorchester. New York: Charles Scribner's Sons, 1909.

Hopkins, Lisa, 'Waltzing with Wellington, Biting with Byron: Heroes in Austen Tribute Texts', in *Jane Austen and Masculinity. Transits: Literature, Thought & Culture 1650–1850*, ed. Michael Kramp, 173–90. Lanham: Bucknell University Press, 2017.

Howard-Smith, Stephanie, "'Hearty Fow Children": The Penrhyns, Pugs, and *Mansfield Park*', *Persuasions* 35 (2013): 191–9.

Howell, Margaret, *Byron Tonight: A Poet's Plays on the Nineteenth Century Stage*. Windlesham: Springwood Books, 1982.

Hubback, J. H. and E. C. Hubback, *Jane Austen's Sailor Brothers*. Cambridge: Cambridge University Press, 2012; first published 1906.

Hunt, James Leigh, *Lord Byron and Some of His Contemporaries*, 2 vols, 2nd edn. London: H. Colburn, 1828.

Hunt, V. G., 'The Village of Chawton in the Time of Jane Austen', *The Jane Austen Society Report 1988 (Collected Reports, 1986–95)*: 101–7.

Hurst, Jane, 'Poor George Austen?', *The Jane Austen Society Report 2004 (Collected Reports 2001–05)*: 348–51.

Huxtable, Sally-Anne, Corinne Fowler, Christo Kefalas and Emma Slocombe, eds, *Interim Report on the Connections between Colonialism and Properties Now in the Care of the National Trust, Including Links with Historic Slavery*. National Trust, 2020.

James, P. D., '*Emma* Considered as a Detective Story', *The Jane Austen Society Report 1998 (Collected Reports 1996–2000)*: 196–200.

Jane Austen House, Chawton, 'Jane Austen Undressed', exhibition, 26 March to 2 October 2022. https://janeaustens.house/stockings-stays-a-new-display/ (accessed 4 December 2022).

Jeffrey, Francis, 'Review of *A Series of Plays*, etc., Vol. 3', *The Edinburgh Review* 19 (1812): 261–90.

Johnson, Claudia L. and Clara Tuite, *30 Great Myths about Jane Austen*. Chichester: Wiley Blackwell, 2020.

Johnson, Samuel, *A Journey to the Western Islands of Scotland: A New Edition*. London: W. Strahan and T. Cadell, 1791.

Kaplan, Laurie, 'London as Text: Teaching Jane Austen's "London" Novels *In Situ*', *Persuasions On-Line* 32, no. 1 (2011). https://jasna.org/persuasions/on-line/vol32no1/kaplan.html (accessed 28 November 2022).

Kelsall, Malcolm, *Byron's Politics*. Sussex: Harvester Press, 1987.

Kenyon Jones, Christine, 'Ambiguous Cousinship: *Mansfield Park* and the Mansfield Family', *Persuasions On-Line* 31, no. 1 (2010). https://jasna.org/persuasions/on-line/vol31no1/jones.html (accessed 13 January 2023).

Kenyon Jones, Christine, '"He is a Rogue of Course, But a Civil One": John Murray, Jane Austen, and Lord Byron', *Persuasions* 36 (2014): 239–54.

Kenyon Jones, Christine, *Kindred Brutes: Animals in Romantic-Period Writing*. Aldershot: Ashgate, 2001.

King, Gaye, 'Catton Hall', *Transactions of the Jane Austen Society of the Midlands* (1991): 61–3.

Kipling, Rudyard, 'The Janeites', in Rudyard Kipling, *Debits and Credits* [1926], ed. Sandra Kemp, np. Harmondsworth: Penguin, 1987. http://www.telelib.com/authors/K/KiplingRudyard/prose/DebtsandCredits/janeites.html (accessed 13 January 2023).

Kirkham, Margaret, *Jane Austen, Feminism and Fiction*. Brighton: Harvester Press, 1983.

Knight, Fanny, *Fanny Knight's Journals*, Knatchbull Manuscript, Kent County Archives, Centre for Kentish Studies, Maidstone, U951, F24, vols 1–10.

Knox-Shaw, Peter, '*Persuasion*, Byron, and the Turkish Tale', *Review of English Studies* 44, no. 173 (1993): 47–69.

Langley Moore, Doris, *Lord Byron: Accounts Rendered*. London: John Murray, 1974.

Lau, Beth, 'Teaching Austen and the Male Romantic Poets', *Romantic Circles*, April 2015, np. http://romantic-circles.org/pedagogies/commons/austen (accessed 21 January 2023).

Le Faye, Deirdre, *A Chronology of Jane Austen and Her Family*. Cambridge: Cambridge University Press, 2006.

Le Faye, Deirdre, *The British Library Writers' Lives: Jane Austen*. London: British Library, 1998.

Le Faye, Deirdre, 'Fanny Knight's Diaries: Jane Austen through her Niece's Eyes', *Persuasions Occasional Papers* 2 (1986): 5–26.

Le Faye, Deirdre, *Jane Austen: The World of Her Novels*. London: Frances Lincoln, 2002.

Le Faye, Deirdre, *Jane Austen's 'Outlandish Cousin': The Life and Letters of Eliza de Feuillide*. London: British Library, 2002.

Le Faye, Deirdre, 'Leonora Austen', *The Jane Austen Society Report 1998 (Collected Reports 1996–2000)*: 182–4.

LeJacq, Seth Stein, 'Rears and Vices: The Austens and Naval Sodomy', *Notches blog*, 13 December 2018. https://notchesblog.com/2018/12/13/rears-and-vices-the-austens-and-naval-sodomy/ (accessed 26 June 2022).

Levy, Michelle, *Literary Manuscript Culture in Romantic Britain*. Edinburgh: Edinburgh University Press, 2021.

Litz, A. Walton, 'Jane Austen: The Juvenilia', in *Jane Austen's Beginnings: The Juvenilia and Lady Susan*, ed. J. David Grey, 1–6. Ann Arbor: UMI Research Press, 1989.

Loche, Renée and Colston Sanger, *Jacques-Laurent Agasse, 1767–1849*, catalogue for an exhibition 15 February–2 April 1989. London: Tate Gallery, 1988.

Looser, Devoney, 'Breaking the Silence: Exploring the Austen Family's Complex Entanglements with Slavery', *Times Literary Supplement*, 21 May 2021, 3–4.

https://www.the-tls.co.uk/articles/jane-austen-family-slavery-essay-devoney
-looser/ (accessed 18 January 2023).

Looser, Devoney, 'Heroics all at Sea', *Times Literary Supplement*, 8 July 2022.
https://www.the-tls.co.uk/articles/jane-austen-brother-slave-trad-essay
-devoney-looser/ (accessed 30 December 2022).

Lucas, Victor, 'Jane Austen's Don Juan', *The Jane Austen Society Report 1992
(Collected Reports 1986–95)*: 255–63.

MacCarthy, Fiona, *Byron: Life and Legend*. London: John Murray, 2002.

Mackintosh, R. J., *Memoirs of the Life of the Right Honourable Sir James Mackintosh*,
2 vols. London: E. Moxon, 1835.

Marchand, Leslie A., *Byron: A Biography*, 3 vols. New York: Alfred A. Knopf,
1957.

'*Marmion; A Tale of Flodden Field*. By Walter Scott Esq.', anonymous review, *The
Edinburgh Review*, 12 (23) (1808): 1–35.

McAleer, John, 'What a Biographer Can Learn about Jane Austen from her
Juvenilia', in *Jane Austen's Beginnings: The Juvenilia and* Lady Susan, ed. J. David
Grey, 7–27. Ann Arbor: UMI Research Press, 1989.

McGann, Jerome J., *Fiery Dust: Byron's Poetic Development*. Chicago: University of
Chicago Press, 1968.

Medwin, Thomas, *Medwin's Conversations of Lord Byron*, ed. Ernest J. Lovell Jr.
Princeton: Princeton University Press, 1966.

Millingen, Julius, *Memoirs of the Affairs of Greece . . . with Various Anecdotes
Relating to Lord Byron and an Account of His Last Illness and Death*. London:
John Rodwell, 1831.

Mills, A. R., 'The Last Illness of Lord Byron', *Proceedings of the Royal College of
Physicians of Edinburgh* 28 (1998): 73–80.

Mitchell, Charlotte and Gwendolen Mitchell, 'Passages to India. Did Joshua
Reynolds Paint a Portrait of Jane Austen's Aunt?' *Times Literary Supplement*,
21 July 2017, 13–14. https://www.the-tls.co.uk/authors/charlotte-and
-gwendolen-mitchell/ (accessed 18 January 2023).

Moore, Thomas, *Letters and Journals of Lord Byron with Notices of His Life*, 2 vols.
London: John Murray, 1830.

Moore, Thomas, *The Letters of Thomas Moore*, ed. Wilfred S. Dowden, 2 vols.
Oxford: Clarendon Press, 1964.

Moore, Thomas, *The Journal of Thomas Moore*, ed. Wilfred S. Dowden, 6 vols.
Newark: University of Delaware Press, 1983–91.

Morgan, Sidney, Lady. *Lady Morgan's Memoirs: Autobiography, Diaries and
Correspondence*, ed. S. Owenson, 2 vols. London: W.H. Allen, 1823.

Morrison, Robert, *The Regency Revolution: Jane Austen, Napoleon, Lord Byron and
the Making of the Modern World*. London: Atlantic Books, 2019.

Mortimer, Ian, *The Time Traveller's Guide to Regency Britain*. London: Bodley
Head, 2020.

Mugglestone, Lynda, '"The Fallacy of the Cockney Rhyme": From Keats and earlier
to Auden', *Review of English Studies* 42, no. 165 (1991): 57–66.

Mullan, John, 'How People Talk in Jane Austen', in *The Jane Austen Society Annual
Report* 2017: 72–88.

Murray, Christopher, 'Elliston, Robert William (1774–1831)', *Oxford Dictionary of National Biography*, 2004. https://doi.org/10.1093/ref:odnb/8724 (accessed 11 December 2022).

Murray, John, *The Letters of John Murray to Lord Byron*, ed. Andrew Nicholson. Liverpool: Liverpool University Press, 2007.

Nelson, Paul David, *Francis Rawdon-Hastings, Marquess of Hastings: Soldier, Peer of the Realm, Governor-General of India*. Madison: Fairleigh Dickinson University Press, 2005.

O'Connell, Mary, *Byron and John Murray*. Liverpool: Liverpool University Press, 2014.

O'Connell, Mary, '[T]he Natural Antipathy of Author & Bookseller: Byron and John Murray', *Byron Journal* 41, no. 2 (2013): 159–72.

Oglivy, Mabell, Countess of Airlie, *In Whig Society 1775–1818*. London: Hodder and Stoughton, 1921.

Ovid, [Publius Ovidius Naso], *Heroïdes and Amores*, trans. Grant Showerman, Loeb Classical Library, vol. 41. Cambridge, MA: Harvard University Press, London: William Heinemann Ltd, 1931. https://www.theoi.com/Text/OvidHeroides5.html#19 (accessed 26 November 2022).

Perlstein, Arnie, 'Jane Austen's Career-Long Fascination with Ovid's Protofeminist *Heroides* Letters'. http://sharpelvessociety.blogspot.com/2016/09/jane-austens-career-long-fascination.html (accessed 23 November 2022).

Polidori, John William, *The Vampyre: A Tale by the Right Honourable Lord Byron*. London: Sherwood, Neely, and Jones, 1819.

Pope, Alexander, *'Eloisa to Abelard': Written by Mr. Pope*, 2nd edn. London: Bernard Lintot, 1720.

Richardson, Alan, 'Byron and the Theatre', in *The Cambridge Companion to Byron*, ed. Drummond Bone, 133–50. Cambridge: Cambridge University Press, 2004.

Sachs, Jonathan and Andrew Stauffer, eds, *Lord Byron: Selected Writings*. Oxford: Oxford University Press, 2022.

Saglia, Diego, 'Touching Byron: Masculinity and the Celebrity Body in the Romantic Period', in *Performing Masculinity*, ed. Rainer Emig and Antony Rowland, 13–27. Basingstoke: Palgrave Macmillan, 2010.

Said, Edward W., *Culture & Imperialism*. London: Chatto & Windus, 1993.

Sandler, Matt, 'Black Byronism', *Byron Journal* 45, no. 1 (2017): 39–53.

Schoina, Maria, 'The Pisan Circle and the Cockney School', in *Byron in Context*, ed. Clara Tuite, 214–21. Cambridge: Cambridge University Press, 2020.

Schuessler, Jennifer, 'Jane Austen Detested Her First Buyer, the Prince', *New York Times*, 25 July 2018, Section C, 1. https://www.nytimes.com/2018/07/24/books/jane-austen-prince-regent.html (accessed 18 January 2023).

Sedgwick, Eve Kosofsky, 'Jane Austen and the Masturbating Girl', *Critical Inquiry* 17, no. 4 (1991): 818–37.

Seymour, Susanne, *The Colour of Money – Slave Trade Legacies*. Information sheet, Newstead Abbey visit, 11 September 2014. https://slavetradelegacies.files.wordpress.com/2014/10/stl-infosheet.pdf (accessed 23 November 2022).

Shelley, Mary, *Frankenstein*, in *Four Gothic Novels: The Castle of Otranto, Vathek, The Monk, Frankenstein*, 449–606. Oxford: Oxford University Press, 1994.

Bibliography

Shelley, Percy Bysshe, *The Letters of Percy Bysshe Shelley*, ed. F. L. Jones, 2 vols. Oxford: Oxford University Press, 1964.

Sheppard, Francis, *London: A History*. Oxford: Oxford University Press, 1998.

Simmers, George and Mary Lister, 'Byron to Murray: An Unpublished Letter', *Byron Journal* 51, no. 1 (2023): 47–56.

Simond, Louis, *Journal of a Tour and Residence in Great Britain: During the Years 1810 and 1811*, 2 vols. London: G. Ramsay, 1815.

Slothouber, Linda, *Jane Austen, Edward Knight and Chawton: Commerce and Community*. Gaithersburg: Woodpigeon, 2015.

Smiles, Samuel, *A Publisher and His Friends: Memoir and Correspondence of John Murray; With an Account of the Origin and Progress of the House, 1768–1843*, 2 vols. London: John Murray, 1891.

Southam, Brian, *Jane Austen and the Navy*. London: Hambledon and London Ltd, 2000.

Southam, Brian, '"Rears" and "Vices" in *Mansfield Park*', *Essays in Criticism* 52, no. 1 (January 2002): 23–35. https://doi.org/10.1093/eic/52.1.23 (accessed 23 November 2022).

Southam, Brian, 'Was Jane Austen a Bonapartist?', *The Jane Austen Society Report 2000 (Collected Reports 1996–2000)*: 312–20.

Spacks, Patricia Meyer, ed., *Pride and Prejudice: An Annotated Edition*. Cambridge MA: Harvard University Press, 2010.

Stabler, Jane, *Byron, Poetics and History*. Cambridge: Cambridge University Press, 2002.

Stabler, Jane, 'Cities', in *Jane Austen in Context*, ed. Janet Todd, 204–14. Cambridge: Cambridge University Press, 2005.

Staël-Holstein, Anne Germaine, baronne de, *Corinne, or Italy,* trans. and ed. Sylvia Raphael. Oxford: Oxford University Press, 1998 (reissued 2008).

Staël-Holstein, Anne Germaine, baronne de, *A Treatise on the Influence of the Passions*. London: George Cawthorne, 1796.

St Clair, William, 'The Impact of Byron's Writings', in *Byron: Augustan and Romantic*, ed. Andrew Rutherford, 1–25, London: Macmillan, 1990.

St Clair, William, *The Reading Nation in the Romantic Period*. Cambridge: Cambridge University Press, 2004.

Stephen, Leslie, 'Humour', *Cornhill Magazine* 33 (1876): 324–5.

Sutherland, Kathryn, 'Jane Austen on Screen', in *The Cambridge Companion to Jane Austen*, ed. Edward Copeland and Juliet McMaster, 2nd edn, 215–31. Cambridge: Cambridge University Press, 2011.

Sutherland, Kathryn, 'Jane Austen's Dealings with John Murray', *The Review of English Studies* 64, no. 263 (February 2013): 105–26.

Sutherland, Kathryn, *Jane Austen's Textual Lives: from Aeschylus to Bollywood*. Oxford: Oxford University Press, 2005.

Tate, Richard, *Alphabetical Catalogue for Godmersham Park, 1818*. https://chawton .org/library/GodmershamCatalogue.html (accessed 18 January 2022).

Teerlink, Amanda, *The Wicked Widow: Reading Jane Austen's* Lady Susan *as a Restoration Rake*. Provo: Brigham Young University, MA thesis, 2018. https://

scholarsarchive.byu.edu/cgi/viewcontent.cgi?article=8100&context=etd (accessed 23 November 2022).

Thomson, Karen, 'Mrs. Musgrave of Newton Priors? Jane Austen and Sir Isaac Newton's Library', *Persuasions On-Line* 38, no. 1 (winter 2017). https://jasna.org /publications-2/persuasions-online/vol38no1/thomson/ (accessed 15 January 2023).

Thorne, Roland, 'Hastings, Francis Rawdon, First Marquess of Hastings and Second Earl of Moira (1754–1826)', *Oxford Dictionary of National Biography*, 2004. https://doi.org/10.1093/ref:odnb/12568 (accessed 18 December 2022).

Tomalin, Claire, *Jane Austen: A Life*. London: Viking, 1997.

Treitel, G. H., 'Jane Austen and the Law', *The Law Quarterly Review* 100 (October 1984): 549–86.

Trelawny, Edward John, *Records of Shelley, Byron, and the Author*, 2 vols. London: Basil Montagu Pickering, 1878.

Tuite, Clara, ed., *Byron in Context*. Cambridge: Cambridge University Press, 2020.

UCL (University College London), *Database of the Centre for the Study of the Legacies of British Slavery*. https://www.ucl.ac.uk/lbs/ (accessed 25 November 2022).

Viveash, Chris, 'Foul-Weather Jack and Jane Austen', *The Jane Austen Society Annual Report 2011*: 167–71.

Viveash, Chris, 'Genius at the Pantomine?', *The Jane Austen Society Report 2002 (Collected Reports, 2001–05)*: 128–32.

Viveash, Chris, 'Jane Austen in Distinguished Company', *Persuasions* 17 (1995): 31–5.

Viveash, Chris, 'Jane's Missing Performances', *The Jane Austen Society Report 2005 (Collected Reports 2001–05)*: 420–5.

Walpole, Horace, *The Letters of Horace Walpole, Earl of Orford*, 4 vols, 1770–97. London: Sherman & Co., 1842. Project Gutenberg, 2004. http://public-library .uk/pdfs/7/553.pdf (accessed 23 November 2022).

Walton, Geri, *Jane Austen's Cousin: The Outlandish Countess de Feuillide*. London: Pen and Sword History, 2021.

Whately, Richard, '*Northanger Abbey* and *Persuasion*', *Quarterly Review* 24 (January 1821): 352–75.

White, Gabrielle D. V., *Jane Austen in the Context of Abolition: 'a Fling at the Slave Trade'*. London: Palgrave Macmillan, 2005.

Williams, Raymond, *The Country and the City*. Oxford: Oxford University Press, 1975.

Wilson, Frances, ed., *Byromania: Portraits of the Artist in Nineteenth- and Twentieth-Century Culture*. Basingstoke: Macmillan, 1999.

Wootton, Sarah, *Byronic Heroes in Nineteenth-Century Women's Writing and Screen Adaptation*. London: Palgrave Macmillan, 2016.

Wootton, Sarah, 'The Byronic in Jane Austen's "Persuasion" and "Pride and Prejudice"', *The Modern Language Review* 102 (January 2007): 26–39.

INDEX

Index

Index

Index